THE JEWS AMONG THE
GREEKS AND ROMANS

ARCH OF TITUS, ROME

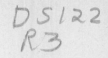

THE JEWS AMONG THE GREEKS AND ROMANS

By
MAX RADIN

PHILADELPHIA
THE JEWISH PUBLICATION SOCIETY OF AMERICA
1915

MATRI MEÆ
PIETATIS ERGO
HOC OPUSCULUM
D. D. D.

PREFACE

It is a counsel of perfection that any historical study should be approached with complete detachment. To such detachment I can make all the less claim as I freely admit an abiding reverence for the history of my own people, and, for the life of ancient Greece and Rome, a passionate affection that is frankly unreasoning. At no place in the course of the following pages have I been consciously apologetic. It is true that where several explanations of an incident are possible, I have not always selected the one most discreditable to the Jews. Doubtless that will not be forgiven me by those who have accepted the anti-Semitic pamphlets of Willrich as serious contributions to historical research.

The literature on the subject is enormous. Very few references to what are known as " secondary " sources will, however, be found in this book. A short bibliography is appended, in which various books of reference are cited. From these all who are interested in the innumerable controversies that the subject has elicited may obtain full information.

There remains the grateful task of acknowledging my personal indebtedness to my friend, Dr. Ernst Riess, for many valuable suggestions. Above all I desire to express my indebtedness to President Solomon Schechter, of the Jewish Theological Seminary of

America, at whose instance the preparation of this book was undertaken. Those who share with me the privilege of his friendship will note in more than one turn of expression and thought the impress of that rich personality.

MAX RADIN

NEW YORK CITY,
   October, 1915

CONTENTS

ILLUSTRATIONS

INTRODUCTION

The civilization of Europe and America is composed of elements of many different kinds and of various origin. Most of the beginnings cannot be recovered within the limits of recorded history. We do not know where and when a great many of our fundamental institutions arose, and about them we are reduced to conjectures that are sometimes frankly improbable. But about a great many elements of our civilization, and precisely those upon which we base our claim to be called civilized—indeed, which give us the word and the concept of civic life—we know relatively a great deal, and we know that they originated on the eastern shores of the large landlocked sea known as the Mediterranean.

We are beginning to be aware that the process of developing these elements was much longer than we had been accustomed to believe. Many races and several millennia seem to have elaborated slowly the institutions that older historians were prepared to regard as the conscious contrivance of a single epoch. But even if increasing archeological research shall render us more familiar than we are with Pelasgians, Myceneans, Minoans, Aegeans, it is not likely that the claims of two historic peoples to have founded European civilization will be seriously impugned. These are the Romans and the Greeks. To these must be added another people, the Jews, whose contribution to civilization was no less real and lasting.

The Greeks and Romans have left descendants only in a qualified sense. There are no doubt thousands of individuals now living who are the actual descendants of the kinsmen and contemporaries of the great names in Greek and Roman history; but these individuals are widely scattered, and are united by national and racial bonds with thousands of individuals not so descended, from whom they have become wholly indistinguishable. We have documentary evidence of great masses of other races, Celtic, Germanic, Slavic, Semitic, entering into the territory occupied by Greeks and Romans and mingling with them, and to this evidence is added the confirmation of anthropological researches. This fact has made it possible to consider Greek and Roman history objectively. Only rarely can investigators be found who feel more than a very diluted pride in the achievements of peoples so dubiously connected with themselves. It is therefore with increasing clarity of vision that we are ordering the large body of facts we already know about Greeks and Romans, and are gathering them in constantly broadening categories.

That unfortunately is not the case with the Jews. Here, too, racial admixture was present, but it never took place on a large scale at any one time, and may always have remained exceptional. However that may be, common belief both among Jews and non-Jews holds very strongly the view that the Jews of to-day are the lineal descendants of the community reorganized by Ezra, nor is it likely that this belief would be seriously modified by much stronger evidence to the contrary than has yet been adduced.[1] The result has been that the place of the Jews in history has been determined upon the basis of institutions avowedly hostile to them. It may be said that historians have introduced the Jews as a point of departure for Christianity, and have not otherwise concerned themselves with them.

There was a time when Greek and Roman and Jew were in contact. What was the nature of that contact? What were its results? What were the mutual impressions made by all three of them on one another? The usual answer has been largely a transference of modern attitudes to ancient times. Is another answer possible? Do the materials at our disposal permit us to arrive at a firmer and better conclusion?

It is necessary first to know the conditions of our inquiry. The period that we must partially analyze extends from the end of the Babylonian Captivity to the establishment of Christianity—roughly from about 450 B. C. E. to 350 C. E., some seven or eight hundred years.

The time limits are of course arbitrary. The contact with Greeks may have begun before the earlier of the two limits, and the relations of the Jews with both Greeks and Romans certainly did not cease with either Constantine or Theodosius. However, it was during the years that followed the return from the Exile that much of the equipment was prepared with which the

Jew actually met the Greek, and, on the other hand, the relations of Christian Rome to the Jews were determined by quite different considerations from those that governed Pagan Rome. It is at this point accordingly that a study of the Jews among the Greeks and Romans may properly end.

THE SOURCES

Even for laymen it has become a matter of great interest to know upon what material the statements are based which scientists and scholars present to them. It is part perhaps of the general skepticism that has displaced the abundant faith of past generations in the printed word. For that reason what the sources are from which we must obtain the statements that we shall make here, will be briefly indicated below.

First we have a number of Greek and Latin writers who incidentally or specially referred to the Jews. However, as is the case with many other matters of prime importance, the writings of most of these authors have not come down to us completely, but in fragments. That is to say, we have only the brief citations made of them by much later writers, or contained in very late compilations, such as lexicons, commonplace books, or manuals for instruction. Modern scholars have found it imperatively necessary to collect these fragments, so that they may be compared and studied more readily. In this way the fragments of lost books on history, grammar, music, of lost poems and plays, have been collected at various times. Similarly the fragments concerning the Jews have been collected, and gathered into

a single book by M. Théodore Reinach, under the title
of *Textes d' auteurs grecs et latins relatifs au judaisme.*
Here the Greek and Latin texts and the French translation of them are arranged in parallel columns, and
furnished with explanatory footnotes. M. Reinach's
great distinction as a classical scholar enables him to
speak with authority upon many of the controverted
questions that these texts contain. Often his judgment as to what certain passages mean may be unques-
tioningly accepted, and at all times one disagrees with
him with diffidence.

Secondly, we have the Jewish literature of the
period; but that literature was produced under such
various conditions and with such diverse purposes that
a further classification is necessary.

Most important for our purposes is that part of
Jewish literature which was a direct outcome of the
contact we are setting forth—the apologetic writings of
the Jews, or those books written in Greek, only rarely
in Latin, in which Jewish customs and history are
explained or defended for non-Jewish readers. Most
of these books likewise have been lost, and have left
only inconsiderable fragments, but in the case of two
writers we have very extensive remains. One of these
men is the Alexandrian Jew Philo, a contemporary of
the first Roman emperors. The other was the Palestinian Jew Joseph, who played an important, if ignoble,
part in the rebellion of 68 c. e.

An estimate of the character of Philo and Josephus
—to give the latter the name by which alone he is

2

remembered—or of the value of their works, is out of place here. Philo's extant writings are chiefly concerned with philosophic exposition, and are only indirectly of documentary value. However, he also wrote a " Defense " of his people, of which large portions have survived, notably the *In Flaccum,* a bitter invective against the prefect of Egypt under Tiberius, and the *Legatio ad Gaium,* a plea in behalf of the Alexandrian Jews made to the emperor Caligula by an embassy of which Philo was himself a member.[2]

An apologetic purpose, for himself more than for his fellow-citizens, is discernible in practically all the extant writings of Josephus. One of them, however, the misnamed *Contra Apionem,* is avowedly a defense of the Jews against certain misrepresentations contained in Greek books. The importance of Josephus' works it is impossible to overrate. For many matters he is our sole authority. But the character exhibited in his own account of his conduct has impaired the credibility of much of what he says, and has provoked numerous controversies. It is impossible to disregard him, and unsafe to rely upon him. However, it is not unlikely that fuller knowledge, which the sands of Egypt and Palestine may at any time offer, will compel us to change our attitude toward him completely.[3]

Besides the apologetic Jewish writings, directed to gentile readers, there was a flourishing literature in Greek (and perhaps in Latin too) intended for Greek-speaking Jews. It may be said that no branch of literary art was quite neglected. The great majority of

these books are lost. Some, however, of a homiletic or
parenetic tendency, attained partial sanctity in some of
the Jewish congregations, and were, under such protection, transferred to the Christian communities that
succeeded them. They may now be found in collections
of Apocrypha and Pseudepigrapha, such as the German collection of Kautzsch and that recently completed
in English by Charles. Examples are the Wisdom of
Solomon, the Jewish Sibyl, the Letter of Aristeas, etc.

All these books were intended for Jewish readers,
but for Jews whose sole mother tongue was Greek. In
Palestine and Syria the Jews spoke Aramaic, and the
educated among them used Hebrew for both literary
and colloquial purposes. There was consequently an
active literature in these languages. Some books so
written were early translated into Greek, and from
Greek into Latin and Ethiopic and have survived as
part of the Apocrypha: Judith, First Maccabees, Tobit,
are instances. It was a rare and fortunate accident that
gave us the Hebrew original of such a book, of Ben
Sira, or Ecclesiasticus.

Again, the highly organized religious and legal institutions of the Jews found literary expression in the
decisions and comments upon them that all such institutions involve. The exposition of the consecrated
ancient literature was also begun in this period. It was
not, however, till relatively late, 200 c. e. and after,
that actual books were put together, so that it is dangerous to accept uncritically references to earlier dates.

The books referred to are primarily the Mishnah and the other extant collections of Baraitot. Besides these, such works as the Megillat Taanit and the Seder Olam must be grouped here. The earlier portions of both Talmuds may be included, perhaps all of the Jerusalem Talmud.

One source of somewhat problematic character remains to be considered. Biblical critics have been at some pains to assign as much as possible of the Bible to the earlier centuries of the period we have delimited. That more than a very slight portion can be so assigned is scarcely probable, but some of it may, especially those books or passages in which Greek influence is clearly noticeable. However, little profit can be gained for our purposes from material that demands such a deal of caution in its use.

Finally, besides literary evidences, which, as we have seen, have wretchedly failed to substantiate the poet's vaunt of being more lasting than brass, we have the brass itself; that is, we have the stones, coins, utensils, potsherds, and papyri inscribed with Hebrew, Aramaic, Greek, Latin, Babylonian, and Egyptian words, which are the actual contemporaries, just as we have them, of the events they illustrate. It is the study of evidences like these that has principally differentiated modern historical research from the methods it displaced, and in the unceasing increase of these fragmentary and invaluable remains our hopes of better knowledge of ancient life are centered.[4]

CHAPTER I

GREEK RELIGIOUS CONCEPTS

The Jew is presented to the modern world in the double aspect of a race and a religion. In a measure this has always been the case, but we shall not in the least understand what the statement of the fact means without a very close analysis of the concepts of race and religion formed by both Greeks and Romans.

The word religion has a very definite meaning to us. It is the term applied to the body of beliefs that any group of men maintain about supernatural entities upon whom they consider themselves wholly dependent. The salient fact of modern religions is that for most men the group is very large indeed, that it vastly transcends all national limits. Christianity, Islam, and Buddhism, all profess the purpose of gaining the entire human race for their adherents, and have actively attempted to do so. The fact that the religions with which we are most familiar are " world-religions," and the abstract character of the predicates of the Deity in them, would seem to make religion as such practically free from local limitation. However, that is not completely true even for our time. In the first place, the bulk of Christians, as of Muslims and Buddhists, are in all three cases bearers of a common culture, and have long believed themselves of common descent. They occupy further a continuous, even if very large, area. Religious maps of the world would show solid blocks of color, not spots scattered everywhere. Secondly, even within the limits of the religion itself national boundaries are not wholly expunged. The common Christianity of Spain and England presents such obvious differences that insistence upon them is unnecessary; nor does the fact that Southern Germany, Belgium, and Ireland are all Roman Catholic imply that all these sections have the same religious attitude.

These are modern illustrations, and they represent survivals of a state of things which in the Greek world was fundamental. As it seems to us axiomatic that an abstractly conceived God cannot be the resident of a limited area on the surface of the earth, just so axiomatic it seemed, at one stage of Greek religious growth, that a god was locally limited, that his activities did not extend—or extended only in a weakened form—beyond a certain sharply circumscribed geographical area. That is probably the most fundamental and thoroughgoing of the differences between Greek religious feeling and that of our day. Opinions may differ widely about the degree of anthropomorphism present at the contrasted periods; and then, as now, the statements made about the nature and power of the Deity were contradictory, vague, and confusing. But one thing it is hard to question: the devoutly religious man of to-day feels himself everywhere, always, in the presence of his God. The Greek did not feel that his god was everywhere with him, certainly did not feel that he was everywhere approachable.[1]

At another point too we are in great danger of importing modern notions into ancient conditions. Judaism, Christianity, and Islam are all book-religions. The final source of their doctrines is a revelation that has been written down, and is extant as an actual and easily accessible book. Moreover, it is the narrative portion of this book that is the best-known part of it, and that is generally associated in the popular mind with it. In the same way, we are prone to think of Greek religion as a series of extraordinarily beautiful myths or narratives of gods and heroes, which have likewise been written down, and are extant in the poems and dramas of which they are the subject. This view has been greatly strengthened by the unfortunate currency of the epigram that Homer was the Greek Bible. No one would be inclined to force, except as a paradox, the analogy upon which the statement rests; yet the phrase is so terse and simple, and the elements of the comparison are so generally familiar, that consciously and unconsciously current conceptions are moulded by it.

Now if the epigram quoted is essentially true, we have at once a measure of Greek religious feeling, since the Homeric poems are as accessible to us as to the Greeks themselves. We should be compelled to reckon with variety in the interpretation of the text, but in the literal signification there would always be a point of departure. And we should at once realize that for divine beings depicted as they are by Homer a devotion of a very different sort is demanded from that which

modern faiths give their Deity. Nor does later literature represent the gods on a loftier moral plane. When
we read Aristophanes,[2] it becomes still more difficult to
understand how the gods could retain their divinity not
only when deprived of their moral character, but even
when stripped of their dignity. So far from raising the
moral character of the divine beings who are the actors
in these legends, the later versions of many quite unex-
ceptionable myths deliberately debase them by subject-
ing most actions to a foully erotic interpretation.[3] The
less offensive narrative, to be sure, survives as well, but
it is to be noted that the divinity of the personages in
question seems to be as unquestioned in the corrupt as
in the purer form of the story.

How might an emotionally sensitive or mentally
trained man pour forth supplication before a guzzling
braggart like the Aristophanic Heracles or an effem-
inate voluptuary like the Apollo of Alexandrian poetry?
It seems hard to discover any other defense than the one
Charles Lamb offered for the dramatists of the Restoration—that the world the gods moved in was a wholly
different one from the human world; a world in which
moral categories had no existence, a Land of Cockayne
without vices, because it was without the sanctions
which vice disregards. No doubt some Greeks felt in
this way toward the myths. But it was not a satis-
factory theory. It introduced a dualism into standards
of conduct that soon became intolerable, when men
reflected seriously upon other sides of the divine nature,
and drew inferences from it.

As a matter of fact, the difficulty we find in addressing words of prayer and praise to such unworthy gods as sat upon the Homeric Olympus is modern, and was probably not felt at all by the vast majority of Greeks, either in Homer's time or later. Not that the fraud, cruelty, faithlessness there exhibited seemed to the Greeks of any epoch commendable or imitable qualities. Even the Homeric Greek was far from being in a barbarous or semi-barbarous state. Civic virtues as between men were known and practised. But the personality of the individual gods in these stories could be disregarded in practice, because they were in no sense a part of the Greek religion. The chastest of men might with a clear conscience worship the lecherous Zeus, because worship did not at all concern itself with the catalogue of his amours. In Homer's time and after, the Greek firmly believed that the Olympians were actually existing beings, but he scarcely stopped to ask himself whether it was literally true that Zeus had bidden Hera be silent under threats of personal violence. What did concern him in his relation with his gods was the disposition in which the god was likely to be toward him or his people. And his religious activity was directed to the end of making that disposition as good as possible.

The matter just set forth is far from being new doctrine; but for the general reader it must be constantly re-emphasized, because it is constantly forgotten. We continually find the Greek myths discussed in terms that would be true only of the Gospel narratives, and we see the Greek gods described as though they possessed the sharpness of personal outline which the Deity has in the minds of believing Christians. It is no doubt the extant literature—a florilegium at best—that is at fault in the matter. This literature, it must be remembered, was not preserved altogether by accident. To a large extent it represents a conscious selection, made for pedagogic purposes. The relative coherence which Greek myths have for us is due to the fact that the surviving poems and dramas which contain them were selected, partially at least, by Hellenistic and Byzantine schoolmasters in order to fit into a set cycle or scheme. Even in what we have there is abundant evidence that the myths about the gods could pretend to no sanctity for anybody, devout or scoffer, for the simple reason that they negated themselves, that widely differing and hopelessly contradictory stories were told of the same event or person.

In reality the Greek myths were not coherent. It is hard to discover in many of them a folkloristic kernel that had to be kept intact. Almost everywhere we are dealing with the free fantasies of highly imaginative poets. So fully was this understood that the stories most familiar to us are generally alluded to in serious Greek literature with an apologetic ὡς οἱ ποιηταί φασι, " as the poets say," or some similar phrase. And as these stories were largely unrelated, so also were the gods of whom they were told, even though they bore the same name. If mythographers had taken the trouble to collect all the stories known of any one god—Hermes, for example—there would be nothing except the common name to indicate that they referred to the same chief actor, and much that, except for the common name, would be referred to different gods. Not even a single prominent trait, not a physical feature, would be found to run through all the myths so collected.

So far we have been dealing with extant literature. But if the more recondite notices of popular superstition are taken into account, as well as the archeological discoveries, we meet such figures as Demeter, Artemis, Apollo,[4] in various and curious forms and associations, so that one might be tempted to suppose that these highly individualized figures of poetry were, in the shrines in which they were worshiped, hardly more than divine appellatives of rather vague content. And on the islands of the Aegean, in Crete and Cyprus, where the continuity between Aegean, Mycenean, and Hellenic civilization[5] was perhaps less disturbed by convulsive upheavals, this seems especially to have been the case.

For cult purposes, then—the primary purpose of Greek religion—there was less difference between gods than we might suppose. Not even the strongly marked personages that poetry made of them were able to fix themselves in the popular mind. Sculptors had been busy in differentiating types, and yet even here the process was not completed. While in general we know of Poseidon-types, Zeus-types, etc., in art, the most thoroughly equipped critics find themselves embarrassed if

they are required to name a statue that is wholly lacking in definite external symbols or attributes, such as
the thunderbolt, trident, caduceus, and others.[6] Even
the unrivaled artistic abilities of Greek sculptors found
it impossible to create unmistakable types of the Greek
gods, for the reason that the character of the god as
portrayed in myth and fable was fluid, and not fixed.

As among most peoples of the time, the essential
religious act was that which brought the god and his
worshiper into contact—the sacrifice. What the real
nature of sacrifice was need not concern us here. The
undoubted fact is that sacrifice and prayer formed a
single act; [7] that it was during the sacrifice that the worshiper ventured to address his prayer to the godhead he
invoked. In doing so he must of necessity use the
god's name, and, as we have seen, the name was of
more general and less specific connotation than is
usually supposed. But the act of worship itself was
specifically occasioned. Even the fixed and annually
recurring festivals related to a specific, if recurring,
occasion in the life of the people. This was eminently
the case in the irregular acts of worship that arose
out of some unforeseen contingency. Whatever the
divine name was that was used, the specific occasion of
its use made it necessary also to specify the function of
the divinity of which the intervention was sought. That
was regularly done by attaching to the name a qualify-
ing epithet. When the rights of hospitality were
threatened with invasion, it was Ζεὺς Ξένιος, Zeus the
Protector of Strangers, that was addressed. In grati-

tude for a deliverance, Zeus or Apollo or Heracles or
the Dioscuri or many another might be invoked as " the
Savior." [8] And it might well be argued that the Greek
who did so had scarcely anything more definite in mind
than a Roman who worshiped Salus, the abstract principle of safety. In very many cases the particular function was especially potent in certain areas, so that a local
adjective applied as a divine epithet would sum up the
power desired to be set in motion.

In the actual moment of prayer or propitiation, it
was often a matter of courtesy to ignore the existence
of other gods. This makes perhaps a sufficiently
definite phenomenon to justify the application to it of
the special name " henotheism " long ago devised by
Max Müller ; [9] and in henotheism we have very likely the
germ of monotheism. But when not actually engaged
in worship, the Greek was well aware that there were
many gods, and that there were differences among
them, and this quite apart from the myths, to which, as
has been said, no very great importance can be attached
in this connection. The differences in power and prom-
inence of deities were perhaps not original, but they had
arisen quickly and generally.

One difference particularly, that between gods and
heroes, seems to have been real to the popular mind. A
difference in the terminology that described the ritual
act, and a difference in the act itself, point to a real distinction between the two divine conceptions. [10]

Who and what the heroes actually were is an
extremely doubtful matter. That some of them were

originally men is a proposition with which legend has made us familiar.[11] We shall recur later to the common heroization of the dead. That some of them were undoubted gods has been amply established.[12] It may well be that they were deities of a narrowly limited territory, knowledge of whom, for one reason or another, remained sharply circumscribed for a long time, so that when they came later within the range of myth-making they could not be readily fitted into any divine scheme. Often the name that appears in some legends as a hero appears in others as an epithet or cult-title of a better-known god. This fact may be variously interpreted. At least one interpretation derives this fusion of names from the fact that the worshipers of the later deity invaded the cult-home of the earlier, and ultimately degraded the latter to accessory rank. Or it may be taken as a compromise of existing claims. At any rate, in some of the heroes we seem to reach an element somewhat closer to the religious consciousness of the Greek masses. And if the gods, or most of them, are heroes who owe their promotion to a fortunate accident rather than to any inherent superiority, we may discover the fundamental divine conceptions of the Greeks in the traits that especially mark the heroes: sharp local limitation, absence of personal lineaments, adoration based upon power for evil as well as for good.[13]

It was because of this last fact that Greek poets could deal freely with gods and heroes in the narratives they created. The divine name possessed none of the ineffable sanctity it has for us by thousands of years of tradition. Except during the performance of the ritual act the god's presence and power were not vividly felt, and it would have been considered preposterous to suppose that he resented as compromising an idle tale from which he suffered no impairment of worship. That the gods really existed, and that honor was to be paid them after the ancestral manner, was more than the essence, it was the totality, of popular Greek theology. Speculation as to the real nature of gods and the world, the mass of citizens would have regarded as the most futile form of triviality.[14]

But there were some who thought otherwise. Many thoughtful men must have felt the absurdities and immoralities of the myths as keenly as we do. Xenophanes [15] protests, and no doubt not first of all men, against them. Further, with the earliest stirrings of cosmic speculation in Ionia, systems of theology are proposed that dispense with demiurges and administrators. Intellectually developed men cannot have been long in ridding themselves of popular conceptions that violated the most elementary reflection. To be sure, the philosopher did not always feel free to carry his conviction to the point of openly disregarding the established forms. To do so would bring him into conflict with other institutions that he valued, and with which religious forms had become inextricably bound up. But his own beliefs took broader and broader ground, and well before Alexander became monotheism, pantheism, or agnosticism.[16]

All these standpoints must be kept in mind when we deal with the conflict between Greek and Jew: the popular one, no doubt rooted in a primitive animism, to which the gods were of indifferent and somewhat shifting personality, but to which the ritual act was vital; the attitude of poetry and folk-lore, in which divine persons appeared freely as actors, but in which each poem or legend was an end in itself unrelated to any other; and finally the philosophic analysis, which did not notably differ in result from similar processes of our own day.

We find the Hellenic world in possession of very many gods. Some of them are found practically wherever there were Greeks, although the degree of veneration they received in the different Greek communities varied greatly. However, such common gods did exist, and their existence involves the consideration of the spread of worships.

It is of course quite possible that the common gods grew out of the personification of natural phenomena, the solar-myth theory, on which nineteenth-century scholars sharpened their ingenuity.[17] It may be, too, that one or more of them are the national gods of the conquering Hellenes, whensoever and howsoever such a conquest may have taken place. Some may have been of relatively late importation. The Greeks lived in territory open to streams of influence from every point of the compass. Of one such importation we know some details—the worship of Dionysus.[18] Of others, such as Aphrodite, we suspect a Semitic origin by way of

Cyprus.[19] It will be noticed that the names of most of the common gods are difficult to trace to Greek roots, a fact in itself of some significance.

We must remember that the wandering of the god is often merely the wandering of a name. That is especially true in those cases in which an old divine name becomes the epithet or cult-title of the intruding deity. Here obviously there was no change in the nature of the god worshiped and no interruption of his worship. It is very likely, too, that very few deities ever completely disappeared, even when there was a real migration of a god. The new god took his place by the side of the old one, and relations of many kinds, superior or inferior, were speedily devised. So at Athens, in the contest between Poseidon and Athena, permanently recorded on the west pediment of the Parthenon, the triumph of Athena merely gave her a privilege. The defeated Poseidon remained in uninterrupted possession of shrine and votaries.

How did the worship of certain gods spread? One answer is obvious: by the migration of their votaries. Locally limited as the operation of the divinity was, in normal circumstances there never was a doubt that it could transcend those limits when the circumstances ceased to be normal. And that certainly took place when the community of which the god was a member changed its residence. The methods of propitiation, as crystallized into the inherited ritual, and the divine name, in which, for the rank and file, the individuality of the god existed, would be continued, though they were subject to new influences, and not infrequently suffered a sea-change.

But migration of all or some of the worshipers of a given deity was not the only way by which the god himself moved from place to place. Exotic rituals, as soon as men became acquainted with them, had attractions of their own, especially if they contained features that made a direct sensational appeal. The medium of transference may have been the constantly increasing commerce, which brought strangers into every city at various times. In all Greek communities there was a large number of " disinherited "—metics, emancipated slaves, suffrageless plebs—to whom the established gods seemed cold and aloof, or who had only a limited share in the performance of the established ritual. These men perhaps were the first to welcome newer rituals, which it was safer to introduce when they were directed to newer gods.[20] They were assisted in doing this by the long-noted tolerance Greeks exhibited toward other religious observances, a tolerance which Christian Europe has taught us to consider strange and exceptional.

That tolerance was not altogether an inference from polytheism itself. Polytheism, to be sure, takes for granted the existencè of other gods in other localities, but it does not follow that it permits the entrance of one god into the jurisdiction of another. And it was not universal. Among communities inhospitable in other respects it did not prevail. But it was the general rule, because the conception of $\dot{a}\sigma\acute{e}\beta\epsilon\iota a$, of " impiety," [21]

was largely the same everywhere. Impiety was such
conduct as prevented or corrupted the established forms
of divine communication. The introduction of new
deities was an indictable offense at Athens only so far
as it displaced the old ones. Where no such danger was
apprehended, no charge would lie. The traditions that
describe the bitter opposition which the introduction of
Dionysus encountered in many places, are too uniform
to be discredited.[22] But the opposition was directed to
the grave social derangements that doubtless attended
the adoption by many of an enthusiastic ritual. The
opposition cannot have been general nor of long duration, since the worship of Dionysus spread with extraordinary rapidity, and covered the whole Greek world.

Religious movements curiously like the " revivals "
of medieval and modern times visited Greece as they
visit most organized communities. One of the most
important of these, which gradually spread over Greece
during the sixth and fifth centuries E. C. E., must be
reserved for later treatment. We may note here merely
that there had been present from very early times the
nuclei of a more intense religious life than any that
could be experienced through the rather perfunctory
solemnities of the state cults. These were the mysteries,
of which the most famous were the Eleusinian in Attica.
Some assign the latter to an Egyptian origin.[23] Wherever they came from, they had assumed a large place in
the imagination of Greeks as early as the eighth century ;[24] and they gained their adherents not so much
by wrapping themselves in impenetrable secrecy as by

promising their participants an otherwise unattainable degree of divine favor. Other mysteries existed elsewhere, possibly modeled upon the Eleusinian. All, however, made similar claims. It was in the form of mysteries that the emotional side of religion was deepened. Further, the organization of these mysteries exercised a profound influence upon all propagandizing movements, whether religious or not. It is not unlikely that the earliest organization of the Christian ecclesiae was, at least in part, influenced by the organization of the mysteries, whether of Eleusis or of some other sort.

It has been said that one commonly worshiped group of heroes were frankly and concededly dead men. It needs no demonstration to make clear that such worship of the dead must of necessity be very old; but at many places in the Greek world this ancient worship of the dead had become much weakened. The Homeric poems, for example, know it only in a very attenuated form.[25] At many other places, on the other hand, it flourished vigorously and continuously from the earliest times. The application of the word ἥρως, "hero," to the dead may have had very ancient sanction. In later times, the term appears very commonly,[26] and undoubtedly claims for the persons so qualified the essential characteristics of other heroes—*i. e.* immortality, the primary divine quality in Homer, and greatly increased power. It involved no difficulty to the Greek mind to make this claim, for it was a very common, perhaps universal, belief that gods and men were akin, that they were the same in nature. Perhaps the very oldest of

transcendental beliefs is that the all-overwhelming
phenomenon of death is not an annihilation, and that
something survives, even if only as a shadow in the
House of Hades. When men began to speculate
actively upon the real results of bodily death, it must
have occurred to many that the vaguely enlarged scope
of such life as did survive was a return to a former and
essential divinity.[27]

But from a hero, limited and obscure, to a god, seated
in full effulgence at the table of Zeus, was a big step,
and bigger yet was the deification of living men. It
may even be that the latter conception was not Greek,
but was borrowed from Egypt or Mesopotamia. There
is no indication of its presence before Alexander. That
a man in the flesh might be translated from mortality
to immortality—*entrückt*—was a very ancient conviction. The son-in-law of Zeus, Menelaos, had been so
privileged.[28] A poetic hyperbole claimed as much for
the tyrannicide Harmodius.[29] There were others, of no
special moment, who by popular legend had walked
among men and were not found, as in later times happened to Arthur and Barbarossa. But they became as
gods only by their translation. We do not meet in
Greece for centuries men who ventured to claim for
themselves in the visible body that measure of divinity.
In Egypt, however, and Mesopotamia the conception
was not new. Certainly Pharaoh did not wait to receive
his divine character from the land of the embalmer.
He was at all times Very God. At both the Euphrates
and the Nile, Alexander found ample precedent for the

assumption of divine honors, to which he no doubt sincerely believed he had every claim. We know how he derived his descent, without contradiction from his mother Olympias. It was novel doctrine for Greeks, but the avidity with which it was accepted and imitated showed that it did not absolutely clash with Greek manner of thought.

After Alexander, every king or princelet who appeared with sufficient force to overawe a town could scarcely avoid the formal decree of divinity. The Ptolemies quietly stepped—though not at once—into the throne and prerogatives of Ra. Seleucus adopted Apollo as his ancestor, and his grandson took Θεός, " the God," as his title. His line maintained a shadowy relation with Marduk and Nebo of Babylon. Demetrius the Besieger had only to show himself at Athens to be advanced into Olympus.

The religion briefly and imperfectly sketched in this chapter was not really a system at all. There is a deal of incoherency in it, of cross-purposes and contradiction. There was no priestly caste among the Greeks to gather into a system the confused threads of religious thinking. Its ethical bearings came largely through the idea of the state, in which religion was a highly important constituent. There was also a personal and emotional side to Greek religion, and in particular cases the adoration of the worshiper was doubtless the sacrifice of a broken and contrite heart, and not the blood of bullocks. But the crudities of animism cropped out in many places,

and in the loftiest of Greek prayers there is no note like
" Thou shalt love the Lord thy God with all thy heart,
and all thy soul, and all thy might." In its most
developed form a Greek's dependence on his god was
resignation, not self-immolation.

CHAPTER II

ROMAN RELIGIOUS CONCEPTS

Roman religious ideas were in many respects like those of the Greeks, partly because they were borrowed from the Greeks and partly because they were common to all the nations of the Mediterranean world. It may even be that some of these common forms are categories which the human mind by its constitution imposes upon some classes of phenomena, *Grundideen,* as ethnologists call them.[1] Among both Romans and Greeks we shall find deities sharply limited in their spheres, we shall find the religious act exhausted in the ritual communion, we shall find evanescent personalities among the gods. But all these things will be found in a far different degree, and at various periods many other matters will demand consideration which the Greeks did not know at all or knew to a slighter extent.

The differences in national development would of themselves require differences of treatment. Greek religion grew up in countless independent communities, which advanced in civilization at very different rates. Roman religion was developed within a single civic group, and was ultimately swamped by the institutions with which it came into contact. Again, it is much more necessary among the Romans than among the Greeks to distinguish clearly between periods. Roman political

history passed through points of obvious crisis, and
many institutions were plainly deflected at these points
into quite new paths of development.

Real comprehension of Roman religion is a matter of
recent growth. During the vogue of comparative
mythology, the Roman myths were principally discussed, and the patent fact that these were mere translations from the Greek seemed a complete summing up
of Roman religion. It is only when the actual Roman
calendar, as recorded on stone during the reign of
Augustus, came to be studied that the real character of
Roman religion began to be apprehended.[2]

The results of this study have made it clear that during the highest development of the Roman state the
official religious ritual was based upon pastoral and
agricultural conditions that could scarcely be reached
even in imagination. Propitiatory and dramatic rites
carried out with painful precision, unintelligible formularies carefully repeated, ceremonial dances in which
every posture was subject to exact regulation, all these
things indicate an anxious solicitude for form that is
ordinarily more characteristic of magic than of religion.
Now, magic and religion have no very definite limits in
anthropological discussions, but most of those who use
the terms will probably agree that magic is coercive,
and religion is not. We shall see at various points in
Roman religion that a coercive idea was really present
in the Romans' relation with the gods, and that it followed in a measure from the way the gods were
conceived.[3]

The personality of the Greek gods was not so sharply individualized as the myths we happen to know would indicate, but the gods were persons. That is, during the act of prayer and sacrifice there was conjured up in the mind of the worshiper a definite anthropomorphic figure, who dealt with him somewhat as a flesh and blood man would do. But what was present in a Roman's mind in very early times—those of the kingdom and the early republic—was probably not at all like this. The name of his deity was often an abstraction, and even when this was not verbally the case, the idea was an abstract one. And this abstraction had so little plastic form that he was scarcely certain of the being's sex to which he addressed words of very real supplication, and wholly uncertain what, if any, concrete manifestation the god might make of his presence.[4]

But it will be well to understand that this abstraction, which the Roman knew as Salus, or Fortuna, or Victoria, was not a philosophic achievement. It was not a Platonic "idea." No one could doubt the fact that in times of danger safety was often attained. The means of attainment seemed frequently due to chance; that is, to the working of unintelligible forces. It was to evoke these forces and set them in operation that the Roman ritual was addressed, and whether these forces acted of their own mere motion, or whether the formularies contained potent spells, which compelled their activity, was not really of moment. That was the nature of the "abstraction" which such words as Fides, Concordia, and the rest signified to Roman minds.

In the early days a great deal of the religious practice was borrowed from the Etruscan neighbors, conquerors and subjects of Rome. The Etruscans, as far as anything can be said definitely about them, were especial adepts in all the arts by which the aid of deities, however conceived, could be secured. How much of actual religious teaching they gave the Romans, that is, how far they actually influenced and trained the emotions which the sense of being surrounded by powerful and unaccountable forces must excite, is not yet determinable. But they gave the Romans, or increased among them, the belief in the efficacy of formulas whether of the spoken word or of action.

Although most of the Roman deities were abstractions in the sense just indicated, many others and very important ones bore personal names. These names could not help suggesting to intelligent men at all times that the god who bore one of them was himself a person, that his manifestations would be in human form, and that his mental make-up was like their own. Genetic relations between themselves and the gods so conceived were rapidly enough established. It is very likely, too, that some of these deities, perhaps Jupiter himself, were brought into Italy by kinsmen of those who brought Zeus into Greece, although the kinship must have been extremely remote. And when the gods are persons, stories about them are inevitable, arising partly as folk-lore and partly from individual poetic imagining. There are accordingly traces of an indigenous Roman or Italic mythology, but that mythology was literally overwhelmed, in relatively early times, by the artistically more developed one of the Greeks, so that its very existence has been questioned.[5]

The openness of the Romans to foreign religious influences is an outcome of a conception, common enough, but more pronounced among the Romans than anywhere else. In most places the gods were believed to be locally limited in their sphere of action, and in most places this limitation was not due to unchangeable necessity but to the choice of residence on the part of the deity. Since it was a choice, it was subject to revocation. The actual land, once endeared to god or man, had a powerful hold upon his affections, vastly more powerful than the corresponding feeling of to-day, but for either god or man changes might and did occur.

Both Greeks and Romans held views somewhat of this kind, but the difference in political development compelled the Roman to face problems in the relations of the gods that were not presented to the Greeks. Greek wars were not wars of conquest. They resulted rather in the acknowledgment on the part of the vanquished of a general superiority. With barbarians, again, the struggles were connected with colonizing activity, and, when they were successful, they resulted in the establishment of a new community, which generally continued the ancient shrines in all but their names. Roman wars, however, soon became of a different sort. The newly conquered territory was often annexed—attached to the city, and ruled from it. To secure the lands so obtained it was frequently found necessary to destroy the city of which they were once a part, and that involved the cessation of rites, which the gods would not be likely to view with composure. The Romans drew the strictly logical inference that the only solution lay in bringing the gods of the conquered city to Rome. The Roman legend knew of the solemn words with which the dictator Camillus began the sack of Veii: " Thou, Queen Juno, who now dwellest in Veii, I beseech thee, follow our victorious troops into the city that is now ours, and will soon be thine, where a temple worthy of thy majesty will receive thee." [6] But besides this legendary incident, we have an actual formula quoted by Macrobius from the book of a certain Furius,[7] probably the contemporary of the younger Africanus. The formula, indubitably ancient and general, is given as Africanus himself may have recited it before the destruction of Carthage in 146 B. C. E., and it is so significant that we shall give it in full:

Whoever thou art, whether god or goddess, in whose ward the people and city of Carthage are, and thou above all, who hast accepted the wardship of this city and this people, I beseech, I implore, I beg, that ye will desert the people and city of Carthage, that ye will abandon the site, the consecrated places and the city, that ye will depart from them, overwhelm that people and city with fear, dread, and consternation, and graciously come to Rome, to me and my people: that our site, our consecrated places, and our city be more acceptable and more pleasing in your sight and that ye may become the lords of myself, the Roman people, and my soldiers. Deign to make known your will to us. If ye do so, I solemnly promise to erect temples in your honor and establish festal games.[8]

What might happen as an incident of warfare could be otherwise effected as well. We have very old evidence of the entry of Greek deities into the city of

Rome. The Dioscuri came betimes; also Heracles and Apollo, both perhaps by way of Etruria. And in historical times we have the well-known official importation of the Great Mother and of Asclepius.[9]

These importations of Greek gods were at the time conscious receptions of foreign elements. The foreign god and his ritual were taken over intact. Greek modes of divine communion, notably the *lectisternium,* or sacrificial banquet,[10] and the games, were adopted and eagerly performed by Romans. When Rome reached a position of real primacy in the Mediterranean, the process of saturation with foreign elements was accelerated, but with it an opposition movement became apparent, which saw in them (what they really were) a source of danger for the ancient Roman institutions. The end of the second Punic war, approximately 200 B. C. E., shortly after a most striking instance of official importation of cults, that of the Phrygian Cybele, particularly marks a period in this respect as in so many others. From that time on, the entry of foreign religions went on apace, but it was somewhat surreptitious, and was carried on in the train of economic, social, and political movements of far-reaching effect.

When the Jews came in contact with the Romans, this point had been long reached. As far, therefore, as the Jews were concerned, their religion shared whatever feeling of repulsion and distrust foreign religions excited among certain classes, and equally shared the very catholic veneration and dread that other classes brought to any system of worship.

The former classes correspond roughly to those of educated men generally. Their intellectual outlook was wholly Greek, and all their thinking took on a Greek dress. But they received Greek ideas, not only through Homer and Sophocles, but also through Plato and Aristotle. Not popular Greek religion, but sophisticated religious philosophy, was brought to the intellectual leaders of Rome. One of the very first works of Greek thought to be brought to Roman attention was the theory of Euhemerus, a destructive analysis of the existing myths, not merely in the details usually circulated, but in respect to the fundamental basis of myth-making.[1] In these circumstances educated men adopted the various forms of theism, pantheism, or agnosticism developed by the Greek philosophical schools, and their interest in the ceremonial of their ancestral cult became a form of patriotism, in which, however, it was not always possible to conceal the consciousness of the chasm between theory and practice.

The other part of the Roman population, which knew Greek myths chiefly from the stage, could not draw such distinctions. What was left of the old Italian peasantry perhaps continued the sympathetic and propitiatory rites that were the substance of the ancient Roman cult. But there cannot have been a great number of these. The mass of the later plebs, a mixed multitude in origin, could get little religious excitement out of the state ritual. What they desired was to be found in the Oriental cults, which from this time on invaded the city they were destined to conquer.

CHAPTER III

GREEK AND ROMAN CONCEPTS OF RACE

During the nineteenth century a peculiar rigidity was given to the conception of race through the application of somewhat hastily formed biological theories. One or another of the current hypotheses on heredity was deemed an adequate or even necessary explanation, and by any of them racial characteristics became determined, fixed: race was an unescapable limiting condition. The Ethiopian could not change his skin. These ideas, when popularized, corresponded crudely to certain other ideas already present in men's minds— ideas that often had a very different basis. Their lowest manifestation is that form of vicarious braggadocio which is known as jingoism, racial or national, and is expressed in the depreciation of everything that concerns other "races."

Many historians have been influenced by this modern and unyielding concept of race, and have permitted themselves to make rather large promises about the destinies of existing groups of men on the basis of it.[1] But as late as a hundred years ago it was not yet in existence. The term race then denoted a sum of national and social traits which it might be difficult to acquire in one generation, but which could readily be gained in two. Even such disparate ethnic groups as

Austrian and Magyar knew of no impassable chasm that good-will on either side could not bridge.

It is the latter racial feeling and not the modern one that classical antiquity knew. Consequently, in the clash of races that took place during the period with which this book deals, " race " must be understood as the centuries before the nineteenth understood it. Racial prejudices, pride of blood, contempt for "slave-nations,"existed and found voice, but the terms are not coextensive with those of to-day.

It is well-known that a primary Greek distinction was that between Hellene and barbarian, and it is equally familiar that the distinction had not been fully formed in the time of Homer. There is no indication that the Trojans were felt to be fundamentally different from the Acheans, although it is likely enough that the allies who attacked the great city of the Troad were of different descent from those that defended it. The one instance found in Homer of the word βάρβαρος is in the compound βαρβαρόφωνος, " of barbarous speech " (Iliad ii. 867), which makes the original meaning of the word apparent. A Greek was one whose speech was intelligible. All others were barbarians, "jabberers." And it is not only incidentally that Homer fails to make the racial division clear. When he of set purpose contrasts the two armies, as in Iliad iv. 422-437, it is the contrast between the silent discipline of the Greeks and the loose, noisy marshaling of the Trojans: "For all were not of one speech or of a single language. Mixed were their tongues, since the men came from far-off lands."

4

It is probably in the course of just such expeditions as the Iliad tells of, a joint movement against a common foe, that a sense of national unity arose, and it is likely that it came to include many tribes of different race. We do not know what real basis there is for the traditional divisions of Ionians, Dorians, and Aeolians. These divisions have not proved very valuable means of classification to modern students of Greek dialects. The generic name of Greek to the East was Yavan, obviously the same as Ionian,[2] and that name indicates where the first contact took place. The struggles of Greeks to establish themselves on the coast of Asia Minor probably created the three traditional groups, by forcing them to combine against threatened destruction. But there is nothing to show that any real feeling of common origin and common responsibility existed even here.

On the continent, again, there were large groups of men whom the Greeks found difficulty in classifying. There were some Epirotes and Macedonians whose claim to be Greeks was admitted. On the whole, however, Epirotes and Macedonians were classed as barbarians, though a different sort of barbarians from Scythian and Phrygian. The first realization of national unity came with the first great national danger, the catastrophe that impended from the Persians.

Even then actual invasion did not succeed in combining the Greeks even temporarily. That was due to the inherent difficulty in interesting Thessalians or Boeotians in the quarrels of Ionians.[3] In spite of them,

the danger was at that time averted, but it did not therefore become less real. The consciousness of this ever-
present danger and the bitter experiences of subjection
created groups that coalesced more solidly than ever
before about certain leaders, Athenians or Spartans.
In the fifth and fourth centuries, the concept of a Greek
race received a real outline, and the feeling of a common race pride became highly developed.

This race pride showed itself principally in an over-
weening confidence in the superiority of Greek arms.
It is a false notion that represents the Greek as careless
or contemptuously indifferent of the races about him.
Never were men more eager for curious tales of out-of-
the-way peoples. Their earliest historians won their
chief success in this way. But Greeks had beaten back
the conquerors of the world, and had maintained themselves aggressively as well. It was very natural that
something of this attitude was apparent in dealing with
barbarians even on terms of comity. The Greeks had
at least colorable ground for believing that in military
matters they were masters wherever they chose.

One phrase of which some Greek writers were fond
need not be taken too seriously. Barbarians, we are
told, are by nature slaves.* It would be an error to
attach much importance to the statement. Greeks did
not really believe that Darius or Datames or Hamilcar
was servile in character or in disposition. The expression was merely the facile chauvinism that military
prestige readily stirs up in any nation. So at certain
times some Englishmen were ready to call the French

cowards, or Frenchmen to call Prussians so. Among
the Greeks the principal basis for the statement was the
fact that the activity of Greek merchants and pirates
filled every city with slaves of all foreign nations.
Indeed the phrase is no more than a generalized assertion of that state of things.

We shall have to qualify similarly the statement now
and then encountered of a natural and permanent hostility between Greeks and barbarians. It is a commonplace of Athenian orators, but it practically always
concerns the real hereditary enemy of Greeks, and
particularly of Athens—the Persians. It is in calling
the Greeks against their ancient foe that Isocrates uses
the phrase,[5] and in Demosthenes[6] it is especially based
upon the hostilities so long maintained between Athens
and Persia and the ancient grudge Athenians bore for
the sack of their city in 480 B. C. E.

The first achievement of united Hellas was the
invasion of Persia, although it was under Macedonian
leadership that this was done, but soldiers of Alexander
appeared as Greeks to the East, and Alexander is מלך יון,
melek Yavan, " king of Greece," in the Book of Daniel.[7]

Just at this culminating point in the development of
Greek nationality, the process of blurring began. Greek
and non-Greek were no sooner sharply contrasted than
by the conscious assimilation policy of Alexander's successors the lines tended to obliterate themselves. At
first Greek culture was dominant, but beneath it Syrian,
Egyptian, and Cappadocian obstinately survived, and
ultimately, under Christian and Mohammedan influ-

ences, regained their place. It is with one phase of this specific problem—the threatened submergence of an Asiatic people by Greek culture—that we are particularly concerned.

The attitude of Romans toward other nations was, as might be expected, even more arrogantly that of masters and conquerors. But where we find among Greeks a certain theoretical importance attached to purity of Hellenic descent [8] (which, by the by, was largely ignored in practice), the Romans scarcely understood what the term meant. A system in which emancipated slaves were citizens, who in the second generation were eligible to high civic honors,[9] and not infrequently attained them—such a system did not tend to encourage claims to purity of blood. That does not mean that foreign origin, real or suspected, could not at any time become a handle for abuse. Cicero fastens on the Celtic strain in Piso's lineage with savage delight, just as Demosthenes' enemies rarely forgot to remind him of his Scythian grandfather.[10] But these are not matters of real significance. The significant fact was that they who were Liby-Phoenicians in one generation were descendants of Romulus in the next.[11]

Sumus Romani qui fuimus ante Rudini, " We are Romans, we who formerly were Rudinians," says Ennius,[12] and the metamorphosis was as complete and as easy if, instead of Italians, they were wholly barbarous elements that were absorbed. In religious matters the Romans more than the Greeks felt the efficacy of form. So in political matters the formula of emancipation and the decree of citizenship were deemed operative of a real change in the persons affected.

The Roman nobility, it is true, often made pretensions to a purity of descent that felt every foreign admixture as a stain.[13] But such claims were absurdly groundless, and cannot really have deceived even those who maintained them. The great majority of Romans had no quarrel with any who desired and tried to be Roman. Even Juvenal's venom is vented only on the avowed foreigners, who as Greeks, Egyptians, and Syrians lolled at their ease, while the ragged Cethegi and Cornucanii munched, standing, the bread of affliction and charity. The leveling tendencies of the autocracy removed a great many of the reasons of this friction, and in part succeeded in giving even the Greek-speaking East and the Latin-speaking West a common culture to maintain. But by that time new movements of population made such race-concepts as were based on blood-kinship too plainly out of accord with the facts to be seriously asserted. At the close of the period we are discussing, every man was either a Roman citizen, with a pressingly heavy share of the burden of maintaining the Roman system, or he was not. Who his ancestors were was wholly forgotten. It had even ceased to be of moment whether he spoke Greek or Latin or Syriac, Punic, or even Gallic,[14] which had never completely died out in their ancient homes.

At no time did a feeling of racial kinship make a strong sentimental appeal. That the whole human race was an extended family was taken as axiomatic. Strik-

ing physical differences did not prevent similarity of
names from proving kinship between Egyptian and
Greek and Persian and Ethiopian. All through Greek
history factions in Greek cities called upon outsiders
against their countrymen. The Phoenicians of Utica
preferred the foreign Romans to their Carthaginian
kinsmen. Similarly the Campanians of Capua chose to
fraternize with the Libyans and Phoenicians of Hannibal's army rather than the closely related Latins.[15]   In
these circumstances nothing will lend itself more easily
to distorting our view of the times than the importation
into them of the modern view of race—of that view, at
least, in which the historians of the nineteenth century
found so easy and adequate an explanation of everything they desired to debase or extol.

CHAPTER IV

SKETCH OF JEWISH HISTORY BETWEEN NEBUCHADNEZZAR AND CONSTANTINE

We have briefly sketched in the foregoing chapters the concepts of race and religion that Greek and Roman applied to the world about them. These concepts were not starkly rigid. They changed considerably and often rapidly in the six centuries our subject covers. They are further to be qualified by the social environment within which they operated. But it was not only the Greeks or Romans who in blood and thought passed through many and profound changes. The Jews, too, developed in many directions, and this development can no more be lost sight of than the corresponding one among their neighbors.

In 586 B. C. E. the kingdom of Judah, which had for some years been a Babylonian dependency, was ended as a political institution, and the majority of its people, at any rate of the nobles and wealthy men of them, were forcibly deported to Babylon. The deportation though extensive was not complete. Some, principally peasants and artisans, were left, but in districts so long wasted by war their condition can only have been extremely wretched. Since the whole region was part of the same huge empire, the old boundary lines were probably obliterated, and those who lived there subjected to the control of imperial governors residing in one or another of the walled cities of Syria or Philistia.

Within the next two generations momentous political changes occurred. The Babylonian empire gave way to a Persian, which, however, can at first have changed nothing except the personnel of the actual administrators. According to a very probable tradition, one of the first acts of Cyrus was to permit, at any rate not to oppose, the remigration of some of the Judean families or clans to their former homes. Within the next hundred years a larger and larger number of the families deported by Nebuchadnezzar likewise returned, though never all of them and perhaps not even a majority of them. Much of the old territory must have been found unoccupied, since otherwise conflicts must have arisen with interests vested within the fifty years and more that had elapsed, and of these we do not hear. But we do hear of immediate conflicts between the returned exiles and those who professed to be the descendants of the Israelites (and Judaites) left by Assyrians (and Babylonians) on the soil. These latter were beginning to gather about Shechem, where they must already have been a dominant element, and where they had created a cult center on Mount Gerizim. The conflict tended to become compromised in time, until the activities of the reformer Ezra, backed by the civil governor Nehemiah, again and permanently separated them.

The returned exiles had from the beginning made the ancient capital their center, and had succeeded in obtaining permission to rebuild their ancient shrine.

But they were at an obvious disadvantage compared with their rivals at Shechem, until the city of David could receive the characteristic of a city—the walls which alone distinguished village or somewhat more densely populated section of the open country from the polis or city proper. These, too, were obtained through Nehemiah, and the prohibition of connubium between the so-called Samaritans of Shechem and the Jews of Jerusalem was the first aggressive act of the now self-reliant community.

The system of government of the Persian empire was not oppressive. The distant king of kings was mainly insistent upon recognition of his sovereignty and regularity of tribute, less as a means of support than as an acknowledgment of submission. Within the provinces the satrap was practically king, and might make his domination light or burdensome as he chose. We have excellent contemporary evidence that he took his responsibilities lightly for the most part. In the mountains of Asia Minor many tribes seem scarcely to have known that they were born vassals of the Persian king.[1] The local satrap rarely attempted to control in detail the administrative affairs of the communities in his charge, particularly when such an attempt would precipitate a rebellion.

In Judea the open plains and low hills rendered it easier for the governor to emphasize the king's authority than it was among the mountains of Cappadocia or the fiords of Cilicia, whose native *syennesis,* or king, retained both title and authority. We have, however, a confused and particularly fragmentary record of what actually happened in the two hundred years that elapsed between Zerubbabel and Alexander. Changes of great moment in the political, social, and religious life of the Jews were undoubtedly taking place, since we find those changes completed a few years later, but we can only conjecture the stages of the process. On the whole our sources, till considerably later, are very imperfect. The Persian period forms the largest gap in the history of the Jews.

A great many Biblical scholars, particularly in Germany, assign to this period an influence nothing short of fundamental. A large part of the texts now gathered in the Bible are placed in this time. The extreme view practically refers the beginning of Jewish history to this date, and assumes that only a very small part of the older literature and institutions survived the Babylonian exile. The new community began its life, it is asserted, with elements almost wholly dependent upon the civilization of Babylon and Persia.

It is extremely unlikely that this theory is correct. Every individual assertion of course must be judged in the light of the evidence presented for it. And on this point it may be sufficient to mention that the evidence for almost every position is of the feeblest It consists largely in apparent inconsistencies of statements or allusions, for which the theory advanced suggests a hypothetical reconciliation. If these hypotheses are to be considered scientifically, they at best present a possible solution and always only one of many possible solutions. But the general theory suffers from an inconsistency much graver than those it attempts to remove.

The inconsistency lies in this: The soil of Palestine, never of high fertility, had greatly deteriorated by the frequent wars of the seventh century and the neglect and desolation of the following centuries. Commerce, because of the absence of ports, was practically nonexistent. Those who returned can scarcely have found time for anything else than the bare problem of living. In these circumstances it is obviously improbable that a literary activity rich and powerful enough to have created the masterpieces often assigned to this period can have existed. The conditions of pioneers do not readily lend themselves to such activities. City life, an essential prerequisite of high achievements in art, was being reconstructed very slowly and was confined almost wholly to Jerusalem. The difficulty is a serious one, and is quite disregarded by many scholars to whom the bleakness of our records of this time affords a constant temptation.

Jewish soldiers fought in the armies of their Persian master wherever these armies went. Some must have been among the Syrian contingent at Marathon and Plataea.[2] The garrisons of the frontiers contained many of them. Recently a fortunate accident has disclosed, at the upper cataract of the Nile, a garrison community of Jews, of which the records, known as the Assuan and Elephantine papyri,[3] have opened up quite new vistas in Jewish history. Perhaps the most important point established is the beginning of the Diaspora.

The existence of communities of Jews outside of Palestine, developing their own traditions and assimilating their appearance and social customs to those of their neighbors, is a matter of capital importance for the history of later Jewry. When such communities multiplied, Jerusalem came more and more to have a merely religious presidency over them, and the constitution of Judea itself became determined by that fact, while the foundations were being laid for the career of religious propaganda later so successfully undertaken.

The virtual autonomy of the Persian period allowed the development of a well-organized ruling caste of priests, in which were perhaps included the Soferim, or Scribes, men learned in the Law, who had no definite priestly functions. The scope of the high priest's jurisdiction, the extent of his powers, may not have been sharply defined as yet. In itself the presence of a high priest as head of the state was not at all unusual in that region. As has been said, the interference of the representative of the Persian sovereign was a variable quantity. In the second half of the fifth century a Jew, Nehemiah, held the office of tirshatha, or viceroy, an accident that was of inestimable value to the growing community, and may have finally secured the threatened political existence of Jerusalem.

One other political event, of which we have dim and confused accounts, was a rebellion—whether in or of Judea—under Artaxerxes Ochus (359-338 B. C. E.). The account of Josephus speaks of feuds in the highpriestly family, the murder of a claimant in the temple precincts, and the intervention of the all-powerful eunuch Bagoas.⁴ That some such thing happened there can be no reasonable doubt, although we cannot recover the details. It is, however, unwarranted to make the incident in any way typical of the fortunes of Judea during Persian rule. There was no tradition in later times of Persian oppression, nor can even this rebellion, if rebellion it was, have involved serious repressive measures, since the Greek invasion a few years later found the Jews loyal to their overlord.

When the Macedonian Alexander changed the face of the East, the Jews were swept along with the rest of the loose-jointed empire built by Cyrus and Darius. Upon Alexander's death, after uncertainties which the whole Levant shared, Palestine fell to Egypt, of which it was a natural geographical appanage as it had been for millennia before. Under the suzerainty of the Ptolemies the Jewish communities in Egypt received very considerable reinforcements, and the home-country became a real national expression, and rapidly attained a relatively high degree of material well-being, since the practical autonomy of Persian days was continued. Seized by Antiochus of Asia in the decrepitude of Egypt, Judea entered with full national consciousness into the heterogeneous kingdom ruled by a singularly fantastic royal house. A blunder in policy of the peculiarly fantastic Epiphanes provoked a revolt that was immediately successful in causing the prompt abandonment of the policy, and was helped by dynastic chaos to a still larger measure of success.

(a. Underwood and Underwood)

RUINS OF THE AMPHITHEATER AT GERASA (JERASH) GILEAD, PALESTINE

The leaders of that revolt, the Hasmonai family, produced a succession of able soldiers. Besides the old
Mattathiah and his heroic son Judah, Jonathan, Simon,
and John, by selling their service dearly to this one or
that one of the Syrian pretenders, by understandings
with the ubiquitous Roman emissaries, above all by
military skill of the first order, changed the virtual
autonomy of Persian and Ptolemaic times into a real
one, in which Syrian suzerainty was a tradition, active
enough under the vigorous Sidetes, non-existent under
the imbecile Cyzicenus.[5]

During all this time Jews, from personal choice and
royal policy, had extended their dispersion throughout the new cities founded by their Seleucid masters.
Until the battle of Magnesia, 190 B. C. E., Asia Minor
was the real center of the Seleucid monarchy; and in the
innumerable cities established there, Jews in large numbers settled. When Judea became independent there
were probably as many Jews outside of it as within it.

With the Hasmonean princes—" high priest " is the
title which the Hebrew legend on their coins gives
them [6]—the country entered upon a career of conquest.
Galilee, Idumaea, the coast cities of Philistia, portions
of Gilead were seized by John, or Aristobulus, or Alexander, so that Judea rapidly became one of the important kingdoms of the East, with which no one could fail
to reckon who became active in the affairs of that
region. Rome had backed the Hasmoneans against
Syria so long as Syria presented the possibility of
becoming dangerous. But that soon ceased. By a

strange paradox of history the Hellenized East found its last champion against the Romans in the Persian kings of Pontus, and when Mithradates was crushed, it could only be a question of the order in which every fragment of Alexander's empire would slip into the maw of the eagles. The Roman liquidator, Pompey, appeared in Asia, and Antioch became a suburb of Rome.

The pretext for clearing their way to Egypt by taking Judea presented itself in a disputed succession. The sons of Alexander Jannai were compelled to accept the arbitrament of the Romans, with the usual result. The loser in the award, Aristobulus, attempted to make good by arms what he had lost in the decision. A Roman army promptly invested Jerusalem, moved by the patent injustice of allowing a capable and vigorous prince to usurp the place of a submissive weakling. The Roman general walked into the inner court of the temple, and peered into the Holy of Holies. He found nothing for his pains, but his act symbolized the presence of the master, and left a fine harvest of hate and distrust for the next generations to reap.

From that time on, the history of Judea is the not uncommon one of a Roman dependency. The political changes are interesting and dramatic but not of particular importance: vassal kings, docile tetrarchs, finally superseded by the Roman procurator with all the machinery of his office. Judea was different only in that her rebellions were more formidable and obstinate. But Rome had developed a habit of crushing rebellions.

Simeon bar Kosiba, known chiefly as Bar-Kochba, was the last Jew to offer armed resistance. With his death the political history of Judea comes to an end.

The religious and social history of the Jews had for many centuries ceased to be identical with that of their country. It was a minority of Jews then living that participated in the rebellion of 58, and perhaps a still smaller fraction that took part in the rising under Trajan and Hadrian. The interest of all Jews in the fortunes of Judea must at all times have been lively and deep, but the feeling was different in the case of non-Palestinian Jews from that of men toward their fatherland.

Meeting for the study of their ancient lore in their "guild-house," the *proseucha,* or *schola,* the Jewish citizens of the various cities of the Roman empire or the Parthian kingdom did not present to their neighbors a spectacle so unique as to arrest the latter's attention at once. They were simply a group of allied cult-communities, sometimes possessing annoying exemptions or privileges, but not otherwise exceptional. An exceptional position begins for them when their privileges are abolished, and their civil rights curtailed, by the legislation of the early Christian emperors.

CHAPTER V

INTERNAL DEVELOPMENT OF THE JEWS DURING THE PERSIAN PERIOD

The Jews took to Babylon a highly complicated body of civil law and religious doctrine. The essence of the latter was an exclusive monotheism, and that belief was not the possession of a cultured few, but the accepted credo of the entire nation. No doubt, among the common people, practices still existed that implied the recognition of polytheism. No doubt, too, words and phrases occurred in common speech, in poetry, and in ritual, which had arisen in polytheistic times, and are fully intelligible only with a polytheistic background. But these phrases and practices do not imply the survival of polytheism, either as a whole or in rudimentary form, any more than using the names of the Teutonic gods for the days of the week commits us to the worship of those gods, or the various funeral superstitions still in vogue allow the inference that our present-day religion is a worship of the Di Manes.

Just as the Jewish religion was in a highly developed form at the time of the Exile, so the Law was very fully developed. That the entire Law, as embodied in the Pentateuch, was promulgated by Moses is not altogether likely, but that any considerable fraction of it is later than 586 B. C. E. is equally unlikely. Interpolations

doubtless occurred often. To insert into an authoritative text an inference from the words which the inter-
polator honestly believed to be true, was not a generally
reprehended practice. Perhaps some of the emphasis
upon sacerdotal organization which parts of the Pentateuch show, may have so been imported into the constituent codes of the Torah. But on how slight a scale
this was can be readily seen by comparing the Pentateuch with any of the apocryphal books consciously
designed to magnify the priesthood.[1] The actual civil
law bears every mark of high antiquity. The religious
law is at least not inconsistent with such antiquity.

Now neither in civil law nor in religious thought did
the community that slowly formed itself about the
acropolis of Zion remain stationary. We must suppose
that the energies of the returning exiles were pretty
well concentrated upon the economic problems before
them. But an actual community they were from the
start, and although the communal life was far from
attaining at once to the richness of former days, it contained all the elements necessary. Without a common
law, *i. e.* a regulation of conflicting claims to property,
and without a common cult, *i. e.* a regulation of the communication between the divine and the human members
of a state, no state was conceivable to the ancient world.
Changed conditions will infallibly modify both, and
some of these modifications it will be necessary to
understand.

We possess in the book known as Een Sira, or
Ecclesiasticus,[2] an invaluable and easily dated record

of life as it appeared to a cultured and wealthy inhabitant of Jerusalem about the year 200 B. C. E. The incidental references to past time and, above all, the inferences which may legitimately be drawn about the origins of a society so completely organized as that of Judea at that time, render recourse to the book a necessity at many points of our investigation. While accordingly we find it a convenient terminus in both directions, we must make large individual qualifications. Ben Sira does not fully represent his time or his people. He belonged to a definite social stratum. His own studies and reflections had no doubt developed conclusions that were far from being generally shared. But he is an eloquent and unimpeachable witness that the Biblical books had already reached a high measure of sanctity, and the division later perpetuated in the tripartite canon of Law, Prophets, and Writings, already existed; and, if nothing else, the single reference to Isaiah as the prophet of consolation renders it probable that even so heterogeneous a corpus as the canonical Isaiah was already extant much as we have it now.[3]

Opinions may differ as to the length of time necessary to permit this development. But that a very few generations could have sufficed for it is scarcely credible. Since even the Secondary Canon, that of the prophets, had already become a rigid one, in which historical differences in parts of the same book were ignored, the Law must have been fixed for an even longer time, and the process of interpretation which every living code requires must have gone on apace for very many years indeed.

We know very little of the actual agencies by which this process was effected. The second great code of the Jews was not finally fixed till 200 c. e. We are, however, measurably familiar with the organization of the judiciary for some two centuries before, but even here there are distressing gaps, and for the time before Hillel the tradition is neither clear nor full. All, therefore, that concerns the organization of the judicial bodies that framed and applied the Law must be conjectured, and the earliest conjectures embodied in Talmudic tradition are perhaps as good as any. The development of " houses of prayer " was a necessity where so many Jewish communities were incapacitated from sharing in the great cult ceremonies at Jerusalem, and these houses became a convenience within Palestine and Jerusalem itself. But the creation of houses of prayer demanded local organization, and with that local organization gradations of members and the establishment of local magistrates. There can be little doubt that the organization of the Greek city-state, familiar to the East for many years, became a model for these corporately organized communities. Now the judicial function inherent in the character of ancient magistrates of all descriptions might easily have been the means of originating that long series of responsa from which the later Mishnah was finally winnowed. With every increase of population, power, and governmental machinery, the judicial system increased in complexity, and the intimate relation which the civil code bore to the ancient sacred code, as well as the close penetration of life by religion, tended to render the complexity still more intricate.

But if the origin of the oral law, in its application at least, can be made clear to ourselves only by means of such imaginative reconstruction, we are helped on the side of Jewish religious development by the possession of at least one fact of prime importance. The religious system of the Bible knows of a life after death, in Sheol, but does not know of a survival of personality. Warlock and witch, by such incantations as were used by Odysseus at the mouth of the dread cave, or by the wise woman at En-Dor, could give the shadowy ghost enough outline to be recognizable under his former name, but for the most part all these flitting spirits were equal and undistinguishable. But about 100 B. C. E. there was current generally, although not universally, a very different belief, to wit, that in Sheol, or the grave, personality was not extinguished, but at most suspended; and that under certain conditions it might, or certainly would, be permanently continued. In other words, between the deportation to Babylon and the culmination of the Hasmonean rule, the belief about life after death had very considerably changed for most people. And the change was of a nature that must inevitably have affected conduct, since the acceptability of man's life could no longer be proved by the naïvely simple method of Eliphaz the Temanite,⁴ nor yet by the austere consciousness of rectitude that was the ideal of the prophets. Transferred to a world beyond perception, reward and penalty gave the Torah a superhuman sanction, which must have been far more powerful than we can now readily imagine.

It is idle to look for the origin of this belief in any one series of influences. For many generations poets and philosophers had swung themselves in bolder and bolder imagery up to the Deity, which they, as Jews, conceived in so intense and personal a fashion. Very many passages in the Bible have seemed to imply a belief in personal immortality and resurrection, and perhaps do imply such a belief. Nor is it necessary to assume that these passages are of late origin. Some of them may be, but one would have to be very certain of the limitations of poetic exaltation to say just what definite background of belief metaphor and hyperbole demand. We shall not go far wrong if we assume that even before the Exile, individual thinkers had conceived, perhaps even preached, the dogma of personal immortality. Its general acceptance among the people occurred in the period previously mentioned. Its official authorization took place much later in the final triumph of Pharisaism.

Personal immortality and resurrection of the body are kindred, but not identical, conceptions. Of the two, resurrection is probably the older, and resurrection, we may note, implies a real suspension of personality, when the body is dissolved in death. But the body may be recombined, and, when that occurs, the personal life is renewed. The exact time must have been very differently conceived by different men. A great many, however, had already very definite fancies—one can hardly say beliefs—as to the great day that would deliver the souls from Sheol. That such a great day would come, on which the whole cosmos would be permanently readjusted, is the essence of all eschatology. It was only natural that all other hopes of the people should tend to be combined with it; and of these hopes the principal one was the Messianic hope.

It is obvious that no adequate discussion of the development of this hope can be given here, even if our fragmentary sources permitted such discussion. The most that can be done is to state the situation briefly. It is all the more important, as the Messianic idea was the source of the most powerful political movements among the people, and the direct occasion of at least one of the desperate insurrections of the Jews.

Many nations look back to a golden age of power and prosperity, and forward to a future restoration of it. The Jews likewise never forgot the kingdom of David and Solomon, and saw no reason to despair of its return. As a matter of fact, the Hasmonean rule at its greatest extent was practically such a restoration. But conditions and people had radically changed between David and Alexander Jannai. In 1000 B. C. E. it was a mighty achievement for the small tribal confederation to have dominated its corner of the Levant, to have held in check the powerful coast cities of Philistia, to have been sought in alliance by Tyre and Egypt. In 100 B. C. E., men's minds had long been accustomed to the rise and fall of great empires. Assyria, Babylonia, Persia, Macedon, Egypt, Syria, Athens, and Sparta, and in the distant west Carthage and Rome, had at different times been lords of many lands. The Judean kingdom itself had arisen from the wreckage of such an empire. It was accordingly a different political ideal that filled the imagination of every nation at this time. To secure and maintain the independence of a few square miles of semi-arid soil between the Jordan and the Sea was no deed to puff men with inordinate pride, however difficult of actual accomplishment it was. As a step toward larger deeds, however, it was notable enough.

What was the larger deed, and how was it to be accomplished? However disproportionate it may seem to us, it was nothing else than the dominion over the whole world, to be accomplished by sudden and miraculous conversion of men's souls for the most part, or by force of arms, if it should prove necessary. And, as was natural enough, it was in the ancient royal line, the stock of David, that the leader, the Anointed of God, was to be found.

The family of David, which was still important and powerful when Zechariah xii. was written (perhaps the fourth century B. C. E.), had evidently since fallen on evil days. It cannot, of course, have entirely disappeared, but no member of undoubted Davidic lineage arises to make political pretensions. It is even likely that, in the absence of adequate records, and with the loss of importance which the family suffered during the fourth and third centuries B. C. E., it had become impossible for anyone to prove descent from David.

None the less, perhaps because of the decline of the family, popular imagination clung to the royal house.

In the bitter days of exile, the writer of Psalm lxxxix. loses no faith in the destiny of David's line:

> I have made a covenant with My chosen,
> I have sworn unto David, My servant,
> Thy seed will I establish forever,
> And build up thy throne to all generations.

So the author of First Maccabees, a loyal supporter of a non-Davidic dynasty, puts in the mouth of the dying Mattathiah the acknowledgment of the ultimate sovereignty of the ancient house: "David for being merciful possessed the throne of an everlasting kingdom" (I Macc. ii. 57).

The certainty of this high destiny grew inversely with the political fortunes of the people. But when even the Hasmoneans fell, and Judea, so far from increasing the possessions of Solomon, found herself a hopelessly insignificant fraction of a huge empire, it was not merely the political side of the Messianic idea that fed upon its non-realization. Obscure economic and religious factors had long been operative, and all these raised popular temper to a point of high and, as it proved, destructive tension. It must always be remembered that those who undertook to lead the people against the Romans did not aim at the restoration of the Hasmonean or even Solomonic kingdom. The establishment of a throne in Jerusalem was the first step of that triumphant march through the world which would inaugurate the reign of the God-anointed son of David. The Judean zealots fought for no mean prize.

The Jews who came into contact with Greeks and Romans were a people whose development had been continuous from the earliest times. The cataclysms of their history had produced disturbances, but no break in their institutional growth. To the civil codes of the ancient polity they were in the process of adding a new body of law based upon judicial decisions. To the ethical monotheism of their former development the popular mind was adding a belief in personal immortality and bodily resurrection. Folk-lore and superstitions on one side, and speculative philosophy on the other, were busy here, as they were busy everywhere, in modifying the attitude of the people toward the established religion.

Finally the Messianic idea was gaining strength and form. In essence a hope for future prosperity, it had united in itself all the dreams and fancies of the people, which had arisen in many ways. It became in the end the dream of a world-monarchy, in which a scion of David's line would be king of kings and give law to the world from Jerusalem. The ushering in of that era soon became a great day of judgment affecting the whole universe and ardently desired to correct the oppressive evils of actual life.

CHAPTER VI
THE FIRST CONTACT BETWEEN GREEK AND JEW

Jews came into the occidental horizon as part of a larger whole. That whole was known as Syria. Unfortunately Syria itself is a very vague term, and is without real ethnographic or geographic unity. It might include Mesopotamia and all the intervening region between the Taurus and Egypt. One might suppose that with such a people as the Phoenicians Greek dealings had been so extensive and frequent that it was impossible to call them out of their name, but Tyrians too are considered and spoken of as branches of the Syrians. The name soon became practically a descriptive epithet, more or less derogatory in its implication.[1]

The lower part of the region between the Taurus and Sinai was known to Greeks as Syria Palaestina, a name almost certainly derived from the Philistine cities whose position on the coast and whose origin made them familiar to traders. The Greeks knew, of course, that variously denominated tribes occupied the hinterland, but what little they knew about them did not until somewhat later get into the literary fragments that have come down to us. Perhaps they would not even have been surprised to learn that here, as in Asia Minor, a very large number of peoples had settled and fought and jumbled one another into what seemed to superficial outsiders a common group of Syrians.

The particular section later occupied by the Jews had itself been the scene of a racial babel. The Israelites were, by their tradition, expressly commanded to dispossess Hittite, Girgashite, Canaanite, Amorite, Perizzite, Hivite, and Jebusite.[2] The recurrence of this enumeration indicates an historical basis for the tradition. It is very likely that nations so named were actually subdued by the invading Hebrews. The fact that the tribes dispossessed are seven in number makes caution necessary in accepting the statement. Perhaps some of these " nations " are different names for the same group. Some of them, *e. g.* Hittite or Amorite, may be vague descriptive terms, like Syrian or even Hebrew.

Then there were the Phoenicians, representing perhaps the first Semitic invasion of this territory. Below them, the Philistines, " from Caphthor," who are very plausibly identified with Cretans or " Minoans," the Keftiu of the Egyptians.[3] During Mesopotamian and Egyptian sovereignty, Mesopotamian and Egyptian infiltration may be safely assumed. The desert never ceased to contribute its share of tribes. Permanent results of such nomad invasions were the settlement of the various Hebrew tribes—Moab and Edom in the southeast and Israel on both sides of the Jordan.

If the analogy of other times and places is to be followed, no one of these groups was ever completely and literally exterminated. Jewish tradition knows of an attempted extermination—that of the Amalekites— only as a very exceptional thing. The resultant nationalities, which in Greek times occupied Palestine, were likely enough to have been of somewhat mixed origin. When the Greeks came to know them well, however, the Jews had long been a well-defined group, frowning upon intermarriage, although it is not likely that the prohibition of connubium had its source in any importance attached to racial purity, or that all Jews everywhere were equally strict in enforcing it.[4]

As has been suggested, the first contact was probably military. Since Jews served in the Persian armies as far south as Elephantine, they probably were equally present in the battalions of Datis and of Mardonius.[5] Another early contact was in the slave-mart, no doubt both as buyers and the bought. Enterprising Tyrian traders had made themselves comfortable in Jerusalem before Nehemiah (Neh. xiii. 6), and human commodities formed the chief merchandise of most commerce. Before him, perhaps before the Exile, Joel reproaches the Phoenicians with the words, " The children also of Judah and the children of Jerusalem have ye sold unto the Grecians."[6] " Syrus " had become a common slave-name in Greece in the fifth century, and Syrus might include anything.[7]

All these scattered and uncertain hints do not tend to present a very clear picture. However, the time was rapidly coming when Greek contact with " Syria " was to be vastly more intimate.

In the spring of 334 B. C. E., Alexander crossed the Hellespont to carry out the cherished vision of Isocrates, a united Hellas drastically stamping out the Persian peril. From the complete success of his efforts we are

wont to date the so-called Hellenistic epoch, the period
in which Greek influences in art, government, and society
were dominant. But Hellenization had in actual fact
begun long ago in the domain of art. It had penetrated
central Asia Minor far back in the seventh century B. C.
E.,[8] and the magnificent " satrap-sarcophagus " at Sidon
shows how thoroughly it was appreciated at the very
borders of Judea well in the middle of the fifth century
B. C. E.[9] A generation before Alexander the king of
Sidon bore a Greek name.[10]

So the "king of Yavan," who received the submission
of Jerusalem, passed, on his way to Egypt, among a
people to whom the name of Greek was quite familiar—
who had long known of Greek skill in craftsmanship,
Greek prowess on the field of battle, and Greek shrewdness in bargaining. The new empire, on the dizzy
throne of which Alexander placed himself, seemed to
all the East commensurate with the whole world, and
to the kinsmen of the new king of kings and lord of
lords all men were ready enough to grant the deference
formerly owed to Persians.

At Alexander's untimely death it could scarcely have
seemed to men that great changes were impending. On
the contrary, the prestige of his literally miraculous
successes, the impress of his powerful and fascinating
personality, continued for a long time. It might be
doubtful—in fact, it must have immediately become
uncertain—whether the persons to whom the actual
administration of affairs would fall, would be of Alexander's blood. The satraps of the old régime had to

some extent been displaced by the great king's generals. Every one of these was convinced that the coveted prize would fall to the strongest or cleverest or quickest; but for a while a short and troubled truce was maintained under the shadow of regal authority embodied in the poor fool Arrhidaeus and the unborn child of Roxane. When the young Alexander was born, the conditions at Babylon challenged the intriguing of every court-parasite. Ptolemy, son of Lagos, satrap of Egypt, was the first to disregard the confused and divided authority of the zany king and his baby colleague. A general débâcle followed. Palestine suffered more than others, because it was unfortunately situated on the road to Egypt. But by about 300 B. C. E. the country was definitely settled as a province of Egypt, and it entered upon a century of extraordinary and varied growth.

It is just about this time that unmistakable knowledge of the Jews themselves, as a separate nationality of Syrians, is evidenced in extant Greek writers. Histories of the nearer and of the remote East, impressions of travel and concatenation of irresponsible gossip of all sorts had long been written by Greeks. Some of these may well have contained reference to the Jews. In the fifth century, Herodotus speaks of the " Syrians of Palestine " in connection with the rite of circumcision, which, he claims to know from the testimony of the Syrians themselves, was derived from Egypt.[11] However, he obviously writes at second hand, so that we have no means of knowing whether or not he refers to Jews. That he knew the name Ἰουδαῖοι is not likely, but the fact that his source was probably a literary one makes it possible to date the acquaintance of Greeks with the practice of circumcision in this region, and therefore perhaps with Jews, at least to the beginning of the fifth century B. C. E.

The peculiar natural phenomena of the Dead Sea attracted the attention of travelers from very early times. Aristotle discusses it, and after him—no doubt before him, as well—the collectors of wonder-tales, of which we have so many later specimens. Interest in the Dead Sea, however, by no means implied interest in those who dwelt on its borders, and the story of the bituminous formation on the water and the curious manner in which it was collected could be and was told without so much as a mention of the name of Jews.[12]

But they are mentioned, and for the first time in extant Greek writers, by the famous pupil and successor of Aristotle, Theophrastus of Lesbos. The passage does not occur in any one of the works of Theophrastus which we have in bulk, such as the Characters or the Natural History. It is a quotation made by the Neoplatonic philosopher Porphyrius, who wrote somewhere about 275 C. E. The quotation may, in accordance with ancient custom, be of substance rather than verbatim. Faulty memory may have further diminished its value for our purposes. When we add to these facts possible uncertainties in the transmission of the text of Porphyrius, we are in a fair way of realizing from what dubious material we must piece our knowledge together.

6

The passage is in itself, except perhaps for one casual phrase, strangely unimportant, but as the earliest plain reference to Jews in a Greek writer it deserves citation in full:

As a matter of fact, if the Jews, those Syrians who still maintain the ancient form of animal sacrifice, were to urge us to adopt their method, we should probably find the practice repellent. Their system is the following: they do not eat of the sacrificial flesh, but burn all of it at night, after they have poured a great deal of honey and wine upon it. The sacrifice they seek to complete rather rapidly, so that the All-Seer may not become a witness of pollution. Throughout the entire time, inasmuch as they are philosophers by race, they discuss the nature of the Deity among themselves, and spend the night in observing the stars, looking up at them and invoking them as divine in their prayers.

As Reinach points out,[13] there is scarcely a correct word in this description considered as an account of actual Jewish sacrificial rites. If we have a correct, or even approximately correct, version of Theophrastus' report, he or his informant was curiously misinformed. This informant obviously could not have been a Jew. No Jew could have been so ignorant of the customs of his people. Nor did his statement come directly from any one who had actually witnessed, from the Court of the Gentiles, even a small part of a Jewish sacrifice. It may well be that we have before us an inextricable confusion between Jewish and other Syrian rites. We are left to wholly uncontrolled speculation, if we are bent on knowing whence Theophrastus derived the assertions he makes here.

The important words of the passage are found in the casual phrase ἅτε φιλόσοφοι τὸ γένος ὄντες, " inasmuch as

they are philosophers by race." The phrasing indicates
that this aspect of the Jews is not wholly new. Word
had come to Theophrastus, and to others before him,
of a Syrian people not far from the coast, whose ritual
in some respects—though the transmission is confused
as to what respects—differed from that of their neighbors, but whose customs were strikingly different in
one particular, that part of their divine observance
was some form of theologic discussion. That, as we
know, was a fact, since " houses of prayer "—we may
call them synagogues—already existed. This reference
to them is the one kernel of observed fact in this whole
description, however indirectly obtained.

Now the Greeks of the fourth century knew of
esoteric religious communities, and they knew of
nations that professed to be especially attached to
religious practices. But groups of mystae engaged in
rapt spiritual converse were never coextensive with
entire nations. And " religious " nations might be simply those among whom an elaborate state cult was
punctiliously performed. Even theocracies were no
unheard-of thing. Sidon was such a theocracy; i. e.
theoretically ruled by the god and administered by his
priest.[14] But that too was largely formal, not strikingly
different from the patronage of Athena over Athens.
The Jewish theocracy was a more intensely real matter
than this, but that fact could not have been apparent to
either merchant or traveler, from whom in the last
analysis the information about Jews before 300 B. C. E.
must have come. If, therefore, Greeks found some-

thing in the religious customs of the Jews that aroused immediate attention, it was the very general interest and participation of the masses in the theological discussion as it was carried on in the synagogues.

This fact alone would justify the use of the term φιλόσοφοι, "philosophers." Theology, the knowledge of the high gods, was an accredited branch of wisdom which the Platonic Socrates strove with a little too palpable irony to elicit from Euthyphro.[15] Those who busied themselves with it were properly termed philosophers, whatever may have been the conclusions they reached. If we venture to assume that the conclusions which the Jews had long reached were actually known, Theophrastus' phrase could only have been confirmed. An exclusive monotheism was in every sense a philosophic and not a popular concept.

A contemporary of Theophrastus was Clearchus of Soli in Cyprus. Of his writings none whatever has survived, except quotations in other books. Among other works he wrote dialogues more or less after the Platonic manner, in which his master Aristotle is interlocutor in place of Socrates. One of these dialogues was marked, no doubt as a subtitle, περὶ ὕπνου, " On Sleep," and in this dialogue an encounter of Aristotle with a Hellenized Jew is described.

We need not seriously consider the question whether such an encounter actually occurred. It is not in the least likely that it did. The only inferences that may be drawn from this passage are those that concern Clearchus.

Aristotle is the narrator, and tells his story, as he takes pains to say, according to the rules formulated in Rhetoric.[16] He had met a man in Asia, a Jew of Coele-Syria by birth, but Grecized in speech and in soul. This Greek or Jew voluntarily sought out Aristotle and his associates, πειρώμενος αὐτῶν τῆς σοφίας, "to find out whether they were really as wise as their reputation." On the whole, however, he had given rather than received edification.[17]

What it was in this man's conversation that so strongly aroused the approval of Clearchus we are not told. Josephus, in whose *Contra Apionem* we find the passage, ends here, to tell us briefly that the rest of Aristotle's story described the man's great strength of character and the admirable self-control of his habits of life. It may be suspected that Clearchus' Jew is little more than a mouthpiece for his own ethical doctrines, a sort of fourth century *Ingénu*, or Candide.[18] But what he does actually say is of great interest.

We have here the first mention of the capital in the form Jerusalēmē, introduced, it may be noted, for its outlandish sound. And we have the statement, curious enough to our ears, that the Jews are descendants of Hindu philosophers, who bear the name of Jews in Syria and Calani in India. Elsewhere Clearchus asserts an exactly similar connection between the Persian magi and the Hindu gymnosophists.[19] It is obvious that Clearchus has the caste organization of the magi in mind, and that his knowledge of Jews is as mediate and remote as that of Theophrastus.

The connection of the Jews with India was evidently a hasty conclusion, arrived at when knowledge came to the Greeks of the existence of castes whose function was principally religious. The statement is repeated by a man who should have known better—Megasthenes, Seleucus' ambassador to India. "All that has been written on natural science by the old Greek philosophers," he tells us, "may also be found in philosophers outside of Greece, such as the Hindu Brahmans and the so-called Jews of Syria." [20] He is of course quite wrong as to the facts. But his statement is evidence of the wide currency of the opinion that the Jews possessed a very special and very profound lore. Megasthenes, it may be noted, does not state or imply that the Greeks were borrowers. If he had done so, the writer in whose book we find the citation, Clemens of Alexandria (about 180 c. e.), would have pounced upon it. Clemens was eagerly searching for demonstration of the thesis set up by many Jews and most early Christians, that all Greek science and philosophy were derived from an imagined early communication between Moses and the first Asiatic philosophers. [21]

Theophrastus, Clearchus, and Megasthenes, all of them belonging to the generation of or immediately after Alexander, hold largely the same views. Influence of one of them upon the others is practically excluded. We may find in them accordingly such knowledge of the Jews as at about 300 b. c. e. had reached educated Greeks.

If we try to imagine how this information reached them, we are reduced to pure speculation. It does not seem to have been a common literary source, although it is likely enough that in the numerous histories of the East, now lost, casual and inaccurate references were made to the Jews. And again it is not likely that the vastly increased communication that followed Alexander's campaign, at once brought the Jews much more prominently within the circle of Greek interest. In those days, the land-passage hugged the sea as closely as the sea-passage hugged the land. Judea was a little inland country, somewhat out of the line of direct communication between the Euphrates and the Nile. If then the current views, expressed as they are by Theophrastus and his contemporaries, had neither a literary source nor one of direct report, it can only have spread as an indirect, filtered rumor, perhaps by way of Phoenicians, Syrians, and Egyptians.

As far as Phoenicians and Syrians are concerned, immediate contact with the Jews must have existed. Tyrians and Sidonians and Philistines are frequently mentioned in the post-Exilic books of the Bible.[22] This contact was not wholly hostile, though it was often so; but if these nations were the sources of Greek information about the Jews, the hostility is not apparent. Perhaps in the generations between Zechariah and Alexander it had disappeared. At all events, it would appear that the Canaanite neighbors of the Jews really knew very little about them, except that the Jews were the residents of the hills about Jerusalem, and that they had highly characteristic religious rites—characteristic principally in the earnestness with which they were performed.

In Egypt, a country that had never ceased to be in communication with Greece from very early times, and particularly since the founding of a Greek city at Naucratis, in Egypt itself, about the middle of the sixth century B. C. E., there had been communities of Jews from times that antedated the Persian conquest. Into the situation here, newly discovered papyri at Assuan and Elephantine allow us a glimpse, but only a glimpse. Even the little we know includes one case of bitter conflict between Jews and Egyptians.[23] No doubt it was not the only case of its kind. Egyptians, we may be sure, knew of the Jews in the communities in which Jews lived, and one might suppose that Greek visitors to Egypt would at some time stumble across Jews there. However, our extant sources, which speak of Egyptians often enough, do not seem to have recognized the presence of foreign elements in the Egyptian population. It was reserved for the papyri to show us Persians, Syrians, Babylonians, and Jews established in the land as individuals and in groups.

The view of the Jews that represented them as a mystical sect did not cease when Judea became an important political factor in the East. One Greek thinker particularly had professed so strange and esoteric a doctrine that his biographers and critics inevitably looked for the source of it in non-Greek tribes and especially in those who had otherwise obtained a reputation for wisdom of various kinds. This was Pythagoras. Some seventy-five years after Theophrastus, Hermippus of Smyrna, in his Life of Pythagoras, ascribed certain definite doctrines of the latter to the Jews and Thracians.[21] Pythagoras as a matter of fact had traveled extensively, and had brought to his Italian home little fragments of exotic lore variously derived. That his philosophy was influenced by them, there is no sufficient proof, much less based upon them, and the general belief that he was so influenced had probably no sounder foundation than the indubitable strangeness of the rites he instituted and his personal mannerisms. But in later times Pythagoras was a name to conjure with for those who were bent on establishing a connection between the Jews and the Greeks. Hermippus had numerous imitators among later Jewish and Christian writers.

We shall of course never be able to discover the particular moment that marked the first meeting of Jew and Greek. The contact that is indicated in the words of Theophrastus or Megasthenes is already of some duration. The term Ἰουδαῖος has a definite meaning for educated Greeks. It denoted a Syrian sect, living together about their rock-citadel and akin in doctrine and probably in blood to the Persian Magi and Hindu gymnosophists. More exact information was scarcely available. The two non-Judean sections where Jews were to be found, Babylon and Egypt, were themselves strange and only partially understood regions to Greeks in spite of their long acquaintance with both of them.

CHAPTER VII
EGYPT

In the relations that subsisted between Jews and Greeks after Alexander, Egypt plays an important part, so that particular attention must be directed to that country.

The influence of Egypt upon Palestine is no new thing in its history. For century after century the mighty empire across Sinai had been the huge and determining fact in the political destiny of all Palestinian nations. Indeed Palestine is much more properly within the Egyptian sphere of culture than the Babylonian. The glamor lasted even when the Pharaoh had become a broken reed. Men's minds instinctively turned in that direction, and the vigor of the relatively youthful Assyria could not hold imaginations with half the force of the remembered glories of Thutmose and Ramses.

Egypt had been in Persian times a turbulent province, subdued with difficulty and demanding constantly renewed subjugation. Shortly before Alexander's conquest, Artaxerxes Ochus had reconquered it with brutal severity. It offered no resistance to the victorious Macedonians. Upon Alexander himself it exercised an undoubted attraction. The ancient gods of this most ancient of countries were those best fitted to confirm his rather raw divinity. From none else than Amon himself, in his isolated shrine in the desert, he claimed to have received revelation of his divine lineage. And at the mouth of the Nile he laid the foundation of the greatest monument he was destined to have, the city of Alexandria.

When Alexander's satraps proceeded to carve out portions for themselves, Egypt was seized by Ptolemy, whose quick brain had grasped at once the advantages accruing from the possession of an inexhaustible granary and from the relative remoteness of his position. The first contests would have to be fought in Asia. To attack Egypt meant a costly and carefully planned expedition, with the hazards of a rear attack. It was attempted, and it failed. Egypt might, as far as the country itself was concerned, breathe freely for a while, and give itself the opportunity of developing its extraordinary resources.

One of Ptolemy's first aggressive campaigns was the seizure of Palestine, the natural geographical extension. Judea and Jerusalem fell into his hands. It is probable, as will be later discussed, that the story of the capture of the city on the Sabbath is apocryphal. But there can be no doubt that one of the immediate consequences of the annexation of Palestine was a greatly increased emigration of Jews, and doubtless of Palestinians generally, to Egypt. There is the tradition of a deportation, but it is feebly supported. However, the emigration was unquestionably vigorously encouraged and stimulated by the king. The new city needed inhabitants, and Egyptians were as yet looked at askance by their Macedonian rulers.

From the beginning, a great number of Greeks, Jews, Persians, Syrians, and Egyptians dwelt side by side in Alexandria. Greeks who now spoke of Jews could do so at first hand, and they could also obtain at first hand accounts of Jews from other nations, especially from the Egyptians. When, therefore, at about this time, Hecataeus of Abdera, a Greek living in Egypt, wrote a history of that country, he had more to say of the Jews than that they were a Syrian caste of strange ritual. Indeed his account of them is so important that it will be briefly summarized.

A pestilence broke out in Egypt, which was popularly attributed to the neglect of the national cult owing to the presence of foreign elements in the population. To propitiate the gods, the strangers (ἀλλόφυλλοι) were expelled. The most distinguished and energetic, as some say, arrived in Greece led by famous chieftains, of whom Danaus and Cadmus are the best known. The mass of the population settled in the neighboring Palestine, which was then a desert.

This colony (ἀποικία) was led by a certain Moses, famous for his wisdom and valor. He founded several cities, of which Ierosolyma is now the best-known. Having organized cult and government, he divided the people into twelve tribes, because he considered that number the absolutely perfect one, and because it corresponded to the number of months in the year.

He made no statues of gods, because he regarded as
God and Ruler of all things the heavens that encircled
the earth, and accordingly did not believe that the Deity
resembled man in form. The sacrifices he instituted,
the manner of life he prescribed, were different from
those of surrounding nations. This was due to the
expulsion they had suffered, which induced Moses
to ordain an inhospitable (μισόξενον) and inhuman
(ἀπάνθρωπον) form of living.

Since the nation was to be directed by priests, he
chose for that purpose men of the highest character and
ability. These he instructed, not merely for their sacerdotal functions, but also for their judicial and governmental duties. They were to be the guardians of law
and morality.

It is for this reason that the Jews have never had a
king, but appoint as ruler the wisest and ablest of their
priests. They call him high priest (ἀρχιερεύς), and
regard him as bearer of the divine commands, which he
announces at the public assemblies and other meetings.
In this matter the Jews are so credulous that they fall to
the ground and adore (προσκονεῖν) the high priest when
he interprets the divine message. At the end of their
laws is written, " These words, which Moses heard from
God, he states to the Jews."

Moses showed much foresight in military matters,
since he compelled the young men to train themselves
by exercises that involved courage and daring and
endurance of privations. In his campaigns he conquered most of the surrounding territory, which was

divided equally among all citizens, except that the priests received larger shares, so that they might enjoy greater leisure for their public duties. These allotments the possessors were forbidden to sell, in order to prevent depopulation by the creation of great estates. As an additional means to that end he compelled every one to rear his children, an arrangement that involved little expense and made the Jews at all times a very populous nation. Marriage and funeral rites were likewise quite different from those of their neighbors.

However, many of these ancient customs were modified under Persian, and more recently under Macedonian, supremacy.[1]

So far Hecataeus of Abdera. The fragment is interesting, not merely as the first connected account of Jews by a Greek, but also from a number of facts that are contained implicitly in his narrative.

We have seen, in the previous chapter, what general knowledge of the Jews educated Greeks had in the latter half of the fourth century. Hecataeus could scarcely avoid being familiar with that version before he came to Egypt. That he ever was in Judea there is no evidence. If he followed his master Ptolemy, he might easily have been there. But the information he gives was almost certainly obtained in Egypt, and the sources of that information will be more closely examined.

It is evident at once that some of his facts must have come from contemporary Jewish sources. His statement of conditions among the Jews is markedly accurate

for the time in which he wrote, although to be sure these
conditions do not date to Moses. The absence of a king,
the presence of a priestly nobility, the judicial functions
of the priests, the compulsory military service, the
supremacy of the high priest, and the veneration
accorded to him, are all matters of which only a resident
of Judea can have been cognizant.

Was the source a literary one? Did Hecataeus, writing at about 300 B. C. E., have before him a translation
of the Bible or of the Pentateuch or a part of it? In the
first place there is very little reason to believe that such
a translation was current or was needed at this time.
Secondly, the matters mentioned are just those that do
not stand out at all in such a rapid reading of the Bible
as a curious Greek might have given it. To obtain even
approximate parallels, single verses of the Bible must
be cited. But the statements of Hecataeus do correspond to actual conditions in the Judea of his time. We
may therefore plausibly suppose that Hecataeus' informant was a Greek-speaking Jew, perhaps a soldier.
Certain inaccuracies in the account would not militate
against such a supposition. Whoever it was from
whom the information came, cannot himself have
been especially conversant with his national history.
The glorious period of Jewish history was that of the
kings, of David and Solomon. For any Jew to have
asserted that no king ever reigned over them is scarcely
conceivable. But that may be an inference of the Greek
and not a statement of the Jew, and that in Egypt there

were Jews crassly ignorant of everything but the facts of their own time, we can readily enough imagine.[2]

Was there any other source of information? Obviously no Jew told Hecataeus that his people were descendants of Egyptian outcasts, at least in the way in which they are here described; no Jew qualified the institutions of his people as " inhospitable and inhuman " ; no Jew represented his kinsmen as credulous dupes. Plainly these stories are told from the Egyptian point of view. The first almost surely is. It constitutes in outline what has often been called the " Egyptian version of the Exodus."

As to that version this question at once arises : What are its sources? Is it a malicious distortion of the Biblical story, or has it an independent origin in Egyptian traditions?

The former supposition is the one generally accepted. We have seen that there is little likelihood that a Greek translation of the Pentateuch existed as early as 300 B. C. E. If then the Egyptian version is consciously based upon the Jewish story, that story must have been known to the Egyptians by oral transmission only. Until recently, imagined difficulties in the way of assuming such a transmission seemed weighty objections, but all these difficulties have disappeared in the light of the Assuan and Elephantine papyri. The existence of Jewish communities in Egypt from pre-Persian times is established by them, and particular interest centers upon one of them, which alludes to the Passover cele-

bration and represents the Egyptian Jewries as referring certain questions to the Palestinian community.[2]

It must be clear that if Passover had been celebrated
in Egyptian surroundings for two centuries, the
Egyptian neighbors of the Jews knew of the feast's
existence and of the occasion it was intended to cele-
brate. In those two centuries the elements that make
this version an Egyptian one may easily have arisen.
Indeed, it would have been strange if stories representing the Exodus as anything but the Jewish triumph
it is depicted in the Pentateuch had not circulated
widely among Egyptians.

The mere celebration of Passover was apt to make
permanent a certain hostility between the two nations.
When we compare Deut. xxiii. 7, "Thou shalt not
abhor an Egyptian," with Ezra ix. 1, where the customs
of the Egyptians are classed as abominations, and where
Egyptian, Moabite, and Edomite are added to the list of
peoples (Deut. vii. 1) to be shunned and avoided, it is
plain that the attitude toward Egyptians had undergone
considerable change in the intervening centuries. It
requires a long period of antagonism to explain the later
Alexandrian anti-Semitism.

At the same time the papyri show other phases of
life as well. They offer instances of amicable relations,
even of intermarriage, as well as instances of hostility,
such as that which resulted in the destruction of the
shrine of Yahu at Elephantine. The latter incident is
too obscure to permit us to draw inferences from it.
But it is clear that it can no more be considered typical

7

than the other examples, which show perfectly free and friendly intercourse.

The story as it appears in Hecataeus, however, does not imply, even in its unflattering aspects, hostility on the part of the Egyptians. It may be remembered that the founders of several Greek nations as well as the Jews were expelled from Egypt on the occasion mentioned. It is easy to see how Egyptians, learning of Greek and Jewish legends that ascribed the origin of those nations to themselves, would accept the ascription, and make it a part of their own stories in a way to flatter the national vanity.

While therefore the supposition that Egyptians based their version on the Jewish story of the Exodus as it became known to them is much the more probable view, the possibility of an independent Egyptian tradition on the subject is not to be dismissed cavalierly.

The Egyptian records that have come down to us do not often mention Jews. Careful study has made it plain that the Pharaoh of the oppression or the Exodus cannot be identified so readily as was formerly done, but they have shown that the popular traditions about the Hyksos had at least so much foundation in fact, that about 1580 B. C. E. Ahmose I did actually drive out the Semitic or half-Semitic conquerors of the country, and these conquerors are quite plausibly identified with the Hyksos. Now during the Hyksos period we hear of a ruler named Jacob-Her, or Jacob-El, and a few centuries after the inscriptions of Mer-ne-ptah show Israel already established in Palestine. If, in the casual selec-

tion of inscriptions that has been made by the lapse
of thirty-five centuries, these facts appear, it is surely
not impossible that in 300 B. C. E. a great many more
facts were known. It is not likely that every Egyptian
priest could read the hieroglyphics, but some could, and
the knowledge of a few could easily become common
possession.

When Greeks came to Egypt in the train of Alexander and Ptolemy, they not only brought Jews there,
but they found them, as well as the story just discussed,
whether two hundred or twelve hundred years old.

When we meet the Egyptian version again, it is in a
form unmistakably malevolent. A very few years after
Hecataeus, an Egyptian priest named Manetho wrote
the history of his people in Greek. His sources were
popular traditions much more than the monuments, but
they were at least partly documentary. Manetho's book
has been lost, and its " fragments," as usual, appear in
the form of quotations in much later books, where we
must estimate the probabilities of wilful and careless
error.

The fragments of especial interest to us are contained in Josephus' apologetic work known as *Contra
Apionem* (§1, 26-27), where unfortunately one cannot
always distinguish between the statements of Josephus
and those of Manetho.

The essential part of Manetho's story, as far as we
can piece it together, is that the Exodus of the Jews
from Egypt was nothing more nor less than the defeat
and expulsion of certain rebellious Egyptians. These

latter had been isolated from their fellow-men as lepers and criminals, and had treasonably summoned to their aid the Bedouin Hyksos from Jerusalem. The Egyptian outcasts were led by a Heliopolitan priest named Osarsiph, who afterwards changed his name to Moses. After a short domination over Egypt, they were defeated and expelled, and pursued to the frontiers of Syria.

If the very indefinite words of Josephus are to be trusted (*Contra Apionem,* i. 26), Manetho expressly asserts that this account is based upon what is popularly told of the Jews (τὰ μυθευόμενα καὶ λεγόμενα περὶ τῶν Ἰουδαίων). Whether Manetho really said so or not, it is extremely unlikely that it was the case. The account seems too finished and detailed to have such an origin. It is much more likely that it is a deliberate invention of Manetho himself, following the Jewish story with a certain amount of care. As has been suggested, the name Osarsiph is simply an Egyptian version of Joseph, the name of Osiris (which often appears as Osar- or Osor- in names)⁴ being substituted for the assumed theophoric element Jo-, a syllable that would be familiar to all Egyptians in such very common Jewish names as Johanan and Jonathan.

The "Egyptian version" as we found it in Hecataeus is far from malevolent. In Manetho it is plainly inspired by hatred. The Jews are represented as the mongrel offspring of Egyptian outcasts and half-civilized Bedouins. The vice of unsociability is reasserted, coupled with a charge of "atheism," a term we shall have to deal with later in detail. Moses, or Osarsiph, forbade the Jews " to have any dealings with anyone whatsoever except their confederates (συνωμοσμένοι). That is, of course, more precise than the words " inhospitable and inhuman manner of life " of Hecataeus, and formed in ancient times a more serious indictment than in our own.

Now Josephus, of course, is roused to considerable heat by the " silly lies " of Manetho, although as testimony to the antiquity of his people the story is grist to his mill. He points out very clearly and correctly that many of the incidents are admissions that the corresponding incidents of the Jewish story are essentially true. These admissions do not prove that Manetho read these matters from the hieroglyphic records, but merely that he knew the Jewish story, and, except for the confusion of Moses and Joseph, that he knew it well.

Nearly all Manetho's details are suggested in some way by the Biblical story. The leprosy of Osarsiph is probably derived from the story of Moses (Exodus iv. 7) ; the convicts in the quarries (οἱ ἐν ταῖς λατομίαις), from the bondage which the Jews acknowledged of themselves (Exodus i. 12-14). Manetho cannot accept Joseph's rule nor Pharaoh's discomfiture at the Red Sea, but, as many other ancient and modern writers did, he will not absolutely deny what he wishes to avoid, but prefers to present it in a form less galling to his pride. Osarsiph did rule over Egypt, but his rule was a chastisement of the Egyptians for the impiety of King

Amenophis, and was effected only by the aid of foreign mercenaries. Pharaoh did advance to " the river " with a picked army and then withdraw before the enemy, but it was a voluntary withdrawal, impelled by his fear of the offended gods.[5]

It is by no means impossible that all the facts implied may have been learned by Manetho through oral acquaintance with the Jewish story of the Exodus. But if Manetho acquired his information so, we should expect confusion in the sequence of events. We should find anachronisms of various sorts. It is therefore more likely that he had an actual book before him. Tradition of strong intrinsic probability assigns the translation of the Pentateuch into Greek to the reign of Philadelphus. Writing at about 270 B. C. E., Manetho may well have read the Pentateuch, at least cursorily. Indeed it would be easy to suppose that it was the circulation in Greek of stories so offensive to Egyptians that specially moved him to publish his own interpretation of those stories. He was hardly likely to have made so much of them, if they were merely legends, scarcely known except to the Jews themselves and their closest neighbors.

The "Egyptian version" may be said to have been the more successful. The leprosy of Moses, the founder of the nation, was constantly girded at by later writers. Tacitus repeats Manetho faithfully in the matter,[6] and one of the latest pagan writers of whom we have fragments concerning the Jews, Helladius, makes allusion to the same thing.[7] The point does not seem to us of capital importance, but among peoples that regarded bodily defects as obvious signs of divine displeasure in the person afflicted, it was likely to have weight.

It may, however, be well to remember that both versions were in equal circulation. To many the Jewish story seemed the more probable. But it is significant that at the very beginning of the period when the Jews took a larger share in the life of the Mediterranean world we find Jews and Egyptians distinctly in conflict. That conflict was destined to become embittered, but it must not be taken as an epitome of Jewish relations generally with other nations.

CHAPTER VIII
JEWS IN PTOLEMAIC EGYPT

Greek civilization was essentially urban. The city-state, or polis, was its highest governmental achievement. When, therefore, under Alexander and Ptolemy, Egypt was to be transferred wholly within the sphere of Greek culture, it was by means of a polis that this was to be effected.

The same was still more largely true for the other parts of Alexander's empire. In Asia and Syria the "Successors" were busy founding, wherever convenient, cities diversely named. However, in these regions they were merely continuing, in a somewhat accelerated fashion, a practice begun long before. In Egypt, on the contrary, it was plain that a modification of that policy was necessary. There was, to be sure, an ancient Greek city at one of the western mouths of the Nile, the city of Naucratis. But that had been founded as an emporium, and due care was taken that it should be essentially nothing more, that it should acquire no supporting territory in Egypt. And however important and wealthy Naucratis became, it remained confined to its foreign trade for its subsistence.[1] Besides, it had considerably dwindled in 330 B. C. E., so that its claims could never have been seriously considered by Alexander, in comparison with his desire to

found a new city and in comparison with the much
superior location of Alexandria.

It is not likely that Alexander himself completed the
plans for the organization of the city. That was left to
Ptolemy, and it was accomplished with a modification
of the Greek system that illustrates both the wariness
and the foresight of this most astute of Alexander's
officers.

The essential part of the polis was its organization as
a commonwealth, *i. e.* as a group of citizens, each of
whom had a necessary function to perform in the state.
From time immemorial the administration of affairs
was assigned to a boulē, or senate, the actual executives
being little more than committees of the boulē; but at
all times an essential element of the constitution was the
confirmation, real or constructive, of all acts of the
boulē by the dēmos, or mass of citizens. The manner in
which the boulē was selected, as well as the extent to
which the check exercised by the dēmos was real, determined the measure of democracy each polis obtained.
However, even in cities which, like Sparta, were in
theory permanent camps, the same view was held of the
necessity of these parts and of their respective functions, so that everywhere, in legal contemplation,
sovereignty resided in the dēmos [1]

It must not be supposed that all men who lived within
the walls of the city were members of the dēmos. That
is a conception of democracy wholly alien to ancient
ideas. The participation of the individual in the state
was a privilege, acquired in the first instance by birth.

Side by side with the citizens was the slave, who was wholly devoid of legal rights, and the metic, or resident foreigner, who had, as a result of a direct compact with the state, acquired the right of residence and personal protection upon the payment of certain specified taxes.

The privilege of citizenship was a complex of rights, to which were attached certain very definite and sharply emphasized obligations. What those rights were depended upon the constitution of the given polis. Where they were fullest, as at Athens, they included voting in the public assembly, the holding of public office, service on the jury, and a claim for certain personal privileges, such as admission to the dramatic performances at the Dionysiac festivals. In other states they were not quite so extensive, but the obligations were everywhere the same, *i. e.* payment of taxes and military service. The state was in the habit of remitting from time to time certain or all of these taxes and other compulsory services, so that we may say that various grades of citizens and metics generally existed.

Now Naucratis was just such a polis as this. So were the various Apameas, Antiochias, Seleucias, Laodiceas, established in Asia and Syria. It is true that the boulē and dēmos of these cities were the merest shadows; and actually the despotism of the monarch was as undoubted as it had been in Persian times. But the shadows were at least a concession to the Hellenic spirit, and as such were immensely treasured; nor can it be denied that as long as they remained the remembrance of free institutions remained as well. At

Pergamon, which the Attalids created, no public act
was done except as the deliberate choice of senate and
people.[3]

But when Ptolemy constituted Alexandria, he deliberately departed from this plan. As has been said,
Naucratis had boulē and dēmos and all the other
appurtenances of a well-regulated polis. So had Ptolemais somewhat later; and many years later, when the
emperor Hadrian founded an Antinois in memory of his
dead minion, he likewise made it a full and complete
Greek city. In Alexandria, on the other hand, there is
no trace, till late in Roman times, of a boulē; and of a
dēmos as little. In the great mass of Greek papyri
that have come from Egypt there is nowhere any indication that a senate ever met, or a people ever assembled,
to parody the deliberations of the Athenian ecclesia.
In other words Alexandria was much less a polis than it
was a royal residence, *i. e.* the site of the king's palace
amidst a more densely gathered group of his subjects.[4]

In externals Alexandria was every inch a city. It
had the high walls, which, as Alcaeus tells us, do *not*
constitute a state. It had the tribe and deme, or district
division, and it had its various grades of citizens, determined by the duties and imposts to which they were
subjected.

Of its tribe and district division we know some
details. There were probably five tribes, each of which
consisted of twelve demes, or districts, which in turn
had twelve phratries, or wards. The tribes were known
by the first five letters of the Greek alphabet. In the

absence of even formal political rights, this division
can have been made simply in the interests of the census
and the police. The obligations to pay taxes and perform military service were very real ones, and their
proper enforcement necessitated some such organization of the city.[6]

Different classes of citizenship were at once created
by the establishment of special taxes and special exemptions. The peculiar Greek fiscal arrangement known
as the liturgy, which made the performance of certain
services to the state a means of compounding for taxes,
was also in vogue. We have records of certain of these
classes of citizens, or inhabitants, and it is at least probable that there were other classes of which we know
nothing.

First of all, there were the Macedones, or Macedonians. These form a specially privileged group,
whose residence was probably by no means confined to
Alexandria. Just what their privileges were we do not
know, but that they lay chiefly in fiscal exemptions of
one sort or another, is almost certain.

Then there were the Alexandreis, or Alexandrians.
We know that there were at least two groups—those
that were enrolled in a given tribe, or deme, and those
not so enrolled. We can only conjecture the purpose of
this division, and one conjecture will be mentioned later.

Besides these, there were other men whose legal right
to residence was unquestioned. They were variously
designated. We find Persians, Jews, and other nationalities, qualified with the phrase τῆς ἐπιγονῆς. which means

literally " of the descent," but the exact force of which is unknown. This classification procured for those so termed certain very much valued exemptions. Native Egyptians also were present, paying a special poll-tax, and no doubt a very large number of metics and transient foreigners. Greek publicists regarded the presence of a large number of metics and foreign merchants as a sign of great prosperity.* We may be sure that no burdensome restrictions made the settling of these classes difficult at Alexandria.

Were the Jews in Alexandria citizens? A great many heated controversies have been fought on this subject, some of which would surely not have been entered into if a clearer analysis had been available of what constituted Alexandrian " citizenship." As we have seen, the question can only be framed thus: Did the Jews of that city appear on the census books as " Alexandreis," with or without the deme and tribe adjective after them, or were they classified as Jews, and did they form a distinct fiscal class by themselves?

The denial of their citizenship is principally based upon distrust of Josephus, who asserts it. But distrust of Josephus may be carried to an extravagant degree. Modern writers with pronounced bias may, of course, be disregarded, but saner investigators have equally allowed themselves to be guided by disinclination to credit Josephus, and have come to the conclusion that the Jews were not citizens of Alexandria.

There were of course very many Jews in Alexandria who were not legally Alexandrians. Josephus' assertion did not and could not mean that every Jew in the city was, by the very fact of his residence, an Alexandrian. Nowhere in the ancient world could citizenship be acquired except by birth or by special decree. Jews who emigrated from Palestine to Alexandria, and were permitted to remain there, were metics, and became Alexandrians only if they were specially awarded that designation. But that was just as true for a foreign Greek or a foreign Macedonian, since at Alexandria " Macedonian " was a class of citizenship, not an ethnic term. Those who assisted in the founding of the city were undoubtedly classified either as " Macedones " or " Alexandreis," and the tradition that Jews were among them is based upon other authority than Josephus. It is not enough, therefore, if one desires to refute Josephus, to show that there were Jews in Egypt who were not " Alexandreis." Undoubtedly there were thousands of them. But if, in the papyri, we do find Jews among the " Macedones " and others among the " Alexandreis," the statements of Josephus on the sub- ject are strikingly confirmed, for he says no more than that there were Jews in both these categories.[1]

Of the two classes of Alexandrians, those enrolled in demes and those not so enrolled, it is likely that the Jewish " Alexandreis " belonged to the latter class. The former either paid a special district tax, or, more likely, were charged with the performance of certain district duties, either religious in their nature, such as the burying of the pauper dead, or of police character. When Alexandrians were constituted, not registered in demes, the purpose can only have been to secure exemption from these local duties, and the example quoted would of itself indicate why the Jews may have been so exempted.

It was not, however, merely in Alexandria that the Jews settled, precisely as it was not merely in Greek cities that Greeks were to be found. That part of Egypt which lay outside the definite civic communities as they were founded from time to time, was organized in nomes, in large agricultural districts containing many villages or even cities. In every instance, however, the administrative unit was the nome.

These nomes had themselves a history of immemorial antiquity. Some of them were surely in boundary coincident with the petty nationalities that antedated the first dynasties. The mass of the population in them had practically always been peasant-serfs, and continued to be so. Beside them, in the villages and towns, there lived in Greek times motley groups of men, whose legal status was determined in a number of ways. Some were citizens of Alexandria, Ptolemais, etc., and merely resident in the nome. Others enjoyed certain military and fiscal privileges, which involved the right of residence. But in all circumstances, in the elaborate financial organization of Egypt every resident had certain precise dues to pay, and was marked by a certain designation.

The military and other settlers whom the Greeks found in Egypt, whether they were Persians, Jews, Syrians, or Babylonians, retained their status, *i. e.* they paid taxes and performed services differing from those of the native Egyptians in part, although no doubt certain taxes were levied upon all. The foreigners whom Ptolemy invited or brought into Egypt must have been settled either in the cities or the nomes, and were given a definite fiscal status. And besides all these various grades, there were metics—a term which may have included emancipated slaves, and of course slaves as well—in huge numbers. There can be little doubt that Jews were to be found in all classes, from the highly privileged nobility of " Macedones " to the slaves.[8]

In most large Greek cities metics of foreign birth or ancestry existed. There were Phoenicians and Egyptians in Athens in very early times. But they were all, together with non-Athenian Greeks, gathered into the general group of metics, and no one group ever became numerically so preponderant that a special class had to be legally constituted of them. In Egypt, however, the general term metic was rarely used. For the nome organization of the country it seemed scarcely applicable. Instead, those foreigners who had acquired legal residence and other rights were known by their national name. So there was a group of Egyptian residents known as Ἰουδαῖοι, as " Jews," which was in their case a legal designation, whereas, when the " Macedones," " Alexandreis," etc., of the same nationality were referred to as Ἰουδαῖοι, the term was merely descriptive.

We do not know whether the Ἰουδαῖοι that had no other classification were more numerous or less numerous than those who had. But it was shortly found advisable to organize the Jewish metics to the extent of superadding upon their own cult-organizations certain royal officers responsible to the king. Of these the chief was the ethnarch, and it is evident that the ethnarch would assume an importance in proportion to the number under his jurisdiction. The right to have an ethnarch seems to have been a prized privilege and was not confined to the Jews. What the relation of the later alabarch ⁹ was to the ethnarch is not clear. The two terms may perhaps designate the same office.

But a complete understanding of the condition of the Jews in Egypt and Alexandria necessitates some account of the synagogue organization.

There is no reason to question the Jewish tradition that the synagogue was Exilic or pre-Exilic in origin. In fact, it is not easily conceivable that it could have been otherwise. Worship was a social act in the ancient world, and properly to be performed in concert. It was inevitable therefore that just as soon as the Jews were removed from those places where the ancestral and traditional ritual was performed without any conscious organization for that purpose, they would combine themselves in groups in order to satisfy the strongly marked religious emotion that characterized them.

Corporate organization, based upon the performance in common of some religious act, characterized the whole ancient world. The state was itself a large corporation of this kind, and the local divisions rapidly assumed, or always possessed, the same form.

8

Obviously members of the same nationality residing in a foreign city would be specially prone to organize themselves into such corporations, and as a rule make the religious bond, which seems to have been a formal requisite, the common worship of one of their own gods. The merchants of Citium at Athens formed a guild for the worship of the Cyprian Aphrodite. It was in this way that Egyptian merchants and artisans made Isis known to the Roman world.[10]

It has been said that the state itself was such a corporation, of which the formal basis was the common performance of a certain ritual act. When new states were founded or new men admitted into old states, a great deal was made of the act. It follows therefore that when Jews were admitted into the newly founded civic communities of Asia, as we know they were, some relation would have to be entered upon between themselves and the religious basis of the state. In most cases, special exemption from participation in these religious acts seems to have been sought and obtained.

In Egypt the conflict between the exclusive worship of Jehovah and the less intolerant worship of the Nile-gods had been in existence for centuries before the Greeks. The pre-Greek Jewish immigrants were perhaps not of the sort that sought to accentuate the conflict, though friction was unavoidable. At the Greek conquest, it must be remembered, no great disposition was shown by the first Ptolemies to accept the native institutions or the native gods. The new god of Alexandria, the mighty Sarapis, was not, as has been generally supposed, a composite of Osiris and Apis, but an out and out Greek god, imported from his obscure shrine in direct opposition to the indigenous gods.[11] Membership in the civic communities or residence in the country districts, can have involved no obligation to share the ritual localized there Every group of foreigners might freely disregard it, and maintain unimpaired their own ancestral forms.

We accordingly find Jewish synagogues—in the sense of cult-organizations, each having its own meeting-house, schola, or proseucha, and organized with magistrates and council, like miniature states— not only in Alexandria but in insignificant little towns of Upper and Lower Egypt.[12] Nor was the legal basis of such organization wanting, *i. e.* the corporate personality, since we find these synagogues enjoying the rights of property and subject to the imposts levied upon it.[13] The extent of each synagogue was limited by the physical capacity of the schola. There must have been in Alexandria very many of them.

Who were members of them? The various classes of Jews in the city and country were divided by social and legal lines. In the synagogue social distinctions cannot have disappeared, but there can be no doubt that in many, if not in all, there would be found Jews representing every class of the community. In other parts of the Greek world it was no strange thing to see citizens, metics, foreigners, slaves, claiming membership in the same cult-organization, and jointly worshiping a native or foreign god. The synagogue likewise con-

tained among its members nobles and slaves. The
tendency for the wealthier classes to become completely
Hellenized, and so completely to abandon the synagogue, did not show itself prominently for some time.

We may readily suppose that the native Egyptians
regarded all the foreign invaders with scarcely discriminating hatred. In most cases, when Greeks and
Jews dwelt in the nomes, they were both exempt from
local dues, and both paid the same special tax. What
the attitude of the Egyptians was to their Greek and
Macedonian masters, we have no need to conjecture.[14]
As under Persian rule, they rose in bloody riots; and
after a century of Greek domination, they were so far
successful that a complete change in the policy of the
Ptolemies was effected. The house had very rapidly
degenerated—a process perhaps hastened by the Egyptian custom of brother and sister marriage, which they
adopted. From the weaker kings of the close of the
third century B. C. E., the Egyptian priests received a
complete surrender. Continuity with the Pharaohs was
consciously sought. The ancient titles in a modified
form were adopted in Greek as well as Egyptian for the
rulers. The hieroglyphics represented Ptolemy as the
living god, sprung from Ra, just as they had done for
Amen-hem-et thousands of years before.[15]

But a Hellenizing process had gone on as well as an
Egyptizing process. The irresistible attractions of Greek
culture had converted even the fiercest nationalists into
Greeks outwardly, and in the horde of Greek names
that the papyri exhibit we have sometimes far to seek,

if we wish to discover unmistakably Greek stock. Inter-marriage and concubinage must have given Egypt a large mixed-blood population, which no doubt called itself Greek. Evidences of Greek aloofness on the subject of marriage have been sought in the denial of connubium by the city of Ptolemais to foreigners.[16] But that applied to foreign Greeks as well, and was a common regulation in most Greek cities.

The Hellenizing process affected the Jews even more. In Alexandria the Jewish community had begun to show signs of the most active intellectual growth, and the results of that growth, naturally enough, wore a Greek dress. But that process had been active in Palestine as well, where the consequences were somewhat more important. It is there that we shall turn for a study of the first conflicts between Judaism and Hellenism.

CHAPTER IX

THE STRUGGLE AGAINST GREEK CULTURE IN PALESTINE

While Palestine was a Greco-Egyptian province, the influences at work over the whole Levant had been as effectually operative there.

In the matter of government no change had been made that was at all noticeable. The internal autonomy of Persian times had been maintained; the claims of the tax-collector and recruiting sergeant were dealt with by the whole community, not by the individual.

Socially and economically, relative peace had permitted considerable progress. At the close of this period the work of Ben Sira is the best of all possible evidence, both of the literary productivity out of which the book arose and of the society which it implies. We are given glimpses of settled and comfortable life, which could scarcely have been attained unless the preceding century had been one of constantly increasing well-being. It is a well-equipped table at which Ben Sira bids us sit. The graces and little luxuries of life are present, and equally the vices that went with these luxuries.[1]

Nor had the character of the whole spiritual culture essentially changed. The language of daily intercourse was Aramaic, the *lingua franca* of the whole region.

But the literary language was still Hebrew. It must have been constantly spoken among educated men, for the changes it continued to exhibit are not such as would occur if it had been quite divorced from life. And the literary activity, which took its forms from the established and already canonical literature, took its substance from the life about it. That this life had been impregnated with Greek elements, there can of course be no manner of doubt.

Not only the old Philistian and Phoenician cities of the coast had acquired a Greek varnish, but Judea was being surrounded by a closer and closer network of new Greek foundations. Ptolemais, Anthedon, Apollonia, Arethusa, and the cities of the Decapolis across the Jordan, brought the external forms of Greek culture so near that even the peasant who went no great distance from his furrow must have encountered them.

What made up the fascination of Greece for the nations she dominated? In the first place it must be insisted upon that there was a national resistance, whether or not it took the form of insurrection. Indeed, insurrection was a thing quite apart from resistance to Hellenism. As we have seen in the case of Egypt, national resistance to the political domination of Greeks did not by any means imply national resistance to the spread of Greek culture. The latter resistance generally took the form of a dull and obstinate clinging to ancestral ritual and language. At Antioch in the fourth century c. e., some men and women still spoke Aramaic, and knew no Greek.[*] It is only within the rather narrow limits set by wealth and education that the Hellenization was really effective. Unfortunately most of our available evidence is concerned with this class.

Among these men, who were naturally open to cultural impressions, the attraction of Hellenism was undoubted, and had been growing slowly for years before Alexander, and it had meant for them all the charm of an intellectual discovery. The mere fact that what the Greeks had was new and different could have been of no real influence. There must have been an actual and evident superiority in Greek life or culture to have drawn to itself so quickly the desires and longings of alien peoples.

In one field that superiority was evident, in the field of art. Whatever may have been the origins of Greek art, from the seventh century on no one seriously questioned that Greek workmen could produce, in any material, more beautiful objects than any other people. Artistic appreciation is no doubt a plant of slow growth, but the pleasure in gorgeous coloring, in lifelike modeling, in fine balances of light and shade, in grouping of masses, is derived immediately from the visual sensation. No peasant of Asia could fail to be impressed by his first glimpse of such a city as the Ephesus and Miletus of even the sixth or fifth century. After the extraordinary artistic progress of the fifth century had vastly increased the beauty of Greek cities, every foreigner who visited them must have found greater and greater delight, as his knowledge grew broader and deeper.

In other branches of art, in music, poetry, dancing, the wealthier Asiatic had a training of his own. But it is likely that even a slight acquaintance with Greek taught him to depreciate the achievements of his own people. Doubtless, in poetic capacity and imagination, Phrygian, Lydian, or Lycian was the equal of Greek. Yet we have no choice but to believe that in sheer sensuous beauty of sound, which made a direct appeal to any partly cultivated ear, no one of the languages could compare with Greek. Nor is it likely that any written literature existed in Asia that could be ranked with Greek.

With the appeal to eye and ear there went an appeal to the intellect. Greek mental capacity was not demonstrably greater than that of the Asiatic peoples to whom the Greeks were perhaps akin, but both imagination and reflection had framed their results in systematic form. The rich narrative material found in every race was available in Greek in dramatic and finished pieces. The philosophic meditation in which others had long anticipated the Greeks was among the latter set forth in clearer and simpler phrasing.

The allurement of all these things was intensified by a franker and fuller exploitation of all physical instincts, and the absence of many tabus and forms of asceticism that existed among non-Greek peoples. A vastly increased freedom over one's body seemed a characteristic of Greek life, and a vastly greater freedom of political action was characteristic of the Greek polis.

It is small wonder therefore that the upper classes of
Asia and Syria had for two or three centuries before
the conquest succumbed to a culture that possessed so
visible a sorcery. Then, with the conquest, came a new
factor. To be a Greek was to be a *Herrenmensch,* a
member of the ruling caste, a blood-kinsman of the
monarch. Syrians, Asiatics, and Egyptians found
themselves under the direct sway of a Greek dynasty,
supported by a Greek court and army. All the tendencies that had made Greek cultural elements attractive for certain classes were intensified by the eager
desire of the Greeks to identify themselves with the
dominant race, and this identification seemed by no
means impossible of achievement.

What had to be given up? As far as language was
concerned, a smattering of Greek was the common
possession of many men. Every trading-post had for
generations swarmed with Greek merchants. Greek
mercenaries were to be found in most armies. It was
no especially difficult matter for those classes which
knew a little Greek to increase their familiarity with it,
to multiply the occasions for its use, to sink more and
more the soon despised vernacular. The latter, we must
repeat, was not and could not be suppressed, but it
became the language of peasants. In the cities men
spoke Greek.

But there were other things—the ancestral god and
the ancestral ritual. These were not so readily discarded. However, the attitude of the Greeks in this
matter made it unnecessary to do so. The gods of

Greece were often transplanted, but rarely more than the name. In Syria and Asia particularly it was only in wholly new foundations that Greek gods and Greek forms were really established. Generally the sense of local divine jurisdiction was keenly felt. Greeks had a wholesome awe of the deity long in possession of a certain section, and in many cases erected shrines to him, invoking him by the name of some roughly corresponding Hellenic god. Frequently the old name was retained as an epithet. Thus Greek and Syrian might approach the ancient lord of the soil in the ancient manner and so perpetuate a bond which it was ἀσέβεια, " impiety," to break.

Since the essentials were maintained, the only step necessary to turn a Syrian into a Greek was to purchase a himation, change his name of Matanbal to Apollodorus, and the transformation was complete. He might be known for several years as " ὁ καὶ Matanbal " —" *alias* Matanbal "; he might suffer a little from the occasional snobbishness of real Greeks, but, especially if he was wealthy, such matters would be of short duration. The next generation would probably escape them altogether, and their children, the young Nicanors, Alexanders, Demetriuses, would talk glibly of the exploits of their ancestors at Marathon or under the walls of Troy.

But there was also no inconsiderable group that combined adoption of the new with loyalty or attempted loyalty to the old. Many Syrians, Egyptians, Phoenicians, and others, conscious of a history not without glory, desired to acquire the undeniably attractive Hellenic culture, while maintaining their racial ties, of which they felt no real reason to be ashamed. That was particularly true of the Seleucid dominions where Alexander's assimilative policy was consistently pursued. Persian or Lydian or Phoenician descent was a thing many men boasted of. It was with a sense of adding something to the culture of the world that natives with Greek training prepared to transmit in Greek forms the history of their people to Greeks and to interpret their institutions to them. And they found a ready enough audience. On many points, especially in religion and philosophy, the Greeks were willing enough to concede a more profound acquaintance to barbarians than they themselves possessed; and often the weariness of civilization made Greeks search among fresher peoples for a sound social life, since that life was tainted, in Greek communities, by many grave diseases.

But people of this class found themselves in a delicate situation, an unstable equilibrium constantly disturbed. It was hard to remain a Grecized Syrian. Generally the temptation to suppress the Syrian was well-nigh irresistible. Now and then, the rise of national political movements would claim some of the younger men, so that the fall was on the native side. In general, the older conservative attitude expressed itself naturally in avoidance of Greeks as far as possible, and precisely in proportion to the value set upon the national and indigenous culture.

The situation of the Jews was only in so far unique that there could be no question among them of gradual steps in the acquisition of Greek culture, but only of partial acceptance of it. The final step of interchanging gods—of accepting the Greek name and maintaining the old rite and of exercising that reciprocity of religious observance which was a seeming necessity for those who lived in the same region—that, as every Jew was aware, could never be taken. The religious development among the Jews had been fuller than elsewhere, and had resulted in a highly specialized form, which by that fact had none of the elasticity of other cult-forms. It was easy to make any one of the Baalim of local Syrian shrines into Zeus Heliopolitanus, Zeus Damascenus, etc. It was not possible to turn the Lord Zebaoth of Zion, the awful and holy God of psalm and prophecy, into an epithet of Zeus or of another.

Consequently Jews who felt the pull of Greek art and literature, who, like other subjects of Greek sovereigns, were eager to gain the favor of their masters, had to realize to themselves the qualifications of their Hellenism, or determine to discard wholly their Judaism. And this latter step, even to enthusiastic Philhellenes, was intensely difficult. For so many generations " Thou shalt have no other gods " had been inculcated into men's hearts that it was no simple thing to undertake in cold blood to bow before the abominations of the heathen.

He who could not do that—and there were many—might feel free to adopt Greek language and dress and name ; but, even more than Babylonian and Egyptian, he was conscious of making a contribution of his own to the civilization of the East. An inherited wisdom, which was in effect closer communion with the Absolute, he believed he had, and, as we have seen, he was generally credited with having. He felt no need therefore of yielding unreservedly to the claims of Greeks, but might demand from them the respect due to an independent and considerable culture.

Barriers to mutual comprehension were created by the Jewish dietary regulations as well as by ritual intolerance. Courtesy and good breeding however might soften and modify what they could not remove, and social intercourse between Greek and Jew certainly existed. Nor need we exaggerate the embarrassments these relations would suffer from the fact that while a Greek might, and doubtless would, assist at the little ceremonies of his Jewish neighbor's household, the Jew might not without sin reciprocate. By judicious absence on occasion—perhaps by little compromises—the average easy-going Jewish citizen of an Asiatic or Egyptian community need not have found himself in constant conflict.

As in the case of other nations, the first Greek-speaking Jews that desired to emphasize their origin while accepting the all-pervading Greek culture, wished primarily to convey to Greeks the facts of their history and institutions. The Septuagint, at least the Penta-

teuch, was probably written in the early part of the
third century B. C. E., and although primarily intended
for Jews, no doubt came within the knowledge of
Greeks as well. But its purpose was utilitarian. The
Greek-speaking synagogues absolutely needed it. If
others were to be acquainted with the history of the
Jews, some other means had to be devised.

About 225 B. C. E., an Egyptian Jew named Demetrius
wrote the history of his people in Greek. Unfortunately we have only such fragments of his work as
Eusebius, the church historian, and Josephus have
chosen to quote; but what we have, permits the conjecture that he wrote in a concise and simple style, without oratorical embellishment, and obviously without
apologetic motives. It seems to have been a sober and
dignified narrative, the loss of which is a serious gap in
our records.[3]

The name of this man, Demetrius, is not without
significance. It contains the name of a Greek deity,
Demeter, so that religious precisians might find in it an
honor—even if only a verbal one—to the Abomination.
But Alexandrian Jews were not likely to be religious
precisians, and we may readily suppose that these
names, attrited by constant use, did not immediately
convey the suggestion of being theophoric. In 238
B. C. E., an Arsinoite slave is named Apollonius or
Jonathas, and about the same time a Jewess is found
with the name of Heraclea.[4]

In the case of Demetrius it was rather the redoubtable Besieger than the goddess that was honored, just

as the very first Jew whom we know by a Greek name, Antigonus of Socho, is probably named after Demetrius' father, the one of Alexander's officers who became so nearly a real Successor. It is to be noted that Antigonus of Socho is one of the earliest doctors of the law, whose fine saying is recorded in Abot i.,[5] and, although we know no Hebrew name for him, there can be no question here of Hellenizing or partly Hellenizing tendencies.

Otherwise Jews in adopting Greek names were prone to translate them approximately. The common Jonathan and Nathaniel became Theodotus, Dositheus, Theodorus, and the like. Phoenicians had long done the same, but there would be of course no difficulty in the case of the latter if they chose to turn Meherbal into Diodorus. That the Jews were scarcely more scrupulous in this matter is a little surprising. It fits in well however with the conclusion that friction in unessentials was rather avoided than invited by the average Jew.[6]

The conflict that was preparing itself in Palestine was not one between Greek and Jew, but between Hellenizing and reactionary elements among the Jews themselves. And the term reactionary is chosen advisedly. In the many centuries that had witnessed the slow spread of Hellenism, and the hundred years or so in which that progress had been immensely accelerated by the political domination of Greeks, a resistance was also preparing itself. In the early years of the movement, before and after Alexander, the numbers affected had been too few to justify active opposition. But the number became constantly greater, and the imminence of a real peril became vividly present to thinking men. The method of opposition was at once indicated. It could be only a conscious restoration of such national institutions as had lapsed into comparative disuse, a recultivation of ancient national practices, and a more intense and active occupation with the traditional sacred literature.

In just this way opposition to the orientalizing of the imperial religion produced the reactionary reforms of Augustus, and much later opposition to an excessive clerical interference with life expressed itself in the very real paganism of the Italian Renaissance. In all these instances the attempt was deliberately made to rebuild with material still present, even if largely discarded, a structure that had fallen into ruins. The success of such movements depends wholly on the amount of material still present. If it has to be painfully gathered and swept together from forgotten corners, success is more than problematic. The Jewish reactionaries were fortunate in that the ancient institutions still held their ground, and in having no huge gap of disuse to fill.

They were also fortunate that the actively Hellenizing party was limited in numbers, and the line of demarcation was the easily noticeable one of wealth and position. Not all men of wealth were in this class. Such a man as Ben Sira, in whose book some have detected Greek elements, betrays no Hellenizing ten-

9

dencies.[7] He is Jew to the marrow, and he can be no
isolated phenomenon. But there had been a rapid
growth of a moneyed class, and this not so much composed of great landowners as of the newer class of
capitalists, who grew rich through the various forms of
financial speculation then open, particularly the tax-
farmers, of whom that magnificent vulture, the Tobiad
Joseph, is a permanent type.[8] The life of these men
involved such an association with king and court that
marked discrepancies of social custom, such as dietary
regulations, or any form of abstinence, as well as differences in dress, were not to be thought of.

It is unfortunate that any discussion of the nature
and character of the opposition involves a controversial
question of the first magnitude, that which concerns the
Hasidim, or 'Assidaei. It were idle to enumerate, much
less to examine critically, the theories that have been
advanced. Our evidence is so scanty that it can be made
to fit into many different schemes, all of which can be
shown to be conceivable. The simplest interpretation
of the extant sources however is by far the best, and it
has further the merit of being the longest-established
and most widely current.

Now concerning the Hasidim we have only three
passages that can be considered even approximately
contemporary, two in the First Book of Maccabees and
one in the Second.

The first passage, I Macc. ii. 41, states that after the
martyrdom of the loyal Jews who had taken refuge in
the desert, there united with Mattathias the συναγωγή

'Ασσιδαίων, "the congregation of Hasidim, a body of great power and influence in Israel, containing all those who were devoted to the Law." In the second passage, I Macc. vii. 12, we read that when the renegade high priest Alcimus and the Greek prefect Bacchides entered Judah with peaceful overtures, they were met by the congregation of scribes, who brought their lawsuits to him, and then recognized his authority. "And the 'Asidaei were the first among the children of Israel, and they also sought peace from them. For they said, "A priest has come of the seed of Aaron with a powerful army, and he will not injure us."

Taken together, these passages are best understood to mean that at the beginning of the Hasmonean revolt an already existing and powerful group, known as the "'Asidaei," or "Hasidim," gave their official support to the Modin rebels, but that upon the arrival of the duly ordained high priest they, or at any rate their officials, put themselves under his authority, to their own undoing. The author of I Maccabees speaks in terms of the highest respect of them, and applies to the treacherous murder of their leaders the words of Psalm lxxix.

In II Macc. xiv. 6, Alcimus replies to the question of King Demetrius as follows: "The so-called 'Asidaei among the Jews, of whom Judas Maccabeus is the leader, maintain the war and sedition, and will not permit the realm to secure peace." It will be seen that this passage is not necessarily in contradiction with those of I Maccabees, since it is here put into the mouth of Alcimus, and is meant to be a wilful misrepresentation of the facts on his part. Like the other passage, it implies that such a definite body with a distinct name existed before the Hasmonean revolt.

To find in Psalms xii., lxxxix., cxlix., and others references to the same group of men is quite gratuitous. The ordinary sense of " righteous " or " saintly " amply satisfies every one of the occurrences of the word Hasid in the Psalms. And the figurative קהל חסידים (Ps. cxlix. 1) no more implies an organized body than קהל מרעים of Psalm xxvi. 5 implies a formal association of evil-doers, a Camorra. We shall be compelled to rely wholly on the passages in Maccabees for any information about the 'Assidaei, or Hasidim, in the sense of a definite organization bearing that title.

Who were these 'Assidaei? That admirable writer and sturdy patriot, the author of I Maccabees, says they were a body of great power and influence in Israel, ἰσχυρὰ δυνάμει, the leaders of the Jews, and, as has been seen, organized before the revolt. Nothing is clearer than that they are not identical with the " scribes," with whom they are grouped in I Macc. vii., among those who acknowledged Alcimus. It is equally clear that they are not at all the same as the Hasmonean partisans, for they join Mattathiah later, and abandon Judah, at least temporarily, early in the struggle. They are characterized by their zeal for the Law, a zeal which naturally manifested itself in strong opposition to Hellenism.

In Palestine, accordingly, for at least a generation before the revolt, the disintegrating tendencies of Hellenism, as evidenced in the apostasy of many wealthy

Jews and in the neglect of many traditional customs on
the part of others, provoked an organized opposition.
Forming themselves into a fraternity or groups of
corporate bodies, to which they applied the name of
" saints," the opponents of the Greeks directed their
efforts to the exact fulfilment of the Torah, and no
doubt carried on a violent polemic against Greek inno-
vations, however harmless and valuable. At about the
same time an exactly similar movement among Egyptians had brought the Ptolemies to terms. It was not
of course to be expected that a single province of the
Syrian-Babylonian monarchy would accomplish the
same result. In the eyes of the Antiochene court their
programme was no doubt treasonable fanaticism. But
it was not, as in the case of Egypt, directly political in
its scope, and it might never have led to armed conflict.

According to Jewish tradition a pupil of Antigonus
of Socho, José ben Joëzer, was a member of this sect of
" saints." [9] And it is significant that, although he is
represented as especially rigorous in all religious
requirements that had a separatist tendency, he was
strikingly liberal in all matters of what might be called
internal religious practice. It is likely enough that the
tradition is accurate and the " saints " were not at
all precisians or fanatics, but that their cohering bond
was simply opposition to Hellenism. As has been said,
it was against the Hellenizing Jews more than the
Greeks that their attack was directed. These latter
had on their side the advantages of wealth and social
position, but they lacked just that which made their

opponents strong, a compact organization. There was no συναγωγὴ Ἑλλήνων, no congregation or fraternity of Philhellenes. They included all shades of Greek sympathizers, from out and out apostates to parvenus, to whom speaking Greek was a mark of fashion. No doubt the feeling between the two groups ran high, and neither side spared bitter abuse and invective.

The conflict was finally precipitated by an act that was one of the commonest occurrences of ancient political struggles. The party defeated, or in danger of defeat, does not scruple to invite foreign intervention. In this case the irreconcilable Hellenists, evidently losing ground in face of the rapid growth of Hasidic conventicles, appeal to the Greek king, whose policies their own efforts were furthering, and of whose sympathy they were assured. That king happened to be the bizarre Antiochus Epiphanes.

CHAPTER X

ANTIOCHUS THE MANIFEST GOD

"And there arose from them [the companions of Alexander] a root of sin, to wit, Antiochus Epiphanes, son of King Antiochus, he who had been hostage in Rome." That to the writer of I Maccabees is a complete characterization of the king whose reign was to be of fateful consequences to the Jews, a ῥίζα ἁμαρτωλός, an ill sapling of a noble tree. Perhaps the writer had in mind the שרש פרה ראש ולענה (Deut. xxix. 17), "a root bearing gall and wormwood." And he had been a hostage in Rome; a man, that is, of no usual character and no usual career.

Except in this general way, he can scarcely be said to have a personality at all to the writers of the Books of Maccabees. He is merely the type of tyrant, proud and presumptuous, unduly exalting himself above God because of his vain and transitory successes, and dying in agony, after an edifying deathbed repentance. No more than the Nebuchadnezzar of the Book of Daniel, is he anything other than an instrument of the wrath of God. It is hard to believe that there was any real feeling on the writer's part.

But Antiochus had a real personality and an especially interesting one. Both in modern and in ancient times characterization of this strange figure has been attempted, and the verdicts have been so widely different that the summary may be given in Livy's words: *Uti nec sibi nec aliis, quinam homo esset, satis constaret,* " So that neither he himself nor anyone else could clearly state what manner of man he was."

The freakish outbursts, which amazed and scandalized his contemporaries, amply justified the common parody of his title Epiphanes by Epimanes, " the madman." [1] Some there were—perhaps his royal nephew and biographer, Ptolemy of Egypt, among them—who regarded him as unqualifiedly demented.[2] It is likely enough, if the stories about him are even partly true, that he had periods of real derangement. But it seems evident that he was a right royal personage, of unusual charm of manner, of undoubted military capacity, quick and decisive in action, fostering a dream of empire whose rude shattering must have been an important contributing cause to his death.

His was a strange blend. Various epochs met in him, and it is not surprising that many incongruities resulted from that fact. First of all he was in every sense a Macedonian despot. Macedonians had always been accustomed to the concentration of supreme power in the hands of a single individual. For four or five generations Antiochus' immediate ancestors had wielded such power over a rabble of nations stretching from the Aegean to the frontiers of India.[3] The emotional reactions which the existence and the possession of this power must have, were present in him. One constant result of it, the absence of any real social life, is an

ANTIOCHUS (IV) EPIPHANES
AFTER A COIN
(From a drawing by Ralph Illgan)

especially fertile source of deterioration, but the worst effects are noticed chiefly in those born to the purple. Antiochus' exile saved him from them. Yet nothing could save him from the consciousness that he might, if he chose, gratify every whim, and yield to every impulse, and his associates found quickly enough that his *bonhomie* and engaging simplicity were moods, which might be succeeded by bursts of quite incalculable and murderous rage.

There was the additional fact that the monarchy founded by Alexander was in legal contemplation the reign of a god made flesh. Seleucus, we may remember, entered almost at once into the titularies of Sumer and Akkad.[4] The second Antiochus was styled "the God," Θεός, *tout simple*. Our Antiochus called himself Epiphanes—which, it need scarcely be said, is to be translated "the Manifest Deity," and not "the Illustrious."[5] And, at any rate at certain moments, the designation was doubtless a real one to him and not a conscious pose. Worship of the king, the foundation of the later Augustus-cult, was an apparent unifying element in the hopeless jumble of gods and rituals. For that purpose it might be encouraged even by hard-headed peasants like Vespasian, or philosophers like Marcus, who had no illusions about the character of their divinity. But that Alexander in all sincerity believed himself to be god can scarcely be questioned, and Epiphanes may often have similarly impressed himself.

Secondly, he was a Greek. Hellenism was to him a real and profound enthusiasm. His early life as a Roman hostage must have immensely stimulated this side of his character. At Rome his associates were the Scipionic circle, to whom Greek culture had come as a revelation. The distinguished Roman families with whom the young prince lived read Greek, spoke Greek, discussed Greek, and were eager to act as the interpreters of Hellenism to their slower-witted countrymen. In these surroundings anyone boasting not only Greek but regal blood must have found his racial self-esteem flattered to an extraordinary degree. Antiochus' first act on his release was to betake himself to the intellectual capital of Greece, to Athens, in whose citizenry he eagerly enrolled himself. In fact, he was an Athenian magistrate—στρατηγὸς ἐπὶ τὰ ὅπλα[6]—when news came to him of the assassination of his brother Seleucus and of the opportunities waiting one who could act quickly.

When he was king, so much of his policy as did not look to the aggrandizement of his empire was directed to the rehabilitation of Greek cities and temples. Megalopolis, Tegea in Arcadia, Delos, Rhodes, were the beneficiaries of his Philhellenic enthusiasm. The truckling Samaritans—at least the Hellenizing party among them—knew that nothing would make a quicker appeal to him than to rename the sanctuary on Gerizim in honor of Zeus Hellenius.[7] He would probably have found it difficult to understand that anyone could seriously maintain the claims of any other culture against that of the Greeks, and no doubt received as a

matter of course the representations of the Jewish Hel-
lenizers that a little impetus would greatly expedite the
Hellenizing process in Palestine.

When we find Antiochus, king of kings, Manifest
God, soliciting the suffrages of the Antiochene burghers
for the office of " market-commissioner," or of " district
mayor," [8] we are not to regard it as an eccentricity of
the same sort that set him wrangling in the public
squares with Hob and Dick, or pouring priceless oint-
ments on his fellow-bathers in the public baths.[9] The
maintenance of the structure of the Greek polis was an
expression of Hellenic pride in a characteristically Hellenic institution. No one, to be sure, was deceived by it
into thinking that Citizen Antiochus could not incon-
tinently change into an irresponsible master at will, but,
comedy as it was, it had a real significance, which did
not escape even the scoffers and, least of all, the king.

Finally there was an ultra-modern side in him.
Antiochus was also a cultivated gentleman, to whom
skepticism was an index of education and sacrilege a
concrete instance of skepticism. He lived in a very
unsettling age. As has been said before, the Greek
culture that found its way into Rome after the Hanni-
balic wars was a sophisticated, disintegrating culture,
to which the ancient institutions had at best a practical
utility, and which acknowledged theoretically no bind-
ing principles in the physical or moral world. It was
in this culture that the young Antiochus was reared.
He was not alone in it. Many of the incidents of this
period show a revolting cynicism on the part of the

actors. One Greek commander erected altars to " Impiety and Illegality." A Spartan brigand called himself " Hybristas," " the Outrager." [10]

Indeed it was as a wanton desecrater of shrines that Antiochus gained an unenviable notoriety. His pillaging of the temple at Jerusalem was only one of a series of similar acts. At Hierapolis, as well as at many other Syrian shrines, and finally at Elymaea, he coolly appropriated the temple treasures, which in most cases involved violence on his part. But it needed his outrageous " marriage " to Diana to set the seal upon his derisive attitude toward his fellow-gods. The sober Polybius attributes his death to his impiety, a conclusion which naturally is warmly supported by Josephus. [11]

It is idle to attempt to reconcile this sort of cynicism with the pretensions to actual divinity which he probably made in all seriousness. The two are of course quite irreconcilable, and represent merely the shifting moods of a complex and slightly abnormal personality. Under almost any king such an outbreak as the Hasmonean revolt might have taken place. Perhaps the conflict was inevitable. But the form the conflict took, the high degree of religious and national enthusiasm which it evoked, and the powerful aid that enthusiasm gave to the propaganda which was preparing itself, were directly consequent upon the character of Antiochus the God Manifest. The rigor and thoroughness with which he strove to suppress the Jewish cult were characteristic of him. His indifference to sacred traditions made his violation of the temple almost a casual act on his part, his Hellenism justified his plans, and his despotic nature, raging under the humiliating rebuff he had received from Rome, found an outlet in the punishment of a disobedient province.

The writer of I Maccabees places the responsibility for the persecution by Antiochus directly upon the Jews themselves. Many, he tells, were persuaded to identify themselves wholly with the Greeks.[12] The first offense to Jewish religious sentiment did not come from the king at all. The men who waited upon Antiochus, and obtained permission to set up a gymnasium at Jerusalem, acted quite of their own volition. Antiochus' direct action in the matter begins with his return from Egypt. "Embittered and groaning," Polybius says, he left Egypt and returned to Syria. Now, just what happened in Judea is not quite clear. First Maccabees tells of an unprovoked pillage of the temple and a massacre of the people. Second Maccabees reports a furious struggle between the two pretenders, Menelaus and Jason, upon a rumor of the king's death. In all likelihood the fight ended with the discomfiture of Antiochus' appointee, Menelaus, and the king immediately proceeded to rescue him. The sack of Jerusalem and a massacre followed. No doubt the massacre was no worse than befell any captured city, since of a special policy of extermination there can as yet have been no question.

Menelaus was restored, the temple treasures were surrendered to the king, and, either directly or after an interval of two years, the programme of forcible suppression of the Jewish cult was announced.

It is for this programme that an adequate explanation is wanting. There is nothing really quite like it in Greek history. Not that religious persecution, or the suppression of an obnoxious cult, was an unheard-of undertaking. The establishment of the worship of Dionysus had encountered vigorous opposition in continental Greece. A probable tradition recounts the attempts at thorough repression with which several Greek communities, notably Thebes, met the intruder.[13] But this movement had as its object the preservation of an ancestral religion, not its destruction. To compel anyone to abjure his national customs, to forsake τὰ πάτρια, must have seemed monstrous to all people in whom the sense of kinship with the deity, and the belief in the god's local jurisdiction, were as strong as they were among the Greeks.

Somewhat later, among the Romans, a successful attempt was made to extirpate the Druidic ritual in Cisalpine Gaul. As far as this was an effort to destroy root and branch an ancient and established form of worship, it presents many analogies to the project of Antiochus. But the persecution of the Druids was based on specific charges of immoral and anti-social practices associated with their ritual, especially that of human sacrifices. That may have been a pretext. The Druids may not after all have been guilty of these enormities. However, the pretext was at least advanced, and the exile of Druidic brotherhoods and the destruction of their sanctuaries were publicly justified only by that.[14]

In the case of the Jews no such assertions are to be
discovered. Antiochus, instigated by renegade Jews,
sets about a systematic obliteration of the distinctively
Jewish ritual. The synagogue services were to be
checked by the destruction of the Torah. Perhaps
periodic reunions in the synagogue were forbidden altogether, since meetings of citizens were proverbially
looked at askance in monarchies.[15] The temple was
rededicated to the Olympian Zeus, and the ceremony of
circumcision was made a capital offense. Observance of
the Sabbath was construed as treason. No detail was
overlooked.

This complete scheme is not to be explained by the
existence of a strong animosity toward the Jews. There
is, in the first place, none of the evidence that was
met with in Egypt, that such animosity existed. And,
secondly, animosity between racial groups expressed
itself in bloody riots, not in a carefully prepared plan
for extirpating a religion while sparing its professors.
Nor can we find in the personal character of Antiochus
a sufficient cause for the persecution. He undoubtedly
exhibited the gusts of passion common enough among
those who wield irresponsible power, but the sustained
and bloody vindictiveness of such a programme is a
very different thing.

It has been frequently suggested that his cherished
policy was the thorough Hellenization of his empire,
that among the Jews only was there a determined
resistance, that upon learning that the basis of their
resistance was a devoted attachment to their ancestral

superstition, he determined to root out the latter. The difficulties with this view are, first, that opposition was not confined to the Jews, but was met with everywhere —a dull and voiceless opposition, which, however, unmistakably existed. Secondly, among the Jews a very large number, we are told, " were persuaded "; and it is highly likely that Antiochus came in direct contact wholly with the latter, or almost wholly, so that the situation in Judea cannot have impressed him as radically different from that of Syria or Babylonia.

But, above all, it is the conclusion that the obstacles to his policy would lead to persecution on his part, which is more than doubtful. No one could have known better than he did himself that ancestral religious customs are not to be eradicated by violence. The Egypt which was so nearly in his grasp might have taught him that, if nothing else could. There the indigenous religion had triumphed. He himself, upon his entry into the kingdom, had crowned himself *more Aegyptico,* "after the Egyptian fashion," [16] that is, with full acknowledgment of the sovereignty of Ptah and Isis over their ancient demesnes.

We shall probably have to look to the Hellenizing Jews not only for the initiation, but for the systematic carrying out, of the policy of persecution. And, as has been suggested, it is one of the commonest phenomena of ancient life. There was scarcely a Greek city in which a defeated faction had not at some time summoned the public enemy into the city, and by their aid taken a cruel vengeance on their opponents. If the

Hellenizing faction in Judea found its influence wan-
ing, its action was from the point of view of ancient
times natural enough. It appealed to foreign aid and
strove systematically to stamp out the institutions it
opposed, just as at Athens the Athenian oligarchs,
placed in power by Spartan arms, tried to maintain
themselves by wholesale proscription and by systematically removing all the democratic institutions that
had developed since Clearchus.[17]

It is likely too that the impelling motive was not
solely the rancor which apostates feel for the faith or
nation they have quitted. They saw themselves in the
presence of a real danger. Among them was to be
found most of the wealth of the community, and no
doubt a great deal of the intellectual culture. Many of
them were already in the third or fourth generation of
Hellenistic Jews. The ancient ritual had for these men
no personal associations whatever. In the various communes they enjoyed the position which wealth necessarily, and in those days especially, brought. That
there was any virtue in poverty or privation in themselves had not yet been preached to the world, and
would have seemed a wild paradox; and although the
vanity of wealth without wisdom was a philosophic
truism, ordinary wits would not always trust themselves
to make the distinction.

When these men, who formed almost a hereditary
nobility, and already cherished a superb aloofness from
the mass, felt their influence and power challenged,
perhaps saw themselves outvoted in the governing

10

councils of the synagogues and communes, and the foundations of their petty glory sapped, they were roused to a counter-effort, of which the results have been indicated. The danger in which they found themselves came from the Hasidim, the group of brotherhoods that made a conscious opposition to Hellenism their bond of union. In Egypt the opposition had found its organs in the caste-like corporations of priests, In Judea the organs had to be created. And that they were successful, the words of I Maccabees testify. They contained the leaders of the nation; their position was already one of dominating influence.

It is unnecessary to detail the course of the Hasmonean revolt. Even the brilliant successes of Judas in the field, and the less splendid but equally solid triumphs of his brothers, would have had fewer political consequences than they had except for the chaos in the Seleucid succession. But of the permanent triumph of the movement there was never any doubt. If the revolt had ended with the death of Judas, the discomfiture of the Hellenists would have been complete. No Macedonian king would ever be tempted to provoke another revolt by a similar project. It could never be a part of a sane ruler's policy to sacrifice valuable military material in order to gratify a local faction. And it must never be forgotten that the Greek rule of the Syrian kingdom was the domination of a military class. Every diminution of the army was a dead loss.

The suggestion may be hazarded that not merely the Hellenistic Jews, but also the Greeks themselves, viewed the progress of the Hasidim with real alarm. We are far as yet from the epoch of real propaganda, but to some extent it may already have begun. Where and when we can only speculate. Perhaps the fervor of Hasidic preaching had touched non-Jewish Syrians; perhaps some of the younger men of the Hellenists " relapsed " under Hasidic stimulation into Judaism. However the case may be. Greeks of influence may have noted that the Grecizing of Coele-Syria was not merely hindered by obstacles in Judea, but that the Judaizing of portions already won was a possibility that was attaining a constantly greater vividness. If this was the case, the persecution by Antiochus was a precaution, insensate and futile, but less at variance with Greek methods than it seems in the usual interpretation of the facts we know.

CHAPTER XI
THE JEWISH PROPAGANDA

The preaching of a gospel seems to us as natural as the existence of a religion. That is because the religions we know best are universal ones, of which the God is a transcendent being, in whose sight human distinctions are negligible. But for the Mediterranean world that was not the case. The religions were not universal; many of the gods were concretely believed to be the ancestors of certain groups of men, and not always remote ones. Local associations played a determining part. If we find an active propaganda here, it cannot be because the spread of a ritual or faith is an inherent characteristic. On the contrary, in normal circumstances there seems to be no reason why one community should change its gods or forms of worship for those of another.

But, as a matter of fact, they did change them. And the change was often effected consciously by the planned efforts of a group of worshipers, and in all the ways that have been used since—preaching, emotional revivals, and forcible conquest. One such carefully planned effort was that of the Jews, but only one of them. The circumstances in which this propaganda was carried out need close investigation.

In discussing Greek religion (above, p. 34) it has been suggested that there was in every community a large number of men who found no real satisfaction in the state cult, and that it was chiefly among them that the proselytes of new and foreign religions were to be found. But that does not make us understand why these foreign religions should have sought proselytes, why they should have felt themselves under obligations to assume a mission. The stranger within the gates might reasonably be expected to do honor to the divine lord of the city: if he remained permanently, his inclusion in the civic family in some way is natural. But what was it that impelled Isis to seek worshipers so far from the Nile, where alone she could be properly adored, or the mysterious Cabiri to go so far from the caves where their power was greatest and most direct?[1]

The movement of which these special missions are phases was old and extensive. It covered the entire Eastern Mediterranean, and went perhaps further west and east than we can at present demonstrate. Its beginnings probably antedated the Hellenes. The religious unrest of which Christian missionaries made such excellent use was a phenomenon that goes back very far in the history of Mediterranean civilization. At certain periods of that history and in different places it reached culminating waves, but it is idle to attempt to discover a sufficient cause for it in a limited series of events within a circumscribed area of Greece or of Asia.

The briefest form in which the nature of this unrest can be phrased is the following—the quest for personal salvation.

We shall do well to remember that the ancient state was a real corporation, based not upon individuals but upon smaller family corporations. The rights of these corporations were paramount. It was only gradually that individuals were recognized at all in law.[2] The desire for personal salvation is a part of the growing consciousness of personality, and must have begun almost as soon as the state corporation itself became fixed.

Within a state only those individuals can have relatively free play who are to a certain extent the organs of the state; that is, those individuals who by conquest, wealth, or chance have secured for themselves political predominance in their respective communities. But these could never be more than a small minority. For the great majority everyday life was hemmed in by conventions that had the force of laws, and was restricted by legal limits drastically enforced. And this narrow and pitifully poor life was bounded by Sheol, or Hades, by a condition eloquently described as worse at its best than the least desirable existence under the face of the insufferable sun.[3]

The warrior caste, for whom and of whom the Homeric poems were written, were firmly convinced that the bloodless and sinewless life in the House of Hades was the goal to which existence tended. But they found their compensation in that existence itself. What of those who lacked these compensations, or had learned to despise them? In them the prospect of becoming lost in the mass of flitting and indistinguishable shadows must have produced a profound horror, and their minds must have dwelt upon it with increasing intensity.

It is one of the most ancient beliefs of men in this region that all the dead become disembodied spirits, sometimes with power for good or evil, so that their displeasure is to be deprecated, sometimes without such power, as the Homeric nobles believed, and the mass of the Jews in the times of the monarchy. These spirits or ghosts had of themselves no recognizable personality, and could receive it only exceptionally and in ways that violated the ordinary laws of the universe. Such a belief is not strictly a belief in immortality at all, since the essence of the latter is that the actual person of flesh and blood continues his identity when flesh and blood are dissolved and disappear, and that the characteristics which, except for form and feature, separated him from his fellows in life still do so after death. The only bodiless beings who could be said to have a personality were the gods, and they were directly styled " the Immortals."

However, the line that separated gods and men was not sharp. The adoration offered to the dead in the Spartan relief [4] is not really different from the worship of the Olympians. From the other side, in Homer, the progeny of Zeus by mortal women are very emphatically men.[5] Whether the Homeric view is a special development, it is demonstrably true that a general belief was current in Greece not long after the Homeric epoch, which saw no impossibility in favored men securing the gift of immortality; that is, continuing without interruption the personal life which alone had significance. This was done by the translations—the removal of mortal men in the flesh to kinship with the gods.⁶

This privilege of personal immortality was not connected, in the myths that told of it, with eminent services. It was at all times a matter of grace. In the form of bodily translation it always remained a rare and miraculous exception. But the mere existence of such a belief must have strongly influenced the beliefs and practices that had long been connected with the dead.

We cannot tell where and when it was first suggested to men that the shadow-life of Hades might by the grace of the gods be turned into real life, and a real immortality secured. It may be, as has been supposed, that the incentive came from Egypt. More likely, however, it was an independent growth, and perhaps arose in more than one place. The favor and grace of the gods, which were indispensable, could obviously be gained by intimate association, and in the eighth and perhaps even the ninth pre-Christian century we begin to hear in Greece of means of entering into that association. One of these means was the " mystery," of which the Eleusinian is the best-known. In these cult-societies, of the origin of which we know nothing, a close and intimate association with the god or gods was offered. The initiated saw with their own eyes the godhead perform certain ceremonial acts; perhaps they sat cheek by jowl with him. It is obvious that such

familiarity involved the especial favor of the gods, and
it is easy to understand that the final and crowning mark
of that favor would not be always withheld. The communion with the god begun in this life would be continued after it. To the mystæ of Eleusis, and no doubt
elsewhere, and to them only was promised a personal
immortality.[7]

It may not have been first at Eleusis. It may have
been in the obscure corners of Thrace where what later
appeared as Orphic societies was developed. But there
were soon many mysteries, and there was no lack of
men and women to whom the promise was inexpressibly
sweet. The spread of Orphism in the sixth and fifth
centuries B. C. E. bears witness to the eagerness with
which the evangel was received.

Outside of Greece, in Persia, India, and Egypt, perhaps also in Babylonia, there were hereditary groups of
men who claimed to possess an arcanum, whereby the
supreme favor of the gods, that of eternal communion
with them, was to be obtained. These hereditary castes
desired no extension, but jealously guarded their
privileges. But among them there constantly arose
earnest and warm-hearted men, whose humanity impelled them to spread as widely as possible the boon
which they had themselves obtained by accident. Perhaps many attempts in all these countries aborted. Not
all Gotamas succeeded in becoming Buddhas.

The Jews seemed to the Greeks to possess just such
an arcanum, and whatever interest they originally
excited was due to that fact. The initiatory rite of cir-

cumcision, the exclusiveness of a ritual that did not brook even the proximate presence of an uninitiate, all pointed in that direction, even if we disregard the vigorously asserted claims of the Jews to be in a very special sense the people of God.

The Jews too had as far as the masses were concerned developed the belief in a personal immortality during the centuries that followed the Babylonian exile (comp. p. 70), and as far as we can see it developed among them at the same time and somewhat in the same way as elsewhere. That is to say, among them as among others the future life, the *Olam ha-bo,* was a privilege and was sought for with especial eagerness by those to whom the *Olam ha-zeh* was largely desolate. Not reward for some and punishment for others, but complete exclusion from any life but that of Sheol for those who failed to acquire the *Olam ha-bo,* was the doctrine maintained, just as the Greek mystae knew that for those who were not initiated there was waiting, not the wheel of Ixion or the stone of Sisyphus, but the bleak non-existence of Hades.[8]

But there was a difference, and this difference became vital. Conduct was not disregarded in the Greek mysteries, but the essential thing was the fact of initiation. Those who first preached the doctrine of a personal salvation to the Jews were conscious in so doing that they were preaching to a society of initiates. They were all mystae; all had entered into the covenant: all belonged to the congregation of the Lord, קהל יהוה. To whom was this boon of immortality, the *Olam ha-bo,* to be giver? The first missionaries, whether they did or did not constitute a sect, had a ready answer. To those to whom the covenant was real, who accepted fully the yoke of the Law.

The sects of Pharisees and Sadducees, whose disputes fill later Jewish history, joined issue on a number of points. No doubt there was an economic and social cleavage between them as well. But perhaps the most nearly fundamental difference of doctrine related to the *Olam ha-bo*. The Pharisees asserted, and the Sadducees denied, the doctrine of resurrection. It is stated by Josephus,' that the Sadducees called in question the *Olam ha-bo* itself. When and where these sects took form is uncertain. The Pharisees at least are fully developed, and form a powerful political party under John Hyrcanus.[16] It is very unlikely that they are related to the Hasidim or are a continuation of them. The latter were a national, anti-Hellenic organization, and contained men of all shades of beliefs and interests. But the Pharisees, like the Hasidim, began as a brotherhood or a group of brotherhoods, however political their aims and actions were in later times. The fact is indicated by the name *Haber*, " comrade," which they gave themselves, and the contemptuous *Am ha-aretz,* ' clod," *οἱ πολλοί*, with which they designated those who were not members of their congregations.

Now the *Haberim,* who preached the World-to-Come, were not in a primitive stage of culture, but in a very advanced one. Their God was not master of a city, but Lord of the whole earth. And they had long main-

tained the principle that merit in the eyes of God was
determined by conduct, both formal and moral, a distinction less profoundly separating than seems at first
to be the case. If that were so, anyone, Jew or Gentile,
might conceivably acquire that merit. How was the
Olam ha-bo to be refused to anyone who had taken upon
himself the yoke of the Law, who did all that the Lord
required at his hands? Jewish tradition knew of several
eminently righteous gentiles, such as Job, in whom God
was well pleased. It was an untenable proposition to
men whose cardinal religious doctrine had for centuries
been ethical and universal that all but a few men were
permanently excluded from the beatitude of life after
death.[11]

Since, however, the promises of the sacred literature
were addressed primarily to Israel, those who were not
of Abraham's seed could become " comrades " only by
first becoming Jews. That conception involved no
difficulty whatever. The people of the ancient world
had empirically learned some of the more elementary
facts of biological heredity; but membership in a community, though determined by heredity in the first
instance, was not essentially so determined. In earlier
times, when the communities were first instituted, not
even the pretense of kinship was maintained. The
essential fact was the assumption of common *sacra.*

That a man might by appropriate ceremonies—or
without ceremonies—enter into another community,
was held everywhere. If, as has been suggested (above,
p. 147), the Hasidim found some of their members

among the non-Jewish population of Syria,[12] it is not likely that the process of becoming Jews was rendered either difficult or long. Abraham, a late tradition stated, brought many gentiles under the wings of the Shekinah, the Effulgence. If this tradition is an old one, it indicates that proselytizing was in early times held to be distinctly meritorious.[13]

The first conquests of the Hasmonean rulers brought non-Jewish tribes under immediate political control of the Jews. Most of them, notably the Idumeans, were forcibly Judaized, and so successfully that we hear of only one attempted revolt.[14] There can of course have been no question here of elaborate ceremonies or lengthy novitiates. The Idumeans were dealt with as shortly as Charlemagne's Saxons, and gave the most convincing demonstration of their loyalty in the time of the insurrections.[15]

This drastic way of increasing the seed of Abraham must have been viewed differently by different classes of Jews. To the Haberim the difference between a heathen and a Jewish aspirant to their communion lay in the fact that the heathen had undergone the fearful defilement of worshiping the Abomination, while the Jew had not. For the former there was accordingly necessary an elaborate series of purgations, of ceremonial cleansing; and until this was done there was no hope that he could be admitted into the congregation of the Lord. But it might be done, and it began to be done in increasing numbers. It would have been strange if, among the many gentile seekers for salvation, Greek,

Syrian, Cappadocian, and others, some would not be found to take the path that led to the conventicles of the Jewish Haberim. This was especially the case when, instead of an obscure Syrian tribe, the Hasmoneans had made of Judea a powerful nation, one of the most considerable of its part of the world.

All the mysteries welcomed neophytes, but none made the entrance into their ranks an easy matter. In some of them there were degrees, as in those of Cybele, and the highest degree was attained at so frightful a cost as practically to be reserved for the very few.[16] In the case of the Jews, one of the initiatory rites was peculiarly repellent to Greeks and Romans, in that it involved a bodily mutilation, which was performed not in the frenzy of an orgiastic revel, but in the course of a solemn ritual of prayer. That fact might make many hesitate, but could not permanently deter those who earnestly sought for the way of life.

The Jewish propaganda was not confined to receiving and imposing conditions on those who came. Some at least sought converts, although it is very doubtful that the Pharisaic societies as a class planned a real mission among the heathen. The methods that were used were those already in vogue—methods which had achieved success in many fields. Books and pamphlets were published to further the purpose of the missionaries; personal solicitation of those deemed receptive was undertaken. Actual preaching, such as the *diatribe* commenced by the Cynics, and before them by Socrates, was probably confined to the synagogue, or meeting within the proseucha, and reached only those who were there assembled.[17]

The literary form of the propaganda was especially active in those communities in which Jews and Greeks spoke a common language and partly shared a common culture. Even books intended primarily for Jewish circulation contain polemics against polytheism and attacks upon heathen custom, which the avowed purpose of the book would not justify.

It is not to be supposed that the literary propaganda was the most effective. It was limited by the very field for which it was intended. Such a book as the Wisdom of Solomon was both too subtle and too finished a product to appeal to other than highly cultivated tastes, and men of this stamp are not readily reached by propagandizing religions. The chief object of attack was the Greek polytheism. "Wisdom" ventures even on an historical explanation of polytheism, which is strangely like that of Herbert Spencer.[18] Now, just for the Greeks, who might read and understand such a book, to refute polytheism was destroying a man of straw. No one of them seriously believed in it. Those who were not agnostics or atheists believed in the unity of the Divine essence, and at most maintained the existence of certain subordinate ministerial beings, who might or might not be identical with the names of the actors in the myths. But many Jews would be ready to admit so much. Indeed that there were subordinate *daemonia,* helpful and harmful, was a widespread belief in Judea, even if without authoritative sanction. Very often the heathen gods were conceived to be not absolute nullities, but demons really existing and evil—a belief which the early Christian church firmly held and preached.[19]

Accordingly the polished society of a Greek city did not need the literary polemics against polytheism to be convinced that monotheism was an intellectually more developed and morally preferable dogma. On the other hand, it was a very difficult task to convince it that the ceremonies of the official cult, granting even their philosophic absurdity, were for that reason objectionable. To make them seem so, there would have to be present the consciousness of sin, and that was not a matter which argumentation could produce.

One other point against which Jewish writers of that time address themselves is the assumed viciousness of Greek life. How much one people has with which to reproach another in that respect in ancient or in modern times need not be considered here. The fact remains that in many extant books sexual excesses and perversions are made a constant reproach to the heathen—which generally implies the Greek—and the extant Greek and Latin literature gives a great deal of color to the charge.[20] This is due not so much to the actual life depicted as to the attitude with which even good men regarded these particular incidents. It is true that we have contemporary evidence that many Jews in Greek communities were no paragons of right living or self-restraint. But it is at least significant that this accusation, continually repeated by the Jews, is not met by a retort in kind. The anti-Jewish writings are not especially moderate in their condemnations. But with viciousness in their lives they do not charge the Jews, and they cannot have been unaware of what the Jews wrote and said.

Polytheism and immorality, the two chief counts in the indictment which Jewish writers bring against heathendom, were not things Greeks were disposed to defend. But it is doubtful whether the books that inveighed against them were valuable weapons of propaganda. We have practically no details of how the movement grew. In the last century before the Christian era it had reached the extraordinary proportions that are evidenced by the satire of Horace as well as by the opposition which it encountered. Jewish apocalyptic literature confidently expects that all the heathen on the rapidly approaching Judgment Day will be brought within the fold.[21] The writers may be forgiven if the success of their proselytizing endeavors made them feel that such a result was well within the range of possibility.

Within the same period the worships of Cybele, of Sabazios, and of Isis, had perhaps even greater success in extending themselves over the Greek and Roman world. The communities they invaded only rarely welcomed them. Even at Rome the official introduction of Cybele was the last desperate recourse of avowed superstition, and it was promptly restricted when success and prosperity returned to the Roman arms. But in all the communities great masses of men were thoroughly pre-

11

pared in mind for the doctrines the Asiatic religions preached. A public preaching, such as the Cynics used, was rarely permitted. But if we recall how many slaves and ex-slaves as well as merchants and artisans were of Asiatic stock, the spread of these cults, including that of the Jews, by the effective means of personal and individual conversion is nothing to be wondered at. The state was perforce compelled to notice this spread. Individuals had noticed it long before.

CHAPTER XII
THE OPPOSITION

The ancient state was based on community of *sacra*, of cult-observances. Anything that tended to destroy them or impair general belief in their necessity, went to the very roots of the state, was therefore a form of treason, and was punished as such. The state rarely was interested in the honor of the gods themselves. Roman law had a maxim, which was very seriously stated, but which makes upon us the impression of a cynical witticism: *Deorum iniuriae dis curae,* " Let the gods attend to their own wrongs." Since the kinship of members of the state was generally known to be a legal fiction, the bond that took its place was common worship. The state could not look without concern upon anything that threatened to weaken its formal structure.

Most Greek states made ἀσέβεια, " impiety," a criminal offense. But just what acts or omissions constituted impiety was in each case a question of fact, to be determined specially in every instance. At Athens various persons of greater and less distinction were prosecuted under that indictment—Socrates, Theophrastus, Phryne. In every one of these cases, the gravamen of the charge was that the defendant did not regard as gods those whom the state so regarded (μὴ νομίζειν θεοὺς οὓς ἡ πόλις νομίζει, Plat. Apol. 24B and 26B), and taught so. In general, individual prosecutions such as these were deemed sufficient to repress the spread of dangerous doctrines. It was not believed necessary to consider membership in any sect or community as *prima facie* evidence of such impiety, punishable without further investigation. In later times, however, even this step was taken. Certain philosophic sects—which, we may remember, were corporately organized—were believed to be essentially impious. The city of Lyctos in Crete forbade any Epicurean to enter it under penalty of the most frightful tortures.[1]

We shall have to distinguish these police measures, which, when aimed at religious bodies, constitute an undoubted religious persecution, from the mutual animosity with which hostile races in any community regarded each other and the bloody riots that resulted from it. In the new city of Seleucia in Babylonia, the Syrians, Jews, and Greeks that lived there were very far from realizing the purpose of the city's founder and coalescing into a single community. Sanguinary conflicts, probably on very slight provocation, frequently took place. Sometimes the Jews and Syrians combined against the Greeks; sometimes the Greeks and Syrians against the Jews, as recounted by Josephus.[2] The situation in Alexandria, where Egyptians hated Greeks, Jews, and doubtless all foreigners with a scarcely discriminating intensity, is peculiar only because we are well informed of conditions there by the papyri. When any one of these nationalities gained the upper hand,

there was likely to be a bloody suppression of its foes,
often followed by equally bloody reprisals. Salamis, in
Cyprus, is a grim witness of the frenzy with which
neighbors could attack each other, when years of
hostility culminated in a violent outbreak.[3]

The attitude of Greek states toward the Jewish congregations in their midst was certainly not uniformly
hostile. But in many cases there could not help being a
certain resentment, owing to the fact that these congregations were by special grant generally immune from
prosecution for impiety, although as a matter of fact
they very emphatically "did not regard as gods those
whom the state so regarded." Of itself this circumstance might have been neglected, but the active and
successful propaganda they undertook made them a
source of real danger to the state. We therefore hear of
attempts made sporadically to abrogate the immunity,
to compel the Jewish corporations to conform to the
local law of ἀσέβεια. Nearly always, however, the immunity was a royal grant and therefore unreachable
by local legislation, a fact that did not tend to alleviate
friction where it existed.[4]

At Rome police measures to suppress irreligion
were long in existence. However, the Roman attitude
toward any form of communion with gods or *daemonia*
was so uniformly an attitude of dread, that prohibition
of religious rites and punishment of participants in them
were not a task lightly assumed by a Roman magistrate. The suppression of the Bacchanalia in 186 B. C.
E. was nothing short of a religious persecution, but the

utmost care was taken to make it appear to be directed against certain licentious practices alleged against the Bacchae, and the senate's decree expressly authorizes the Bacchic rites, under certain restrictions deemed necessary to insure their harmlessness.[5] Very early the Isiac mysteries and other Eastern cults came within the animadversion of the urban police.[6] Here too the theory was that the crimes and immorality of the communicants were the sole objects of punishment, especially that species of fraud which took the form of magic and unofficial fortune-telling. In reality, however, all these pretexts covered the fact that the Romans felt their state ritual endangered, not by the presence, but by the spread, of such rituals among Romans; and in this their alarm was very well grounded indeed. But to proceed openly and boldly against any manifestation of a divine numen, was more than the average Roman board of aediles ventured to do.

If the official attitude of various communities toward outside cults and toward the Jews in particular can be brought under no general rule, we may be sure that the personal attitude of individual Greeks toward them varied from enthusiastic veneration to indifference and determined antagonism. In certain cities the Jews as foreigners could not hope to escape odium nor the jealousy of competing individuals and organizations. In Egypt particularly, the feud between Egyptians and Jews existed before the coming of the Greeks there, and grew in intensity as time went on. As far as definite attacks upon the Jews and their institutions went, many of them had an Egyptian origin, and many others were wholly confined to that country.

These attacks are not essentially different from the methods that generally obtained when one group of men found itself in frequent opposition to another group on the field of battle or otherwise. The populace needs no rhetorical stimulation to represent its enemies as wicked, cowardly, and foolish. That is a human weakness which exists to-day quite as it has existed for many centuries. However, even for the populace, such phrases were accepted conventions. They were not quite seriously meant, and could be conveniently forgotten whenever the former foe became an ally.

Among professional rhetoricians this particular method of argumentation formed a set rhetorical device, one of the forms of *vituperatio* as classified in the text-books. Certain τόποι, "commonplaces," were developed concerning all nations, and used as occasion required. Historical facts, popular gossip, freely imagined qualities, were all equally used to support the statements made or to illustrate them. Now it is in the works of professional rhetoricians that most of the attacks on the Jews are to be found. Further, we have their works wholly in the form of citations taken from the context. We cannot even be sure to what extent the authors themselves were convinced of what they said. Wherever we meet what is plainly a rhetorical τόπος, we have little ground for assuming that it corresponds to any feeling whatever on the writer's part. Often it was mechanically inserted, and has all the effect of an exercise in composition.

With a laughter-loving people one of the first resources in controversy is to render the opponent ridiculous. It was especially on the side of religion that the Jews maintained their difference from their neighbors, and claimed a great superiority to them. A Greek enemy would be much inclined to heap ridicule, first on the pretensions to superiority, and then on the religious form itself. That may be the basis of a story, which soon became widely current, to the effect that the Jews worshiped their god in the form of an ass.

The story is of Egyptian origin. Just where and when it began, cannot be discovered. Josephus in combating Apion refers to a writer whose name the copyists have hopelessly jumbled. It is not unlikely that he was a certain Mnaseas, perhaps of Patara in Lycia, or Patras in the Peloponnesus, a highly rhetorical historian of the second century B. C. E. [8] He wrote therefore before the establishment of the Maccabean state. Wherever he was born, he was a pupil of Eratosthenes, and therefore a resident of Alexandria.[9]

We have his words only at third hand, in Josephus' account of Apion's reference. Each citation is of substance, not the *ipsissima verba;* and, besides, of this part of Josephus we have only a Latin translation, not the original. The story, whether it is Mnaseas' or Apion's, is to the effect that a certain Idumean, named Zabidus, duped the Jews into believing that he intended to deliver his god, Apollo,[10] into their hands, and contrived to get into the temple and remove " the golden head of the pack-ass."

The uncertainty and indirectness of the citation makes it dubious whether Mnaseas understood this ass to be the actual divine symbol or, as others said, merely one of the figures of a group. The absurdity of the story seems so patent that its existence is almost incredible. It indicates the extreme strictness with which gentiles were excluded from even the approach to the temple at Jerusalem that the baselessness of the ass-legend was not immediately discovered.[11]

Josephus' indignation and his frequent reference to the "pretended wit" of Apion or of Mnaseas make the tone and intention of the story quite plain. It can have had no other purpose than that of holding the Jews up to ridicule. But just what the point of the jest is, is by no means quite so easy to discover. We cannot reconstruct even approximately the words of Mnaseas. It is, however, at least likely that if he had attributed the adoration of an ass to the Jews, a somewhat less equivocal statement to that effect would appear. Other writers do make that statement plainly enough. The point of Mnaseas' raillery seems rather to be the easy credulity of the people, a characteristic that was at all times attributed to them in the ancient world, from the earliest references, as they are found in Hecataeus, to the latest. It is curious that this quality, which to Greeks and Romans seemed the most striking trait of the Jews, is the very last that modern observers would ascribe to them.

If we follow the story as it appears in later writers, we shall meet it next in the history of the Syrian Posi-

donius, who lived about 100 B. C. E.   Again, we have his
statement only in quotation, this time in a fragment of
the work of Diodorus, a Sicilian contemporary of
Augustus.   Posidonius does no more than make the
assertion that the innermost shrine of the temple contained the statue of a long-bearded man, assumed to
be Moses, riding on an ass (λίθινον ἄγαλμα ἀνδρὸς
βαθυπώγωνος καθήμενον [sic] ἐπ' ὄνου).¹² This is very far
from accusing the Jews of worshiping an ass.   Indeed
it is likely enough that nothing was further from the
mind of the writer.   Perhaps Mnaseas too told the same
or a very similar story, since his anecdote would fit in
just as well with the account of Posidonius as with the
later version.

The story appears again in the writings of Molo, the
tutor of Caesar and Cicero; but Molo's statement is
wholly lost.   In the next generation we find it in the
writings of the Egyptian Apion, and in Damocritus, of
whom we know nothing, but who, it is likely enough,
was a resident of Alexandria.¹³

Here the statements are unmistakable.   According to
Damocritus, if he is accurately cited by the late Byzantine lexicographer Suidas, the Jews adored the gilded
head of an ass (χρυσῆν ὄνου κεφαλὴν προσεκύνουν).   Apion,
in the Latin translation of Josephus, asserts that the
Jews "adored this ass' head, and worshiped it with
much ceremony" (*id* [*i. e. asini caput*] *colere ac
dignum facere tanta religione*).¹⁴

Probably from Apion it got to Tacitus, 120 C. E., who
in his Histories (v. 4) uses the words, *effigiem* [*asini*]

penetrali sacravere, " they consecrated the figure of an ass in their inner shrine." Tacitus expressly avoids the allegation of worshiping this statue. He probably intentionally modified the words of Apion to fit the statement into the then abundantly proven fact that the Jews worshiped an imageless and abstract deity (Hist. v. 5).

The Greek essayist Plutarch, almost a generation before Tacitus, makes a similar reference, though in his case without the least hostile or satiric intention. The ass is according to him the animal most honored among the Jews (τὸ τιμώμενον ὑπ' αὐτῶν μάλιστα θηρίον), a statement which, it may be said incidentally, is by no means without foundation.[15]

It is generally assumed that the use of an ass as an object of adoration necessarily aroused derision. That would probably be true of our own times in Europe or in America, but it would not obtain in the ancient world. Veneration of an ass was no more extraordinary to a Greek than veneration of any other animal symbol. Nor was the ass associated in men's minds only with contemptuous and derisive images. He played a large part in the economy of the people, and was in many places correspondingly esteemed. The very first reference to him in Greek literature is in the Iliad (xi. 558), where Ajax's slow retreat is compared to the stubborn and effectual resistance of an ass in the fields—surely no dishonoring simile. The ass was a part of the sacred train of Dionysus,[16] long before the latter was identified with the Phrygian Sabazios. Again, the ass was transferred to heaven, where he still shines as a constellation. At Lampsacus and Tarentum he was a sacrificial animal.[17]   At Rome he was associated with Vesta, and crowned at the Consualia.

Among the Jews, as among all the people of that portion of Asia, his importance is such as to justify in a large measure the words of Plutarch.   Generally in the Bible he is preferred to the horse (Prov. xxvi. 3; Psalm xxxii. 9).   In the ancient song of Deborah (Judges v. 10) those who sit on white asses are the princes of the people.   The Anointed of God would ride into the city upon an ass.   It is not without meaning that asses, but not horses, appear on Assyrian sculpture.

In Egypt, however, the ass was a symbol of evil.   He was associated with the demoniac Typhon, and was an object of superstitious fear and hatred.[18]

For most of the Mediterranean nations the worship of an ass was only in so far contemptible as the worship of any animal was so considered.   Romans and Greeks take very lofty ground indeed when they speak of Egyptian theriolatry, although innumerable religious practices of their own were associated in some way or other with animals.[19]   It is not likely accordingly that the allegation of this form of fetichism against the Jews arose among Greeks or Romans or Syrians or Palestinians.   For Egyptians, on the contrary, this particular story would charge the Jews with "devil-worship," or, at least, the veneration of a deity hostile to them. In Egypt, and in Egypt alone, the story would have a special point.

It may further be noted that in Manetho's account the Jews are brought to Avaris, a site consecrated to Typhon.

As it appears in Posidonius, perhaps in Mnaseas and Molo, and certainly in Plutarch, the story is based upon a real Jewish tradition and actual custom. In Democritus and Apion, on the other hand, it is a malicious slander, needing no basis in observed fact. It is one of the many developments of the mutual hatred of Jew and Egyptian, of which there is such a wealth of other evidence.

This story has been dealt with in some detail because it illustrates in very many ways the character, sources, and methods of the literary anti-Semitism of ancient times. Wholly without basis from the beginning, it becomes almost an accepted dogma, as well grounded as many another facile generalization in those days and ours. Further, it will be observed that it does not everywhere necessitate the inference of hostility on the part of the writer. The historians of those days were *ex professo* rhetoricians. Every form of literary composition had as its prime object a finished artistic product. Since the subject of literature, or artistic verbal expression, was human life, history, which is the record of human life, was eminently the province of the word-fancier, the rhetorician. The trained historian has no words of sufficient contempt for the mere logographer whose object is the recording of facts. That " pretty lies " do not in the least disfigure history, is the opinion of the Stoic Panaetius and his pupil and

admirer Cicero. And that was particularly the case
when the history was, as it often became, an expanded
plea or invective, in which case the tricks of trade of the
advocate were not only commendable but demanded.[20]

Most of the accounts of the Jews or the fragments
of such accounts come to us from just these rhetorical
historians. If the whole book were extant in any case,
we should be in a position to determine the occasion for
the account and the source of its color. As it is, we
are on slippery ground when we endeavor to interpret
the fragments in such a way as to discover the facts of
which they present so distorted an image.

Not all historians, however, were of this type. Even
among the rhetors, many had, or at any rate professed
to have, a passion for truth. And among the others
there is manifested from time to time a distinct historical conscience, a qualm as to the accuracy of the
assertion so trippingly written.

It is for this reason an especially painful gap in our
sources to find that portion of Polybius missing in
which he promised to treat at length of the Jews.
Polybius of Megalopolis, a Greek who lived as an
Achean hostage in Rome, in the second third of the
second century B. C. E., was the nearest approach the
ancient world had to an historian in the modern sense,
one whose primary object was to ascertain the truth
and state it simply. Polybius could, for example, feel
and express high admiration for Roman institutions
and at the same time do justice to the bitter hater of the
Romans, Hannibal. And this too in the lifetime of men

who may themselves have heard the dreadful news of Trasimene and Cannae.

In his sixteenth book, Polybius briefly relates the conquest of Judea among other parts of Coele-Syria, first by Ptolemy Philometor's general, then by Antiochus the Great. "A little while after this, he [Antiochus] received the submission of those of the Jews who lived around the temple known as Jerusalem. About this I have much more to tell, particularly because of the fame of the temple, and I shall reserve that narrative for later."

An evil chance has deprived us of that later narrative. If we possessed it, we should probably have a very sane and, as far as his sources permitted, an accurate account of the condition of the Jews during the generation between Antiochus the Great and the Maccabees. Polybius, however, wrote before the establishment of the Jewish state and the spread of its cult had focused attention upon the people, and roused opposition. And he wrote, too, at the very beginning of Roman interference in the East, which reduced Egypt to a protectorate before another generation. When he speaks therefore of the "great fame of the temple" ($\dot{\eta}$ $\pi\epsilon\rho\grave{\iota}$ $\tau\grave{o}$ $\iota\epsilon\rho\grave{o}\nu$ $\epsilon\pi\iota\phi\acute{a}\nu\epsilon\iota\alpha$), he is an especially important witness of what the name meant to the Romans and Greeks, for whom he wrote.[11]

CHAPTER XIII

THE OPPOSITION IN ITS SOCIAL ASPECT

If the rivals and opponents of the Jews had nothing more to say of them than that they worshiped the head of an ass, it is not likely that their opposition would have been recorded. But they would have put their training to meager use, if they could not devise better and stronger terms of abuse.

The very first Greek historian who has more than a vague surmise of the character and history of the Jews is Hecataeus of Abdera (comp. above, p. 92). As has been seen, his tone is distinctly well-disposed. But he knows also of circumstances which to the Greek mind were real national vices. He mentions with strong disapproval their credulity, their inhospitality, and their aloofness.

Credulity is not a vice with which the Jews were charged in later times. That may be due to Christian tradition, in which of course the sin of the Jews is that they did not believe enough, as stated in Christian controversial writings. But Greeks and Romans were quite in accord, that the Jews were duped with extraordinary facility; especially that they were the victims of the deception of their priests, so that they attached importance to thousands of matters heartily without importance. We may remember Horace's jibe, *Credat*

Iudaeus Apella, "Tell it to the Jew Apella";[1] and nearly two hundred years later Apuleius mentions the *Iudaei superstitiosi,* "the superstitious Jews."[2]

Among the Greeks particularly the quality of εὐήθεια, "simplicity," had rapidly made the same progress as the words "silly" and "simpleton" have in English.

Sharpness and duplicity were the qualities with which non-Greek nations credited the Greeks, and whether the accusation was true or not," "naïveté," εὐήθεια, excited Greek risibilities more quickly than anything else. The εὐήθεια of the Jews lay of course not in their beliefs about the Deity. On that point all educated men were in accord. But it lay in believing in the sanctity of the priests, and in the observance of the innumerable regulations, particularly of abstention, which had already assumed such proportions among the Jews. The line of Meleager of Gadara, about his Jewish rival,

ἔστι καὶ ἐν ψυχροῖς σάββασι θερμὸς Ἔρος,[3]

Even on the cold Sabbaths Love makes his warmth felt,

contains in its ψυχρὰ σάββατα, "cold Sabbaths," an epitome of the Greek point of view. ψυχρός, "cold," was almost a synonym for "dull." That a holiday should be celebrated by abstention from ordinary activities and amusements seemed to a Greek the essence of unreason. Their own religious customs were, like those of all other nations, full of tabus, but they were the less conscious of them because they were wholly apart from their daily life. Jews avoided certain foods, not merely as an occasional fast, but always. Their myths were not

12

irrelevant and beautiful stories, but were firmly believed
to be the records of what actually happened. The pre-
cepts of their code were sanctioned, not merely by expediency, but by the fear of an offended God.

An excellent example of how the rhetorical τόπος of
"naïveté" was handled is presented by Agatharchidas
of Cnidus, who wrote somewhere near 150 B. C. E.'

He tells us of Stratonice, daughter of Antiochus
Soter and wife of Demetrius of Macedon, who was
induced by a dream to remain in a dangerous position,
where she was taken and killed. The occasion is an
excellent one to enlarge upon the topic of superstition,
and Agatharchidas relates in this connection an incident
that is said to have happened one hundred years before
Stratonice, the capture of Jerusalem by Ptolemy Soter
through the fact that the Jews would not fight upon the
Sabbath. "So," says Agatharchidas, "because, instead
of guarding their city, these men observed their senseless rule, the city received a harsh master, and their law
was shown to be a foolish custom." One cannot repro-
duce in English the fine antitheses of the related words
φυλάττειν τὴν πόλιν balanced by διατηρούντων τὴν ἄνοιαν, νόμος
answering to ἐθισμόν; but, besides the artificiality of the
phrases, the total absence of any attempt to make the
words fit the facts is shown by the conclusion to which
Agatharchidas, by rule of rhetoric, had to come. Now
a "harsh master" is just what Ptolemy was not to the
Jews, and Agatharchidas of all men must have been
aware of that fact, for he wrote not only at Alexandria, but at the court of Philometor, an especial patron
of the Jews individually and as a corporation.

The practice of the Sabbath was one of the first things that struck foreigners. It is likely that the congregations of Sabbatistae in Asia Minor were composed of Jewish proselytes.[5] The name of the Jewish Sibyl Sambethe,[6] the association of Jewish worship with that of the Phrygian Sabazios,[7] were based upon this highly peculiar custom of the Jews. But its utter irrationality seemed to be exhibited in such instances as Agatharchidas here describes, the abstention from both offensive and defensive fighting on the Sabbath.

Whether the incident or others of the same kind ever occurred may reasonably be doubted. The discussion of the question in Talmudic sources is held at a time when Jews had long ceased to engage in warfare.[8] Their nation no longer existed, and their legal privileges included exemption from conscription, if they chose to avail themselves of it. In the Bible there is no hint in the lurid chronicles of wars and battles that the Sabbath observance involved cessation from hostilities during time of war, and the supposition that no resistance to attack was offered on that day is almost wholly excluded. It is not easy to imagine one of the grim swordsmen of David or Joab allowing his throat to be cut by an enemy because he was attacked on the Sabbath.

That any rule of Sabbath observance which demanded this had actually developed during the post-Exilic period is likewise untenable. The Jews served frequently in the army under both Persian and Greek rule. This is amply demonstrated by the Aramaic papyri of Elephantine and the existence of Jewish mercenaries under the Ptolemies.⁹ The professional soldier whose service could not be relied upon one day in seven would soon find his occupation gone.

Several passages in the Books of Maccabees have often been taken to imply that the strict observance of the Sabbath was maintained before the Hasmonean revolt, and deliberately abrogated by Mattathiah (I Macc. ii. 30-44; II Macc. viii. 23-25). But upon closer analysis it will be seen that the incidents there recorded do not quite show that. The massacre of the loyal Jews in the desert was a special and exceptional thing. They were not rebels in arms, but hunted fugitives. Their passive submission to the sword was an act of voluntary martyrdom (I Macc. ii. 37). ἀποθάνωμεν οἱ πάντες ἐν τῇ ἁπλότητι ἡμῶν: μαρτυρεῖ ἐφ᾽ ἡμᾶς ὁ οὐρανὸς καὶ ἡ γῆ ὅτι ἀκρίτως ἀπόλλυτε ἡμᾶς, "Let us all die in our innocence. Heaven and earth bear witness for us that ye put us to death wrongfully."

Again, it is not Mattathiah, but the sober reflection of his men, that brings them to the resolution that such acts of martyrdom, admirable as they are in intention, are futile. The decision is rather a criticism of their useless sacrifice than anything else.

Similar acts of self-devotion on the part of inhabitants of doomed cities were not uncommon. As final proofs of patriotism on the part of those who would not survive their city, they received the commendation of ancient writers.¹⁰ But to kill oneself or allow oneself to be killed for a fantastic superstition, could have seemed only the blindest fanaticism.

Now there is no reason for doubting the essential accuracy of the report in I Maccabees, to the effect that one group of Jewish zealots chose passive resistance to the attempt of Antiochus, and by that nerved the Hasmoneans to a very active resistance. And it is very likely that in this event we have the basis for the stories that related the capture of Jerusalem—almost in every case—on the Sabbath. The story is told of the capture by Nebuchadnezzar, by Artaxerxes Ochus, by Ptolemy, and by Pompey. It is a logical inference from the non-resistance of the refugees mentioned in I Maccabees. The conditions of ancient warfare make it highly improbable that it was more.

The rationalist Greek or Roman felt it a point of honor to hold in equal contempt the " old-wives' tales " of his own countrymen as to the supramundane facts with which the myths were filled," and the vain and foolish attempts by which barbarians, and Greeks and Romans too, sought to dominate the cosmic forces or tear the secret from fate. These attempts generally took the form of magic, not, however, like the primitive ceremonies, of which the real nature had long been forgotten, but in the elaborate thaumaturgic systems which had been fashioned in Egypt, Persia, and Babylon. In their lowest forms these were petty and mean swindling devices. In their more developed forms they contained a sincerely felt mysticism, but under all guises they aroused the contempt of the skeptic, to whom the most

ancient and revered rites of his own cult were merely
ancestral habits which it did no harm to follow. The
tone such men adopted toward the complicated Oriental
theologies and rituals was very much like that of modern cultivated men toward the various " Vedantic philosophies," which at one time enjoyed a certain vogue.
Those who seriously maintained that by the rattling
of a sistrum, or the clash of cymbals, or by mortifica-
tions of the flesh, influences could be exerted upon the
laws that governed the universe, so as to modify their
course or divert them, were alike insensate fools, whose
chatter no educated man could take seriously. The
Jews, who observed, even when they were less rigorous,
a number of restrictive rules that gravely hampered their
freedom of action, who seriously maintained that they
possessed a direct revelation of God, were fanatics and
magicians, and exhibited a credulity that was the first
sign of mental inferiority.

" Senseless," " nonsense," ἀνοητός, ἄνοια, are terms
that are principally in the mouths of the Philopator of
III Maccabees and the Antiochus of IV Maccabees, in
whose words we may fairly see epitomized all the current abuse as well as criticism which opponents to
the Jews, from philosophers to malevolent chauvinists,
heaped upon them.

Hecataeus says of Moses that he instituted an " inhospitable and strange form of living." [12] The two words
μισόξενον and ἀπάνθρωπον form a *doublette,* or rhetorical
doubling of a single idea. That idea is " inhospitality,"
lack of the feeling of common humanity, a term which

for Greeks and Romans embodied a number of conceptions not suggested by the word to modern ears.

The word ξένος, which is the root of the words for
"hospitality" and its opposite, has no equivalent in
English. A ξένος was a man of another nation, who
approached without hostile intent. The test of civilization was the manner in which such a ξένος was dealt
with. The Greek traditions, even their extant literature, have a very lively recollection of the time when
hospitality was by no means universal, when the ξένος
was treated as an enemy taken in arms or worse. The
one damning epithet of the Cyclops is ἄξενος, "inhospitable."[13] The high commendation bestowed upon the
princely hospitality of the Homeric barons itself indicates that this virtue was not yet a matter of course,
and that boorish nations and individuals did not possess it.

Legally, of course, the ξένος had no rights. Such
claim as he could make for protection rested upon the
favor of the gods, especially of Zeus, who was frequently addressed by the cult title of Ξένιος, the Protector of Strangers. The uncertain aid of the gods was
soon displaced by personal relations between individuals
and groups of individuals in different states, who were
mutually πρόξενοι to each other, a title that always
created a very definite moral obligation and soon a legal
one as well. So, when Alexander destroyed Thebes, he
spared the πρόξενοι of his own family and of the Macedonians in general.[14]

The institution and the development had practically gone on in similar ways all through the Mediterranean world. The Bedouins still maintain the ancient customs of their fathers in that respect. The Romans had the word *hospes,* of which the history is a close parallel to that of ξένος.

Of the Jews the same thing may be said. The Bible enjoins the protection of strangers as a primary obligation. They were the living symbols of the Egyptian bondage. So Exodus xxiii. 9, " Also thou shalt not oppress a stranger, for ye know the heart of a stranger, seeing ye were strangers in the land of Egypt." One of Job's protests of righteousness is his hospitality (Job xxxi. 32).

In these circumstances just what could the charge of μισοξενία, of " inhospitality," have meant? We shall look in vain in Greek literature for an injunction to hospitality as finely phrased as the passage just quoted from Exodus. To understand the term as applied to the Jews we shall have to examine the words that are used for the acts connected with hospitality.

In Homer the word ξεινίζω [15] is frequently found. Strictly of course it means simply "to deal with a stranger," but it is used principally in the sense of " entertain at dinner." The wandering stranger might as such claim the hospitality of the people among whom chance had brought him, and claim it in the very concrete sense that food and lodging at the master's table were his of right. Indeed it would almost seem that he became *pro hac vice* a member of the family group in

which he partook of a meal, protected in life and limb
by the blood-vengeance of his temporary kinsmen.

That however seems to have been the general rule in
the older communities of the East, in Palestine just as
in Greece and Asia. There was no feeling against entertaining a stranger at table among the Jews, although
the relation could not well be reversed. And there was
the rub. It was not in Palestine (where the Jew was
likely always to be the host), but in the communities in
which Jew and non-Jew acknowledged the same civic
bond that the refusal of the Jew to accept the hospitality
of his neighbor would be a flagrant instance of μισοξενία,
of dislike of strangers. We need not suppose that it
needed careful investigation and the accumulation of
instances to produce the statement. A few incidents
within anyone's experience would suffice. We shall
have to remember further that we are dealing with a
literary tradition in which many statements are taken
over from the writer's source without independent conviction on his own part.

However, among the great masses the general feeling that the Jews disliked strangers, and so were properly to be termed μισόξενοι, was in all likelihood based
on an observation of more obvious facts than dietary
regulations. It is principally in meat diet that the separation is really effective, and meat diet was the prerogative of the rich. Then, as now, the great majority
of the people ate meat rarely, if at all, and surely could
take no offense at a man's squeamishness about the
quality or nature of the food he ate. But what every-

body was compelled to notice was that the Jews deliberately held aloof from practically all public festivities, since these were nearly always religious, and that they created barriers which seemed as unnecessary as they were foolishly defended. That in itself could be interpreted by the man in the street only as a sign of deep-rooted antipathy, of μισοξενία.

This accusation, as has been shown, was more than the reproach of unsociability. The vice charged by it was of serious character. Those individuals who in Greek poetry are called inhospitable are nothing short of monsters. It implied not merely aloofness from strangers, but ill-usage of them, and that ill-usage was sometimes assumed to be downright cannibalism. So Strabo (vii. 6) tells us that the "inhospitable" sea was called so, not only because of its storms, but because of the ferocity of the Scythian tribes dwelling around it, who devoured strangers and used their skulls for goblets. That was of course to be inhospitable with a vengeance, but the term covered the extreme idea as well as the milder acts that produced at Sparta and Crete frequent edicts of expulsion (ξενηλασίαι)[16] and a general cold welcome to foreigners.

In very many cases, especially in the rhetorical schools, "inhospitality," "hatred of strangers," was a mere abusive tag, available without any excessive consideration of the facts. And when intense enmity was to be exhibited, the extreme form of "inhospitality" was naturally enough both implicitly and expressly charged against the objects of the writer's dislike.

GREEK INSCRIPTION, FOUND ON SITE OF TEMPLE AREA, FORBIDDING
GENTILES TO PASS BEYOND THE INNER TEMPLE
WALLS AT JERUSALEM

(Now In the Imperial Ottoman Museum Constantinople)

There are many instances in which the hereditary enemy was credited with human sacrifice or cannibalism. Indeed it was currently believed that cannibalism had universally prevailed at one time, and with advancing civilization was gradually superseded.[17] As far as human sacrifice was concerned, many highly civilized states knew of vestiges or actual recurrences of it in their own practice. Rome is a striking example. But in Rome such things were rare exceptions, employed in times of unusual straits to meet a quite unusual emergency.[18] In Greece there were many traces frankly admitted to be such—if not actual instances of such sacrifices. But here, as at Rome, the act was admittedly something out of the ordinary, a survival of primitive savagery.[19]

Accordingly when Greeks and Romans spoke of human sacrifices, it was not of an inconceivable form of barbarity, which placed those who took part in it quite out of the human pale, but as a relic of a condition from which they had themselves happily grown, and to which they reverted only in extremities. Its presence among other tribes was a demonstration that they were still in the barbarous stage, and especially was it deemed to be so when all strangers who chanced to come upon the foreign shore were the selected victims of the god.

That charge, as we know, was made against many Scythian and Thracian tribes. The story of Iphigenia in Tauris is an example of it. It was made against the Carthaginians, at least in the early stages of their history. The Gauls, according to both Greek and

Roman writers, had made of it a very common institution.[20] We do not know very much of the evidence in the case of the Thracians, Scythians, and Gauls. It is not impossible that customs like certain symbolic rites found in many places were misinterpreted. Or it is highly likely that, if human sacrifices existed, they were, as among Greeks and Romans, a rare form of expiation. For the Carthaginians the story is almost certainly a by-product of national hatred, and rests upon the same foundations as the "cruelty" and "perfidy" of Hannibal.

Human sacrifices, similar to those of Greece and Rome, existed in Palestine. Children were sacrificed to the nameless god or gods that bore the cult title of *melech, i. e.* "king." As in the rest of the Mediterranean world such sacrifices were exceptional and grisly forms of expiation, used when ordinary means had failed. Among the Jews, on the other hand, they seem to have been prohibited from the very beginning of their history as a community. It is a purely gratuitous theory that makes *melech,* or *molech,* a cult-title of Yahveh in Israel. There is simply no evidence of any kind that it was so. On the contrary, the oldest traditions of the Jews represent the abolition of human sacrifices as one of the first reforms instituted by the founders of their faith. The Mosaic code made these sacrifices a capital offense (Lev. xviii. 21 ; xx. 2). The very name *molech* indicates an intense abhorrence, if, as has been plausibly suggested, it is simply מלך, or "king," with the vowels of בשׁת, "the Abomination."[21]

With so old a tradition on the subject, the Jews must
have felt, as peculiarly irritating, the transference of
this vituperative tag to them. That it might be so
applied was of course an inevitable expansion of
the belief that the Jews were μισόξενοι, " haters of
strangers." However, it must not be supposed that the
statement was widely current. On the contrary, we
have only two references to it. Damocritus, who lived
perhaps in the first century B. C. E., as quoted by the late
Byzantine compiler Suidas,[22] asserts that the Jews captured a stranger every seven years, and sacrificed him to
their god ; and Apion, in the first century C. E., relates the
circumstantial story of the captured Greek who was
found immured in the temple by Antiochus Epiphanes.

The latter story is an amusing instance of rhetorical
method. Of its baselessness of course no proof need be
adduced. It is almost certainly the concoction of Apion
himself, perhaps based upon some such statement as
this just quoted from Damocritus. Its melodramatic
features, the fattening of the stranger, the oath sealed
by blood, are highly characteristic of Apion's style.

It cannot be said that this particular charge against
the Jews had any real success. The later writers do not
mention it. Tacitus and Juvenal, both of whom are
very likely to have read Apion, pass by the story in
silence. And Juvenal, who in his Fifteenth Satire
expresses such detestation of a similar act among the
Egyptians he abominated,[23] would certainly not have let
off the Syrian fortune-tellers, whom he equally disliked,
with an allusion to their unsociability.

Non monstrare vias nisi eadem sacra colenti,[24] " They are instructed not to point out a road except to those who share their rites." It might almost seem as though even rhetorical animosity demanded more for its terms of abuse than the authority of Apion.

The tragic importance of the " ritual murder " in the modern history of the Jews since the Crusades has given the account of Apion a significance to which it is by no means entitled. The least analysis will show that the " ritual murder " of modern times is not really like the ancient story at all. The latter is simply an application to the Jews of the frequent charge of ξενοθυσία, " sacrifice of strangers," such as was made against the Scythians. And Apion's fable found practically no acceptance. There is of course no literary transmission between Apion and the chroniclers of Hugh of Lincoln, but we cannot even suppose that there was a popular one. In the fearful struggles of the rebellions under Hadrian and Trajan, it is impossible to believe that the mutual hatred, which found such expression as the massacre at Salamis and the reprisals of the Greeks, would have failed to register this charge against the ἀνόσιοι Ἰουδαῖοι, " the wicked Jews," if it were known.

The early Middle Ages, at any rate from the Crusades on, devised the " ritual murder " without the aid of older authorities. It is one of the many cases in which parallel developments at different times and in different places produce results that are somewhat similar, although only superficially so.[25]

CHAPTER XIV

THE PHILOSOPHIC OPPOSITION

A favorite adjective in describing the Jews was "superstitious." Strangely enough, another, perhaps even more general, was "irreligious." The Jews were frequently stigmatized as ἄθεοι, a word generally translated "atheist," and undoubtedly often used in the sense of the modern term. It remains to be seen whether the term meant, in its application to the Jews, all that the corresponding modern term implies. That is particularly necessary here, since to the modern world the devotion of the nation to its Deity is its most striking characteristic, and at least one of the key-notes of its historical development. Upon us it has almost the effect of a paradox to read that this people impressed some Greeks as a nation of "atheists" or "godless."

The modern term and the ancient partly cover each other. Both often denote the speculative negation of a supernatural direction of the world. Now it simply cannot be, in view of the wide distribution of the Jews and their successful propaganda, that even the unthinking could associate the people whose claims to direct divine guidance were so many and so emphatic, with a term that implied the non-recognition of any god. We may remember how even the very first contact had seemed to emphasize the religious side of the Jewish communal life.

The usual explanations will not bear analysis. It is frequently asserted that " atheist " was applied to the Jews because of their imageless cult. The natural inference, we are told, from the fact that there were no statues was that there were no gods. But that is to assign to the statue a larger importance in ancient religious theory than in fact belonged to it. We meet, to be sure, cases where the identification of the statue and the resident deity seems to be complete. Especially in such scoffers as Lucian,[1] or in the polemics of the philosophic sects, or in those of Jews and Christian writers, Romans and Greeks are often charged with the adoration of the actual figure of stone or bronze. That, however, was surely not the general attitude of any class. The passages that seem to show it are generally figurative and often imply merely that the god had taken his abode within the statue, and might leave it at will.

Indeed, just for the masses, the most intense and direct religious emotions were always aroused, not by the great gods whose statues were the artistic pride of their cities, but by the formless and bodiless spirits of tree and field and forest that survived from pre-Olympian animism. And these latter, if adored in symbolic form, were represented generally by pillars or trees, and not by statues at all.

Nor were the Jews the only imageless barbarians whom the Greeks and Romans encountered. Most of the surrounding nations can scarcely have possessed actual statues at first. And the Greeks or Romans drew no such inference as atheism from the fact that they found no statues of gods among Spaniards, Thracians, Germans, or Celts. On the contrary, we hear of gods among all these nations, many of them outlined with sufficient clearness to be identified promptly with various Greek deities. What a Greek would be likely to assume is rather that these barbarians lacked the skill to fashion statues or the artistic cultivation to appreciate them. If it occurred to him to explain the imageless shrine at Jerusalem at all, he would no doubt have offered some such statement, especially as it was quite common to assume lack of artistic skill in barbarians.

Atheism as a philosophic doctrine was relatively rare. Diagoras of Melos, a contemporary of Socrates, and Theodore of Cyrene,[2] a contemporary of the first Ptolemy, were said to have held that doctrine, and the former was known from it as " the Atheist." However, even in this case we cannot be quite sure of our ground. Some of the poems of Diagoras seem to have a distinct, even a strong, religious feeling. Josephus asserts that Diagoras' offense in Athenian eyes was scoffing at the mysteries.[3] If that is true, he received his sobriquet less from atheism, as we understand it, than from the same facts that brought Protagoras, Anaxagoras, and Socrates himself within the ban of the Athenian police. That is, he was charged rather with contempt of the actually constituted deities of the Athenian state than with a general negation of a

divinity. The term itself, ἄθεος, is not necessarily negative. In fact, Greek had very few purely negative
ideas. In Plato's Euthyphro⁴ the only alternatives that
are admitted are θεοφιλές and θεομισές, *i. e.* what the
gods hate and what the gods love. So the various Greek
adjectives compounded with "*a* privative," ἀνωφελής,
"useless," ἄβουλος, "thoughtless," are really used in a
positive sense contrary to that of the positive adjective.
So ἀνωφελής is rather "harmful" than merely "useless"; ἄβουλος is "ill-advised"; etc. The word ἄθεος
would, by that analogy, rather denote one that opposed
certain gods than one who denied them. A man might
be ἄθεος in one community and not in another. Indeed
his "atheism" might be an especial devotion to a divine
principle which was not that recognized by the state.

In ordinary literary usage ἄθεος is denuded even of
this significance. It means little more than "wicked."
It is used so by Pindar, by Sophocles, and in general by
the orators. Often it runs in pairs with other adjectives
of the same character. Xenophon calls Tissaphernes
(An. II. v. 29) ἀθεότατος καὶ πανουργότατος, "most godless and wicked," in which the superlative is especially
noteworthy. As a matter of fact it is often used
of a man whom the gods would have none of, rather
than one who rejects the gods. Αθεος, ἄφιλος ὀλοίμαν,
cries the chorus in Oedipus Rex, "May I die abandoned
by gods and men."⁵

When it is first used of the Jews by Molo, it is as part
of just such a group; ἄθεοι καὶ μισάνθρωποι, he calls the
Jews, "hateful to gods and men," and other rhetoricians

follow suit. As a term of abuse, ἄθεος was as good as
any other.

But there may have been a more precise sense in
which the Jews might by an incensed Greek be properly
stigmatized as ἄθεοι. To the thoroughgoing mono-
theists, the gods of the heathen are non-existent. They
are not evil spirits, but have no being whatever. The
prophets and the intellectual leaders of the Jews held
that view with passionate intensity. But even they used
language which readily lends color to the view that these
gods did exist as malignant and inferior *daemonia*.
The "devils" of Leviticus xvii. 7 are undoubtedly the
gods of other nations.⁶ The name "Abomination,"
which for the Jew was a cacophemism for "god,"
equally implies by its very strength a common feeling of
the reality of the being so referred to. Likewise the
other terms of abuse which the Jews showered upon
the gods of the heathen indicate a real and fiercely personal animosity.

Hatred and bitterness formed almost a religious
duty. An implacable war was to be waged with the
abominable thing, and it is not likely that dictates of
courtesy would stand in the way. The retort of ἄθεος
would mean no more than a summary of the fact that
the Jew was the declared enemy of the constituted
deity, whose anger he provoked and whose power he
despised.¹

Something of this appears in the statement of the
Alexandrian Lysimachus, that the Jews were enjoined
to overturn the altars and temples which they met

(Josephus, Contra Ap. i. 34), and in the phrase of the elder Pliny (Hist. Nat. XIII. iv. 46), *gens contumelia numinum insignis,* " a race famous for its insults to the gods."

Most of the phrases that have been quoted have been taken from works where they were little more than casual asides imbedded in matter of different purport. Rhetoricians, in attempting to establish a point, use some phrase, either current through popular usage or a commonplace in their schools. In this respect the Jews fare no better and no worse than practically all nationalities of that time. Individual writers disliked or despised various peoples, and said so in any manner that suited them. Slurs against Romans, Athenians, Boeotians, Egyptians, Cappadocians are met with often enough. The Cretans were liars, the Boeotians guzzlers, the Egyptians knaves, the Abderitans fools; antiquity has furnished us with more than one entertaining example of national hate and jealousy.[8] The epithets which the Acheans showered on their Aetolian rivals certainly leave nothing to be desired as far as intensity is concerned.[9] The various panders of Roman comedy often are represented as particularly choice specimens of Agrigentine character.[10] Cicero particularly knew from his rhetorical masters how to use national prejudices in the conduct of his business. If Celts are the accusers of his client, as they were in the case of Fonteius, they are perjurers, murderers, enemies of the human race. " Tribes," he says, " so far removed from other races in character and customs that they fight, not for their religion, but against the religion of all men."[11] If they are Sardinians, these are a "tribe whose worthlessness is such that the only distinction they recognize between freedom and slavery is that the former gives them unlimited license to lie."[12]

To take this seriously is to misconceive strangely both the functions of an advocate and the license of rhetoric. Now the abusive paragraphs directed against the Jews are quite of this type. And it is in the highest degree extraordinary that these phrases, which, in the instances just cited, are given no weight in determining national attitude, should be considered of the highest importance in the case of the Jews. Whether it was Syrian, Greek, or Celt that was attacked, the stock epithet means no more than the corresponding terms of our own day mean.

But besides these occasional flings there were whole books directed against the Jews, and to that fact a little attention may be given.

It is a relatively rare thing that a writer should nurse his bile against a particular people to the extent of expanding it into a whole book. We must of course remember that a " book " was sometimes, and especially in this polemical literature, a single roll, and we are not to understand it in the sense of a voluminous treatise. However, there were such books and these we must now consider.

What such a book was like, recent anti-Semitism has made it very easy to imagine. There is no reason to suppose that this type of pamphlet was appreciably

different in those days. It consisted of a series of bitter
invectives interspersed with stories as *pièces justifica-
tives.* Now and then an effort is made to throw it into
the form of a dispassionate examination. But even in
very skilful hands that attitude is not long maintained.

Of several men we know such treatises. All have
already been mentioned—Apollonius Molo, Damocritus, and probably Apion.

Apollonius, either son of Molo, or himself so named,
was one of the most considerable figures of his day.
He taught principally, but not exclusively, at Rhodes,
and numbered among his pupils both Cicero and Caesar.
As a rhetorician he enjoyed an extensive and well-
merited influence. It was during his time that the reaction against the florid literary style of Asia culminated
in the equally artificial simplicity of the Atticists—a
controversy of the utmost importance in the history of
Latin literature no less than Greek. The doctrine of
mediocritas, "the golden mean," set forth by Molo,
moulded the style of Cicero and through him of most
modern prose writers. The refined taste and good
sense which could avoid both extremes justify his
repute and power.

He was a voluminous writer on historical and rhetorical subjects. Only the smallest fragments remain, not
enough to permit us to form an independent estimate of
his style or habits of thought. Just what was the incentive for the pamphlet he wrote against the Jews it is
impossible to conjecture. But it is not likely that it contained many of the specially malignant charges. To

judge from Josephus' defense, it seems to have concerned itself chiefly with their unsociability, and may
have been no more than a sermon on that text. Josephus'
charge against him is that of unfairness. There is none
of the abuse in Josephus' account of Molo which he
heaps upon Apion. We may accordingly infer that
Molo's pamphlet was considerably less offensive. It
may have been, in effect, a mere *declamatio,* a speech
in a fictitious cause, or the substance of an oration
delivered in an actual case. Or perhaps a single instance of personal friction produced it as an act of
retaliation. The rhetoricians of those days were essentially a *genus irritabile,* and their wrath or praise was
easily stirred.

Of Damocritus we know almost nothing. Suidas, a
late Byzantine grammarian mentions a short work of
his on Tactics, and one as short, or shorter, on the Jews.
The reference to human sacrifice (above, p. 189), might
be supposed to indicate a strong bias. While it is likely
enough that it was hostile in character, that single fact
would not quite prove it, since we do not know whether
Damocritus represented these human sacrifices as an
ancient or a still-existing custom.

The third name, Apion, has become especially familiar from the apology of Josephus. The latter refers
to him throughout as an Egyptian, and in spite of certain very warm and modern defenders he very likely
was of Egyptian stock. From the Oasis where he was
born, he came to Alexandria where he established a
great reputation. Undoubtedly possessed of fluency

and charm as a speaker, he was a most thoroughgoing charlatan, a noisy pedant wholly devoid of real critical skill. He boasted of magical power, through which he was enabled to converse with the shade of Homer. His vanity prompted the most ludicrous displays of arrogance. Tiberius Caesar dubbed him the *cymbalum mundi,* " the tom-tom of the world," a characterization that seems to have been generally accepted.[13]

In the appeal of the Jewish residents of Alexandria against the maladministration of the prefect Flaccus, argued before the emperor, he represented the Alexandrian community, whose acts were the basis of the charge made by the Jews. As such he no doubt delivered an anti-Jewish invective, and it is at least likely that this speech formed the substance of his book on the subject, just as the defense of the Jews and the attack upon Flaccus are contained in the two extensive fragments of Philo, the *Legatio ad Gaium,* and the *In Flaccum.*

It has been doubted whether he really wrote such a book, although there are express statements that he did. It is true enough that those who assert it may easily have been misled by the fact that certain books of his History of Egypt may have contained these anti-Jewish passages or most of them. None the less, the fact that he must have prepared a set speech in the case mentioned, coupled with the statements of Clemens of Alexandria and Julius Africanus, renders the older view the more probable.[14] There would of course be nothing strange if the books of the History of Egypt and a special monograph contained essentially the same material.

As to other similar pamphlets, we hear of a περὶ Ἰουδαίων by a certain Nicarchus, son of Ammonius, which may have had an " Egyptian " bias, in that Moses is said to have been afflicted with white scales upon his body—an assertion that seems to be a revamping of Manetho's "leprous outcasts." But the title of the book does not point to a wholly hostile attitude, nor does the passage referred to necessarily imply such an attitude.[16]

Taking all these passages together, from Manetho to Apion, one thing must be evident: Manetho himself, Mnaseas, Agatharchidas, Chaeremo, Lysimachus, Apion, are either Egyptians or are trained in Alexandria, and represent the Egyptian side of a bitter racial strife, as intense and lasting as was generally the case when the same community contained several compact groups of different political rights and privileges.

The conditions of the population of Alexandria have been previously discussed. It was the great market center of the East, and as such of the Mediterranean world, since the commercial and intellectual hegemony was always east of the Aegean Sea. The population had been a mixed one since its foundation. The warped notions that have often been held of the position of the Jews there are due to a failure to realize concretely how such a city would be likely to grow. The Greeks and Macedonians that were originally settled there

undoubtedly constituted a real aristocracy, and made
that attitude very thoroughly felt. One thing further
is clear, that the native Egyptians, who probably formed
the mass of the populace, looked upon these Greeks as
they did upon all foreigners, with intense dislike. We
have a document in which a Greek suitor in court
impugns the credibility of Egyptian testimony against
him because of the well-known hatred Egyptians bear
toward Greeks.[16]

Egyptian animosity toward Jews had been of longer
standing simply because intercourse in close proximity
was much older. Further, the Jewish colonies from
early Persian times had always represented the foreign
master. It was as natural, therefore, for this animosity
to express itself in street-conflicts in Alexandria as for
anti-Greek feeling to be manifested there. Those
modern investigators who have confidently asserted that
Alexandrian " anti-Semitism " was of Greek origin and
leadership have permitted the rattle of the *cymbalum
mundi* to confuse their minds. For it is Apion and
Apion alone that makes the claim that the Jews are
especially embittered against Greeks, and seeks to
create a general Greek feeling against them. His
motives are too apparent to need comment, and there is
no evidence whatever that he was successful.

Further, it is the Egyptians Manetho and Apion
whose tirades have a fiercely personal coloring. The
Greek Alexandrians make their anti-Jewish polemics on
the basis of general theories, and particularly lay stress
on what was to them the perfectly irrational separatism

which the Jews had made a part of their religion. As
has been frequently shown, the relatively small fragments of these writers do not enable us to say how far
this Jewish characteristic is used to point a moral, much
as the modern clergy takes chauvinistic commonplaces
to illustrate the evil results of doctrines they are
attacking.

In the case of two Greeks, Posidonius of Apamea in
Syria, and Molo, no Egyptian influence can be shown.
Both were among the most influential men of their
time. Molo's career and importance have been briefly
sketched. To Posidonius must be assigned a still more
powerful intellectual influence over his generation and
those that followed." The leader of the Stoic school or,
as it may well be called, sect, he so reorganized its
teaching that the Stoa became nothing else than the
dominant faith among cultivated men, a situation perhaps paralleled by Confucianism in China, which is also
an ethical philosophy that finds it possible to dwell on
terms of comity with various forms of cruder popular
belief.

What Molo's philosophic affiliations were is not easy
to determine. The Stoics were nearer than most other
schools to rhetoricians and grammarians, but many men
of these professions acknowledged allegiance to the
Academy, to Epicureanism, or even to the revived
Pythagoreanism of the first century B C. E. Of the
extensive writings of the Rhodian rhetorician there is
not enough left to give even a probable answer.

But most philosophic sects laid stress on the universality of their teachings, and were marked by an intense
intellectual rationalism. The crude psychology of those
days made the formation of categories a simple thing.
Thinkers could scarcely be expected to admit that
inherited instincts could qualify the truth of a philosophic dogma. More particularly, the philosophic
movements were powerful solvents of nationalism.
Even the distinction between Greek and barbarian did
not exist in theory for them.[18] The notion of the state
and the maintenance of its ancestral rites became for
them a meaningless but innocuous form, which men of
common sense would not despise, but to which one
could attach no great importance.

Face to face with congregations like those of the
Jews, which enforced their separation by stringent
religious prohibitions, the Stoics more than others found
their opposition roused. More than others, because many
Stoics adopted from the Cynical school the methods of
the diatribe, the popular sermon, and, indeed, made an
active attempt to carry the universality of their principles into practice. And the Stoics, more than others,
would find the height of irrationality in the stubborn
insistence on forms for which only an historical justification could be found.

A highly interesting document, which gives a certain
phase of the controversy, or perhaps even fragments of
an actual controversy, between the general philosophic
and the Jewish doctrine, has come down to us in the
tract known as the Fourth Book of Maccabees. The

author announces his purpose of setting forth a most philosophic thesis, to wit, whether the pious reason is sovereign over the passions. The philosophic argument, which fills the first three chapters, is Stoic in form and substance. Then, to illustrate his point, he cites certain vaguely remembered stories of II Maccabees, which he expands into highly detailed dramatic forms. In the mouth of Antiochus Epiphanes are placed the stock philosophic arguments against the Jews, which are triumphantly refuted by the aged Eleazar and the seven sons of Hannah.

So we hear Epiphanes reasoning with Eleazar and urging him to partake of swine's flesh (IV Macc. v. 8 seq.) :

For it is obviously a senseless proceeding to refrain from enjoying those pleasures of life which are free from shame : it is even wicked to deprive oneself of the bounties of nature. And it seems to me that your conduct will be still more sense-less, if you provoke my anger because of your zeal for some fancied principle. Why do you not rid your mind of the silly doctrine of your people? Discard that stupidity which you call reason. Adopt a form of thought that suits your age, and let your philosophic principle be one that actually serves you. . . . . Further consider this : If in the Deity you adore there is really a power that oversees our deeds, it will grant you full pardon for all transgressions which you have been forced to commit.

To a Greek, and no doubt to many modern men, the reasoning is conclusive. It presents the Greek point of view very well indeed, and is doubtless the epitome of many conversations and even formal disputes in which these matters were discussed between Greek and

Jew. And just as the argument of Epiphanes seems strangely modern in its appeal to common sense and expediency, so the answer of Eleazar rings with a lofty idealism that is both modern and ancient:

We, whose state has been established by God, cannot admit that any force is more powerful than that of the Law. Even if, as you assume, our Law were not divine, yet, since we suppose that it is, we durst not set it aside without gross impiety.

Eleazar then proceeds to elaborate upon the Stoic paradox that the slightest and the greatest transgressions are equally sinful; [19] and that in so far as abstention is a form of self-control, it is an admirable and not a contemptible act. After a detailed account of the hideous sufferings heroically endured by the priest, the author breaks out into a panegyric of him as a maintainer of the Law, in which the fundamental Stoic proposition with which he begins is less prominent than his intense Jewish piety.

For us, however, the prime importance lies in the sharp contrast between the Greek and the Jewish attitude. Upon the philosophically cultured man, the reasoning of Epiphanes could not fail to produce a certain impression. In the case of the seven sons of Hannah, while many elements are repeated (IV Macc. viii. 17 seq.), the writer has in mind the appeal to the flesh, which Hellenism made. "Will you not change your mode of life for that of the Greeks and enjoy your youth to the full?" asks Antiochus (*ibid*. viii. 8); and that no doubt was the whisper that came to the heart of many a young man, surrounded by the bright and

highly colored life of the Hellenic communities in
which he dwelt. There is no exchange of vituperation.
The denunciations hurled against Antiochus are im-
personal, indeed are generic. He is the type of tyrant,
another Busiris or Phalaris, a bowelless despot. And
the one word which alternates with " senseless " in the
mouths of Antiochus and his executioners is " mad."

The actual events described are of course quite unhis-
torical. But we do not find here any of the various
forms in which racial animosity or personal spleen
exhibited itself against the Jews. In spite of the setting, the controversy is, judged by disputation standard-
ards, quite decorous. The terms that qualify the
Jewish doctrine as " irrational " are almost controversial commonplaces. The martyrs do not resent the
epithet. They seem to accept it as the logical inference
of the carnal philosophy of their oppressors and claim
to be justified by a higher wisdom.

Jewish and Greek life began to touch each other
at many points in the six or seven generations that
intervened between Alexander and Caesar. Hellenism
dominated the political and social culture of the Eastern
Mediterranean, although the nationalities it covered
were submerged rather than crushed. In Egypt the
indigenous culture maintained itself successfully, and
forced concessions from the conqueror, which made the
Hellenism of that country a thing quite different from
that of the other lands within the sphere of Greek
influence. The resistance of the Jews also took the
form of successful insurrection, and in their case

enabled an independent political entity to be constituted.

The dispersal of the Jews was already considerable at this time. It differed from the dispersal of the Syrians in the fact that the bond of union of the Jewish congregations existed in the common cult and the common interest in the fortunes of the mother-country. On the other hand, the Syrians of Rome and of Naples shared nothing except the quickly effaced memory of a common racial origin.[20]

The propaganda of the Jews was also well under way. Since it was believed that they possessed a mystery, initiation into which gave promise of future beatitude, they were strong rivals of the Greek and Oriental mysteries that made similar claims. It was chiefly among the half-educated or the wholly unlettered that these claims would find quickest belief. However, the Jewish propaganda had also its philosophic side, and competed with the variously organized forms of Greek philosophic thought for the adherence of the intellectually advanced classes as well.

Through the Diaspora and this active propaganda an opposition was invited. In Egypt the opposition was older, because the presence of Jews in Egypt was of considerably earlier date than the period we are considering. The occasions for its display were various, but the underlying cause was in most cases the same. That was the fact of religious separatism, which in any given community was tantamount to lack of patriotism. It does not appear, however, that this opposition found voice generally except in Egypt. Elsewhere racial friction was relatively rare.

The literature of the opposition falls into two classes: first, that which scarcely knows the Jews except as a people of highly peculiar customs, and uses these customs as illustrations of rhetorical theses; and second, that which is inspired by direct animosity, either personal or, in the case of the Egyptians, racial in its character.

CHAPTER XV
THE ROMANS

We have been concerned so far almost wholly with Greeks and the Greek attitude toward the Jews. It will be necessary at this point to turn our attention to a very different people, the Romans.

If we desire to trace the development of this all-overwhelming factor in our reckoning, it will not be possible to go back very far. During the fifth century B. C. E., in which Greek genius is believed to have reached its apogee, it is doubtful whether even the faintest whisper had reached Greeks that told of the race of Italic barbarians destined so soon to dominate the world. Little as was known of the Jews by Greeks of this period, the Romans were still less known. The eyes of men were persistently turned east.

Rome, however, even then was not wholly insignificant. Many centuries before, there had grown up, on the south bank of the Tiber, a town of composite racial origin. It is possible to consider it an outpost of the Etruscans against Sabine and Latin, or a Latin outpost against the Etruscans. Whatever its origin, at an indeterminate time, when the Etruscan hegemony over central Italy was already weakened, this town of Rome became a member of the Latin Confederation, a group of cities of which the common bond was the shrine of Jupiter Latiaris on the Alban Mount.

There may have been rude hamlets upon this site from times very ancient indeed. But from the beginning of its existence as a real city Rome must have been a considerable community. Her strategic position upon seven hills, the commercial advantages of her location upon a navigable stream, conspired to this end.

The Latin Confederation had long been under the real or titular presidency of the city of Alba. At some time before our records become reliable, Rome had obtained a decidedly real leadership in the league, and unscrupulously used the latter's resources for the furtherance of her own power and wealth. Without a definite programme of conquest, and with military skill and personal hardihood very little, if at all, superior to that of their neighbors, the Romans had, by steadfastness and native shrewdness, developed a policy which it is difficult to put in precise terms, because it was never even approximately formulated, but which may be said to consist of unremitting vigilance and long memory, combined with special alertness to profit by the mistakes or division of the foe. It may be that the indubitably mixed character of Rome's population produced that result. Certainly in these respects no other ancient community was its equal.

The legendary history of Rome is as generally familiar as the commonest household stories of the race. Modern investigators have abandoned the attempt to find out even partially the line at which its history ceases to be legendary. Fairly correct accounts of Rome begin with the permanent contact of the city with a literate community of which the records have survived, namely, the Greeks.[1]

The Greeks had founded cities along the southern coast of Italy and the eastern half of Sicily as early as the ninth century B. C. E. With some of these cities it was inevitable that Rome should be in frequent communication, but the communication did not impress itself for many years upon that class of Greeks which, in the extant books, speaks for the whole people. Not till the time of Alexander (330 B. C. E.) do our Greek records begin to deal with Romans. At that time Rome was already the dominant power in central and in the interior of southern Italy, succeeding roughly to the empire of that great Tuscan League of which she was once the subject. And yet, Alexander's teacher, the encyclopedically learned Aristotle, had only vaguely heard of Rome as an Italian city overrun by marauding Gauls.[2]

The position occupied then by Rome would of itself have made active participation in Mediterranean affairs a necessity. The embroilment of Romans in the conflicts in which international politics is expressed was precipitated by the ambition of the restless Diadochi and their successors. It was a kinsman of the lurid Demetrius the Besieger, the Epirote prince Pyrrhus, who undertook to save the Greek civilization of the coast cities from the Italian barbarians. Pyrrhus ultimately retired with his tail between his legs, after hav-

ing dragged the Romans into Sicily and brought them
face to face with the Carthaginians. The succeeding
three generations were occupied in the mortal grapple
between these two. It ended with the triumph of
Rome.

So far Rome had dealt only with the West, but with
the permanent eastward bent of men's minds the lord of
the Western Mediterranean was, as such, a power in the
East as well. Scarcely a single generation passed before
it became the sole power in the East, so that future
political history becomes the act of officially recording
successive realizations of that fact. And yet, this extraordinary people, which had in an astoundingly short
time secured the primacy over a considerable fraction
of the earth, was apparently possessed of slighter intellectual endowments than many of its subjects. It had
not succeeded in giving such culture as it had developed
any artistic form. And before it had taken any steps
in that direction, it came into immediate contact with
nations of much older culture, which had done so; in
one case, a nation which had carried artistry of form
to a degree never subsequently attained by any single
people. First, the Etruscans had given in bulk a mass
of finished cultural elements especially in religion and
constructive crafts, and had otherwise exercised an
influence now wholly undeterminable. Secondly, by
Etruscan mediation and afterwards directly, the
Romans became the intellectual vassals of the Greeks, a
fact that lends some justification to the modern tendency to treat classical antiquity as a single term.

The Romans obtained their very earliest knowledge of the Jews when the political and social development just outlined was practically complete.

The treaty cited in I Macc. viii. 22 seq. is perhaps apocryphal, but the substantial accuracy of the chapter is scarcely doubtful. " And Judas had heard the name of the Romans," we read, and this statement is followed by a lengthy recital of the recent conquests of Rome. After the first Hasmonean successes the little knowledge that Roman and Jew had of each other may be so summed up. On the Roman side, the responsible senatorial oligarchy learned with undisguised satisfaction that a previously unknown tribe of Syrian mountaineers, grouped about a famous temple-rock not far from the Egyptian frontier, had successfully maintained themselves against a troublesome and unaccountable tributary king. On the Jewish side, the leaders of the victorious rebels, conscious of the precarious nature of their success, turned at once to that mighty people— known as yet scarcely by report—which from far off directed men's destinies. Even at that time the Roman policy of *divide et impera,* " divide and rule," was well understood and consciously exploited by all who could do so. The embassy sent by Judas—there is no real reason for questioning its authenticity—presented to curious Romans in 162 B. C. E. an aspect in no way different from that of other Syrian embassies long familiar to the capital. And if it is true that some of that train or of a later embassy of Simon took up permanent residence in Rome, that fact was probably scarcely noticed from sheer lack of novelty.

Generally speaking, the Roman attitude to the Jews, as to all other peoples, was that of a master : the attitude of the Goth in Spain, the Manchu in China, the English in India. No one of these analogues is exact, but all have this common feature, that individuals of the dominant race can scarcely fail to exhibit in their personal relations with the conquered an arrogance that will vary inversely with the man's cultivation. It is so very easy to assume for oneself the whole glory of national achievements. No doubt every Italian peasant and artisan believed that it was qualities existing in himself that commanded the obedience of the magnificent potentates of the East. The earliest attitude of Roman to Jew could not have been different from that toward Syrians or foreigners in general. If in 150 B. C. E. the term *Iudaei* had reached the ears of the man in the street, it denoted a Syrian principality existing like all other principalities at sufferance and upon the condition of good behavior.

For nearly a hundred years this state of things remained unchanged. Then the inevitable happened. Syria became Roman, and the motives that had won Roman support for the Jews no longer existed. Roman sufferance was withdrawn, and Judea's good behavior ceased. That Gnaeus Pompey encountered serious resistance on his march from Antioch to Jerusalem is doubtful. The later highly-colored versions of his storming of the temple are probably rhetorical inventions. The Psalms of Solomon, which are very plausibly referred to this period, are outbursts of passionate grief at the loss of the national independence; for no recognition of Hyrcanus' rank could disguise the fact of the latter's impotent dependence upon the senate, and the limitations openly placed upon the vassal-king's authority show that the Romans were at no pains to disguise the fact.[3]

When the Romans added Asia to their dominions, as they had in the generation preceding the occupation of Jerusalem, they annexed with Asia many hundreds of Jewish synagogues in the numerous cities of Asia. Jews lived also in Greece, in Italy and Rome itself, and in Carthage. Egypt, which contained many hundreds of thousands, was still nominally independent. Roman officials had long known how to distinguish the *Iudaei* from others of those ubiquitous Syrians who, as slaves, artisans, physicians, filled every market-place of the empire. More than one provincial governor must have collected a few honest commissions from a people indiscreet enough to collect sums of considerable magnitude, as the Jews did for the support of the temple.

That they were classed as Syrians did not raise the Jews in general, and particularly in Roman, esteem. The Syrians, to be sure, were one of the most energetic, perhaps mentally the quickest, of the races then living, but they were the slave race *par excellence; i. e.* the largest number of slaves were and had long been derived from among them. The vices of slavery, low cunning, physical cowardice, lack of self-respect, were apparent

RUINS OF AN ANCIENT SYNAGOGUE AT MERCM, GALILEE,
PALESTINE
(Roman Period)

enough in those Syrians who were actually slaves, and were transferred to all men of that nation. " Syri " is nothing less than a term of contempt applied to any people of unwarlike habits.[4]

Unwarlike the Jews of that day were not. All that had commended them to Roman notice was their military successes over the troops of Antiochus and Demetrius. Pompey may not have found Aristobulus and his Nabatean allies really formidable, but he did have to fight, and did not meet that docile crawling at his feet which he had encountered elsewhere. That made considerable difference in Roman eyes, and may have caused the unusual tenderness they manifested as a rule for what they loftily termed the Jewish superstition.

As has been said, we have reason to believe that a Jewish community already existed at Rome, and we shall see that it must have been fairly numerous. As a city, Rome was probably the least homogeneous in the world. It may have contained at this time something less than a million people, perhaps much less; but this population was of the most diverse origin. Not only had the capital of the world attracted to it all manner of adventurers; not only was it teeming with slaves of every imaginable blood and speech; but the thronging of the city with the refuse of the world had been a conscious policy of the democratic and senatorial rings, to whom modern " colonization " was a familiar and simple process. When we recall that the accepted governmental theory was still that of the city-state, we shall see that mere residence made to a certain extent a Roman of everyone who lived within the walls. Various measures of expulsion, such as the Lex Junia Penni and the Lex Papia of 65 B. C. E., were wholly ineffective.

As a matter of fact, the governmental apparatus of the city-state was quite unable to cope with the situation that presented itself. Until 200 B. C. E., the turning-point in Roman history, the city was small and mean; the population, though composite, was still almost wholly Italian in character. A rapid increase in wealth and a consequent increase in glaring inequalities of fortune began at this point. The governing council of ex-magistrates, whose office had in practice become almost hereditary, found itself confronted by a needy and exigent proletariat, which it could neither overawe nor purchase.

The urban tendency of the population of Italy was due largely to the failure of the small farms to support their man. Free labor was subjected to the constant drain of military levies, and temporary suspension of cultivation was ruinous. The obvious remedy was a forced and unprofitable sale to the agrarian capitalists, whose leasehold interest in the great public lands had long been so nearly vested that it was almost sacrilege to attack it. To migrate to the city was then the only course open to the peasant, but in the city the demand for free labor was never great. The new arrivals joined the great mass of landless rabble, sinking soon into an idle and pauperized mob.

But at the same time infusions of foreign blood came into the city. The rapid rise in wealth and power had poured into Rome a constant stream of the commonest of wares, viz. human chattels. These slaves, Greek, Thracian, but above all Syrian, were directly consequent upon the imperative demand for skilled labor, which they alone could satisfy. But the very number of these slaves, and the changes in personal fortunes, which were then even more frequent than now, made them often a liability rather than an asset to their master.

Enfranchisement was encouraged by another consideration. The Roman law, determined by a very ancient patriarchal system, was apparently very rigid as to the extent of the master's *dominium*. The slave was, in law and logic, a sentient chattel indistinguishable from ox and ass. But in other respects the Roman law was extraordinarily liberal. For practical purposes the slave could and did acquire property, the so-called *peculium*, and could and did use it to purchase his freedom.

Further, the newly-made freeman became a full citizen, a *civis Romanus*. His name was enrolled in the census books; he possessed full suffrage, and lacked only the *ius honorum*, the right of holding office. Even this, however, his children acquired. Sons of slaves who held magistracies are frequent enough to furnish some notable examples; *e. g.* Cn. Flavius, the secretary to Appius Claudius; P. Gabinius, the proposer of the Lex Tabellaria of 139 B. C. E.[8] It is for this reason that indications of servile origin have been found in names nothing less than illustrious in Roman history.[9]

With this steady influx of dispossessed peasants and enfranchised Greek and Asiatic slaves, the urban population was a sufficiently unaccountable quantity; and in this motley horde, constantly stirred to riot by the political upheavals, which quickly followed each other from the Gracchan period onward, all manner of strange and picturesque foreigners lived and worked. To the Roman of cultivation they were sometimes interesting, more often repellent, especially if he found himself compelled to reckon with them seriously on the basis of a common citizenship. Even for foreigners Roman citizenship was not very difficult to acquire, and was, as we have seen, obtained with especial facility through slavery. The emancipated slave was as such a *civis Romanus*. His son had even the *ius honorum;* he might be a candidate for the magistracy. This process had been accelerated after the Social War, which admitted an enormous and quite unmanageable number into citizenship. The popular leaders were especially lavish, and no doubt many ward politicians took it upon themselves to dispense with the formalities when a few votes were needed.

We are very fortunate in possessing for this period records of quite unusual fulness and variety. The last century of the Roman republic was rich in notable men, with some of whom we are especially familiar. In literary importance and in permanent charm of personality, no one of them can compare with the country squire's son, Marcus Tullius Cicero, who achieved the impossible in his lifetime, and attained posthumous fame far beyond his wildest dreams. He was consul of Rome in the very year in which Jerusalem was captured, and was in the throes of the same political uncertainty that marked his whole later career. The most brilliant pleader in the city or the world, he was feared, loved, and hated for his mordant wit his torrential fluency of speech, and his remarkable power and skill in invective. Although his personal instincts had always inclined him to the gentlemanly aristrocracy that made up the majority of the senate he had won his first successes in politics on the other side, and reached the summit of his ambition, the consulship, as a popular candidate, receiving the support of the senate only because he was deemed the least dangerous of three.

In the year 59 B. C. E. Cicero, conceded y the leader of the Roman bar and still more concededly the social lion of the day, undertook the defense of Lucius Valerius Flaccus, former governor of Asia, who was charged with maladministration and oppression. The counts in the indictment were numerous. Among them was the following allegation: That Flaccus as praetor had seized certain sacred funds; to wit, the moneys which Asiatic provincials, Jews in origin, had, in accordance with ancient custom, collected and were about to transfer to the temple at Jerusalem. By so doing Flaccus had doubled embezzlement upon sacrilege, for the sanctity of the temple was established by its antiquity, and confirmed by the conduct of Pompey, who had ostentatiously spared it and its appurtenances.

It will be necessary to examine in some detail the circumstances of the entire case. Flaccus was a member of the reactionary wing of the senatorial party, which until recently had held Cicero aloof as an upstart provincial. His birth and training were those of an aristocrat. A certain portion of Cicero's defense is occupied in descanting on the glories of the Valerian house, to which Flaccus belonged. The prosecution of Flaccus, again, was a political move of the popular opposition, now at last, after the futile essays of Lepidus and Catiline, finding voice and hand in the consummate skill of Gaius Julius Caesar.

Shortly before this date a powerful combination had been made, which enlisted in the same scheme the glamour of unprecedented military success in the person of Gnaeus Pompey, the unlimited resources of the tax-farmers and land-capitalists represented by Marcus Crassus, and the personal popularity of the demagogue Caesar. Each no doubt had his own axe to grind in this coalition, and the bond that held them was of an uncertain nature, opposition to the senatorial oligarchy. Further, only in the case of Caesar was the opposition a matter of policy. In the case of the other two, it was the outcome of nothing loftier than pique. None the less, when the strings were pulled by Caesar, this variously assembled machine moved readily enough.

In 59 B. C. E. this cabal had been successful in winning one place in the consulship, that of Caesar himself. Lucius Flaccus had earned Caesar's enmity by his vigorous action against the Catilinarians in 63 B. C.

E., so that when an influential financier, C. Appuleius Decianus, complained of Flaccus' treatment of him, the democratic leader found an opportunity of gratifying his allies, of posing as the protector of oppressed provincials, and wreaking political spite at the same time. A certain Decimus Laelius appeared to prosecute the ex-governor of Asia.

Of Flaccus' guilt there seems to be no reasonable question. He was plainly one of the customary type of avaricious nobles to whom a provincial governorship was purely a business proposition. No doubt he was no worse than his neighbors His guilt seems to have been especially patent. "Cicero," says Macrobius, "secured the acquittal of Flaccus by an apposite jest, although the defendant's guilt of the charges made was perfectly apparent." [7] And indeed on the principal counts Cicero has no evidence except exaltation of Flaccus' personal character, and abuse of the witnesses against him, whom he characterizes as lying and irresponsible Greeks. His peroration is a flaming denunciation of the prosecution and an appeal to the jury not to permit the supporters of the dead traitor Catiline to win a signal triumph.

The speech was successful. Flaccus was acquitted, and the acquittal may have hastened Cicero's own banishment. But for us the particularly interesting part of this brilliant effort is contained in §§ 66-69. After he has disposed of the various charges of peculation and extortion, he turns to the charges made by the Jews:

Next comes the malicious accusation about the gold of the Jews. No doubt that is the reason why this case is being tried so near the Aurelian terrace. It is this count in the indictment, Laelius, that has made you pick out this place, and that is responsible for the crowd about us. You know very well how numerous that class is, with what unanimity they act, and what strength they exhibit in the political meetings. But I shall frustrate their purpose. I shall speak in a low tone, just loud enough for the jury to hear. There is no lack of men, as you very well know, to stir these fellows up against me and every patriotic citizen; and I have no intention of making the task of such mischief-makers lighter by any act of mine.

The facts are these: Every year it has been customary for men representing the Jews to collect sums in gold from Italy and all our provinces for exportation to Jerusalem. Flaccus in his provincial edict forbade this to be done in Asia.

Now, gentlemen, is there a man who can honestly refuse commendation to this act? That gold should not be exported is a matter which the senate had frequently voted, and which it did as recently as my own consulship. Why, it is a proof of Flaccus' vigorous administration that he took active steps against a foreign superstition, as it is an indication of a lofty sense of duty that he dared defy, where the public weal was concerned, the furious mass of Jews that frequently crowd our meetings.

But, we are told, when Jerusalem was captured, the conqueror Gn. Pompey touched nothing in that shrine. And that was very wisely done on Pompey's part, as in so many other acts of that commander. In so suspicious and slanderous a city as ours, he would leave nothing for his detractors to take hold of. But I do not believe, and I cannot suppose you do, that it was the religion of such a nation as the Jews, recently in arms against Rome, that deterred our illustrious general. It was rather his own self-respect.

In view of these considerations, just wherein does the accusation lie? You do not anywhere charge theft; you do not attack the edict; you admit due process of law; you do not deny that the moneys were openly confiscated upon official investigation. The testimony itself discloses that the whole matter was carried on by men of rank and position. At Apamea, Sextus Caesius, a Roman knight and a gentleman of whose honor and integrity there can be no question, openly seized and weighed out in the forum at the feet of the praetor a little less than a hundred pounds of gold At Laodicea an amount somewhat more than twenty was seized by Lucius Peducaeus, a member of this very jury; at Adramytus, ... by the governor's representative, L. Domitius. A small quantity was also seized at Pergamon. The accounts of the gold so seized have been audited. The gold is in the treasury. There is no charge of theft. The purpose of the charge is to excite odium against my client. It is not the jury that the prosecution is addressing, but the audience, the crowd about us.

Religious scruples, my dear Laelius, are primarily national concerns. We have our own, and other states have theirs. And as a matter of fact even while Jerusalem was standing, and the Jews were at peace with us, there was very little in common between the religious customs of wh ch their rites are examples and those which befit an empire as splendid as ours, or a people of our character and dignity. Our ancestral inst tutions are as different from theirs as they well can be. Now, however, there surely can be all the less obligation upon us to respect Jewish religious observances when the nation has demonstrated in arms what its feelings are toward Rome, and has made clear how far it enjoyed divine protection by the fact that it has been conquered, scattered, enslaved

There are a number of difficulties with the passage. The text of the final sentence is doubtful—but the d s- cussion of that point will be reserved for the Notes.*

We cannot suppose that Cicero was guilty of delib- erate misstatement on matters about which he could be immediately confuted. We must therefore accept his assertion that this count in the indictment did not charge theft or malversation, but merely public con- fiscation of the funds in question. It is undoubtedly a

15

fact that the exportation of the precious metals had been frequently forbidden, although the senatorial resolution to this effect was far from being a law, but with this precedent and even without it no one could very well deny that it was within the imperium of a proconsul to make such a regulation if he saw fit.[9]

One may well ask with Cicero, *Ubi ergo crimen est?* The point seems to be that previous officials had interpreted the rule to refer to exportation for commercial purposes, and had exempted from its operation contributions for religious purposes. Doubtless the self-imposed temple tax of the Jews was not the only one of its kind. If custom had sanctioned that exemption, Flaccus' act would be felt as an act of oppression, since the strict or lenient enforcing of the edict on this point was purely a matter of discretion.[10] Flaccus' successor, Quintus Cicero, a brother of the orator, seems to have reverted to the former practice.

In one other respect the seizure of these sums may have seemed an act of arbitrary tyranny. The sum seized at Apamea was said to be one hundred pounds of gold—about 72 English pounds—and must have equaled about 75,000 Roman denarii or Athenian drachms. As the temple tax was a didrachm, that would imply over 35,000 heads of families, or a total Jewish population for Apamea of 170,000. That number is quite impossible. It is, however, very likely that the Jews of the various synagogae paid their didrachm with their other dues to the corporation *arca,* or treasury, and that it was the whole treasury that was seized.

That would give the Jews of these cities a very real grievance, and make their animus against Flaccus easy to explain.

The importance of the passage, however, is in no way concerned with the justice or injustice of the accusation against Flaccus. It lies first in its picture of the Jewish community at Rome, and secondly in its indication of Cicero's personal views.

The very insertion of the charge proves that a considerable Jewish element existed, whose aid the prosecution was anxious to enlist. Cicero's own statements show this directly. Here and here only in his speech he refers to the popular odium sought to be incited against his client, and speaks of the number and power of the Jews *in contionieus*,[1] " in the political meetings," and in the crowd about him. Part of this, the *summissa voce*, " low tone,' for example, is the veriest acting. Cicero was really not afraid to say loudly what he wished to say, and if the jury could hear him, part of the crowd could hear as well. But although the Roman Jews were probably not so redoubtable as Cicero would have his jury believe, they must have formed a large contingent. Where did they come from?

We have the statement of Philo that it was not until the capture of Jerusalem by Pompey in 63 B. C. E. that Jews were brought to Rome in large numbers.[2] These, it is supposed, were enfranchised shortly after, and are the people here referred to. That may be said to be the general view.

There are, however, serious difficulties in it that escape those who hold it, simply because they fail to follow in detail the implications of their view. Pompey did not arrive in Rome till January, 61 B. C. E. His army had been previously dismissed, but was to assemble for the great triumph that took place in September, 61. The trial of Flaccus was held in August, 59 B. C. E. Some months must have been spent in preparing the case against him. Accordingly we are to suppose that thousands of Jewish captives were brought to Rome, sold there, enfranchised, learned Latin, became politically organized, and developed formidable voting strength, all within less than two years! The mere question of language makes the hypothesis impossible. Pompey's captives were Palestinian Jews, of most of whom the native language was Aramaic, not Greek.[13] Without command of Greek or Latin the ready acquisition of either was nothing short of miraculous, and the immediate political activity is only less so.

But the chief difficulty lies in another matter. The phrase "taken prisoners" immediately suggests the conditions of modern warfare, in which whole armies are surrendered and transferred in bulk great distances for safe-keeping. It is to be feared that some such idea was suggested to modern writers by the words of Philo. But that is not at all what occurred in ancient times. Prisoners taken on the field of battle were sold immediately at the nearest market. Slave-dealers followed the army. Caesar's account of his campaign in Gaul affords numerous instances of this immediate dis-

posal of captured foes; *e. g.* the case of the Atuatuci
and Veneti.[14] If they were assigned as loot to individual
soldiers, they were disposed of in the same way. Here
and there a soldier would, for one reason or another,
retain his prisoner as a personal slave, but in general
he had almost no facilities for providing or caring for
a number of them. A few of the distinguished captives
were reserved by the commander for a triumph.

Now Pompey's army had just finished a five years'
campaign. It had marched through Asia and Syria,
winning battles that were not very bloody, but must
have been immensely lucrative. The Jews formed only
a small portion of the total prisoners taken. If all those
prisoners actually accompanied their captors to Rome,
the question of transportation and provision for such a
horde must have been tremendous. What could have
induced a general or private to assume this enormous
expense and care, when the greatest slave-market in the
world, viz. that at Alexandria, was relatively near by,
is inconceivable. If they got to Rome, the city's population must have swelled visibly under the process.
There is no record that it did, and it could scarcely have
escaped notice, had such a thing taken place.

And finally, even if we assume that such a wholly
unprecedented and inexplicable incident occurred, how
are we to explain the immediate and wholesale enfranchisement of so large a number? Ransom by
wealthy coreligionists at Rome is excluded by the
hypothesis. Similar action by Jews outside the city
would demand a much longer time. The reasons gener-.

ally assigned are based upon the assumed uselessness of Jewish slaves for ordinary purposes because of their dietary laws and religious intransigeance. But that is a purely dogmatic assertion. Papyri and inscriptions have shown that in spite of a bitter racial opposition and perhaps economic strife as well, Jew and non-Jew could live quite peaceably together. The dietary laws would not render his master's meals obnoxious to a Jewish slave, because he did not eat at his master's table, and might consume his scanty vegetable food where and how he pleased. If a master actually chose to force attendance at the sacrifice, the compulsion of necessity would have been a valid excuse for all but those of martyr stuff, and we cannot suppose that every Jewish soldier had in him the zeal of a martyr. Besides, for such compulsion the slave would in no sense be responsible, and it is with disadvantages moving from him that we are concerned.

It is simply impossible to imagine what could have induced Pompey's soldiers or those who purchased from them to enfranchise immediately slaves transported from such a distance and at such expense.

Philo's statement is at best a conjecture, made without any better acquaintance with the facts than we ourselves possess, and contradicted by the necessary inference from Cicero's words.

We must therefore assign the settlement of Jews in Rome to a much earlier date. The tradition that some of the train of Simon's embassy had remained in Rome is, as we have seen, probable enough. To that nucleus there was added, by a perfectly natural and even inevitable infiltration, a group of Jewish freedmen, artisans, and merchants who were establishing themselves all over the Mediterranean. Jews are met with at Delphi a hundred years before the delivery of this speech.[1]

We have therefore, in 59 B. C. E., an established Jewish community, necessarily organized in synagogues and chiefly of servile origin. The use of foreigners at the polls by the political leaders had led to the Lex Junia Penni of 80 B. C. E. and the Lex Papia of 65 B. C. E., which ordered foreigners to leave the city. But these measures were wholly ineffective, and in any case could have only partly served those who proposed them, since the mass of the democratic strength lay in the proletariat, and the proletariat was largely composed of undoubted citizens, although freedmen. The Jews formed, as we see, an active and troublesome element in the turbulent city populace. Their attachment to the democratic leader, Caesar, is well attested, and Caesar's marked favor toward them has all the appearance of the payment of a political debt, as in the case of the Cisalpine Gauls.[16]

As far as Cicero was concerned personally, we may assume that his attitude was the contempt which he no doubt honestly felt for the *infima plebs* and for Syrian barbarians in particular. He probably voices the sentiments of the optimates,[17] with whom, though still hesitant, he had already cast his fortunes. The abuse arises from the necessities of the case. As previously pointed out, it is in this very speech that we have fine examples of the device of abusing your opponent's witnesses when arguments give out. These phrases show no special animus. Just as Greeks are liars if they are on the other side, and men of honor on his own, as exhibited almost in successive paragraphs of this speech,[18] so we may be sure if Cicero were prosecuting Flaccus, a few eloquent periods would extol the character of those ancient allies and firm friends of Rome, the Jews.

How much Cicero really knew of the Jews is not certain. He is aware that in point of religious observance the Jews are strikingly different from other tribes. The contrast he emphasizes in his speech may be an allusion to the imageless cult of the Jews and the inference of meanness and poverty of ceremonial which Romans would draw from it. And the taunt *quam dis cara,* "how dear to the gods," seems an unmistakable fling at the claim of the Jews, loudly voiced in their propaganda, to possess in a high degree the favor of the Divinity, or even a special communion with the Deity in their mysteries.

All this Cicero might have learned from his surroundings. It is doubtful that he learned it from Posidonius and Molo, both of whom he knew well. In these two appear stories which Cicero could hardly have overlooked if he knew them. When we remember what he says of Sardinians in the Scauriana, of Gauls in the Fonteiana,[19] he surely would not have omitted to catalogue the tales treasured up by these two Greek teachers of his; to wit, the ass-god, the scrofulous prophet, the savage inhospitality and absurd fanaticism Molo and Posidonius ascribe to the Jews.

One other phrase which Cicero applies to Jews would deserve little attention if it were not for the extraordinary general inferences some have drawn from it. In May, 56 B. C. E., Cicero has an opportunity to vent his venom on his enemy Gabinius, consul in 59 B. C. E., whom he held personally responsible for the humiliation of his exile. Gabinius, in 56, was governor of Syria, and seems to have been rather short with the tax-farmers, whom, to the delight of the provincials, he treated with contumely and no doubt with gross injustice. The persistent favor he showed to all provincial claims against these men, many of them Cicero's personal friends and at all times his supporters, caused the orator, to exclaim:

As far as the unfortunate tax-farmers are concerned—and I count myself equally unfortunate to be compelled to relate their misfortunes and sufferings—Gabinius made them the chattel-slaves of Jews and Syrians, races themselves born to be slaves.

The concluding phrase is simply the application of the rhetorical commonplace of Greeks that barbarians as such were slaves by nature. It was applied to Syrians with a certain justice, as the slave name Syrus testifies. From that standpoint, however, it was obviously absurd to assert that it was true of Jews. Cicero's inclusion of them is due to the fact that, as governor of Syria, Gabinius would have had many occasions to favor Jewish litigants against the publicans, probably in pursuance of his party's policy. Gabinius, we may recall, was a very obedient servant of his masters, the triumvirs, and the interest of the leading spirit of the coalition in the provinces has been previously pointed out.[20]

Allusions of this type made in the course of vehement advocacy or invective are really of little meaning even as an indication of personal feeling. It is true, however, that Cicero shows very little sympathy in general with the Roman masses or with the provincials, despite the Verrine prosecution. That he could have felt any interest or liking for Syrian barbarians in or out of the city is very improbable.

None the less, within Cicero's own circle, the same elements in Jewish customs which had impressed Greeks, such as Theophrastus and Clearchus, could not fail to strike such Romans as made philosophic pretensions. The fame of the shrine at Jerusalem had reached Rome a century earlier, as we have seen from Polybius. Pompey's capture of the city formed no inconsiderable item in his exploits. Cicero refers to him jestingly as *noster Hierosolymarius,* " Our Hero of Jerusalem." [21] We can tell from Cicero's own words the emphasis that Laelius had laid on the fame of the temple and its sanctity when he denounced Flaccus. As a matter of fact it was a constant practice of Romans to find, in those institutions of barbarians which could be called severe or simple, the image of their own golden age of simplicity, before the advent of Greek luxury. So Cicero's learned friend and correspondent Varro is quoted by Augustine [22] as referring to the Jews among others as a people whose imageless cult still maintains what the Romans had abandoned. There may be very little sincerity in this regret of a simple-living past, but it is an indication that the exceptional character of Jewish religious customs might in Cicero's own *entourage* be characterized in terms somewhat different from those of the Flacciana.

We shall have reason to distinguish very sharply between the attitude of Romans of rank and cultivation and that of the great mass. However, that is true not only in this relatively minor detail but in thousands of other matters as well. The Roman gentleman was distinct from the mass, not merely in political principles, but in his very speech. In the following generations social readjustments of all sorts frequently modified the position of the Jews in Rome, but until the increasing absolutism of the monarchy practically effaced distinctions, the cleavage just indicated largely determined the point of view and even the terms used.

CHAPTER XVI

JEWS IN ROME DURING THE EARLY EMPIRE

We are all familiar with the assertion that both Greeks and Romans of the last pre-Christian century were in a state of complete moral and religious collapse, that polytheism had been virtually discarded, and that the worn souls of men were actively seeking a new religious principle to take its place. This general statement is partly true, but it is quite inadequate, if it is made to account for the situation at Rome at that time.

The extant literature of the time makes it quite clear that there was no belief in the truth of the mythology. But it is doubtful whether there ever had been, and mythology was no part of religion. This was particularly true at Rome. For some thousands of years the inhabitants of central Italy had performed ceremonies in their fields in connection with their daily life. A great many of these ceremonies had become official and regulated in the city of Rome and many other Italic civic communities. It was the practice of educated Italians to devise aetiological stories for these practices and to bring them into connection with Greek myths. In this way a Roman mythology was created, but more even than in the case of the Greeks it was devoid of a folkloristic foundation.[1] For the masses these stories can scarcely be said to have existed. But the cere-

monies did, and their punctilious performance and the
anxious care with which extraordinary rites of purga-
tion were performed satisfied the ordinary needs of
ordinary men.

Mention has been made of the religious movement
which from the seventh century B. C. E. spread over the
Eastern Mediterranean, and which was concerned with
the demand for personal salvation and its corollary, a
belief in personal immortality. In the Greek-speaking
world the carriers of that movement were the Orphic
and Dionysiac mysteries. In the non-Greek East there
was abundant occasion for beliefs of this kind to gain
ground. The great world monarchies introduced such
cataclysms in the smaller nations that a violent read-
justment of relations with the divinity was frequently
necessitated, since the god's claim to worship was
purely national. No such profound political upheavals
occurred in Greece. Here, however, a fertile field for
the spread of mysteries and extra-national means of
divine relations was found in the rapid economic degeneration caused by the slave system. Attachment to the
state was confined to those who had a stake in it. The
maxim that a man's fatherland was where his fortune
brought him seemed less a bold and cynical aphorism
than the veriest commonplace for all but a few idealists.[2]
To save the personality that individual misfortunes
threatened to overwhelm, recourse was had to every
means and especially to the vague and widespread doctrine of other and fuller existences beyond the confines
of mortality.

In Rome the obvious hinge in the destinies of the
people from almost every point of view was the Hanni-
balic war.   For a short time disaster seemed imminent,
and the desperate reaching out to the ends of the earth
for divine support could not fail to make a deep impression upon thousands of men.   In that moment of
dreadful stress, it was not the Etruscan Triad on the
Capitol nor Father Mars, but the mystic Ma, the
Ancient Mother of Phrygia with her diadem of towers,
her lion-chariot and her bloody orgies, that stayed the
rush of the Carthaginian.   It is true that the city's
ultimate triumph caused a reaction.   An increased
national self-consciousness made Romans somewhat
ashamed of their weakness, but they could not blot out
the memory of the fact.

The city's increase in total well-being went on with
tremendous strides, but the disintegrating forces of
a vicious economic system were present here too.
Besides, the special circumstances that tended to
choke the city with people of diverse origin were intensified.   In the next few generations we hear of the
threatening character of foreign mysteries, of surreptitious association with the Cybele worshipers, of Isis
devotees gaining ground.   Shortly after the Second
Punic War occurs the episode of the Bacchic suppression.   One can scarcely help noticing how strikingly
similar were the accusations directed against the Bac-
chanales and those later brought against the Christians,
and wondering whether they were any truer in the
one case than in the other.   The whole incident can

easily be construed as an act of governmental persecution, which, it may be noted, was as futile as such
persecution generally is. The orgiastic Dionysus was
not kept from Italy, though he always remained an
uncomfortable god for Romans of the old type. One
reason has already been referred to ; viz , the constant
recruiting of the *infima plebs* from enfranchised foreign slaves. The lower classes were becoming orientalized. The great Sicilian slave revolt of 134 B. C. E.
was almost a Syrian insurrection, and was under the
direct instigation of the Syrian goddess Atargatis.[3]

During the civil wars and the periods of uncertainty
that lay between them, all political and social life seemed
as though conducted on the edge of a smouldering vol-
cano. Innumerable men resorted to magic, either in its
naïve form or in its astrological or mathematical refine-
ments. Newer and more terrific rites, stranger and
more outlandish ceremonials, found a demand constantly increasing. And the Augustan monarchy
brought only a temporary subsidence of this excitement. Order and peace returned, but Augustus could
not cure the fundamentally unsound conditions that
vitiated Roman life, nor did he make any real attempt to
prevent Roman society from being dissolved by the
steady inpour of foreign blood, traditions, and non-
Roman habits of mind. The need of recourse to foreign
mysteries was as apparent as ever.

In this way the internal conditions of Roman society
impelled men to the alien forms of religion. And
external impulses were not lacking. There were present

professional and well-equipped missionaries. Our information about them is fullest with reference to the philosophic schools, which consciously bid for the support of educated Romans. These groups of philosophers were nearly all completely organized, and formed an international fraternity as real as the great International Actors Association and the similar Athletic Union.[4] It was scarcely feasible to stand neutral. A man was either an Academic, or Stoic, or Epicurean, or Neopythagorean, and so on. So skilful a trimmer as Cicero's friend, the astoundingly shrewd Atticus, was enrolled as an Epicurean.[5] Even skepticism classified a man as an Academic, as Cicero himself was classed despite occasional exhibitions of sympathy for the Stoa. And the combat was as intense and as dogmatic as that between competing religious sects. That is precisely what they were, and they bandied their shibboleths with the utmost zeal and unction.

Some of these philosophic sects, the Cynics and Stoics, reached classes of lower intellectual level. And there they came in conflict with astrologer and thaumaturg, with Isis and with Atthis devotees, and with Jews. The popular sermon, the diatribe, was an institution of the Cynics, and was directed to the crowd. Indeed the chief object of Cynic jibes was the pretension of philosophers to possess a wisdom that was in any way superior to the mother-wit of the rudest boor.[6] The Stoics too used the diatribe with success. It must not, however, be supposed that either Stoic or Cynic was a serious rival of the dramatic and sensationally attractive rites of the Eastern cults. The latter counted their adherents by the hundreds where the preaching philosopher might pick up an occasional adherent. The importance of the philosophers for the spread of non-Roman beliefs lies chiefly in the fact that they reached all classes of society, and, different as they seem from the cult-associations of the various foreign deities, they really represented the same emotional need as the latter.

These had literary support as well. We have recently had restored to us some astrological pamphlets, such as that of Vettius Valens,[7] and we can only guess from what arsenal Isiac or Mithraist drew those arguments with which he boasted of confuting even Stoics and Epicureans. But we may safely assume that tracts existed of this sort.

As far as the Jews are concerned, their propaganda may have begun with their first settlement in Rome. Cicero does not mention it, but Cicero was not interested in what went on among the strata of society in which the Jews then moved. In the next generation their propaganda was so wide and successful that it must have been established for a considerable time.

Further, from what has been said it is clear that this propaganda must have been directed primarily to the plebs, to the same classes, that is, as those who received Isis and Cybele, Mithra and the Cabiri. At first it practically did not reach the intellectually cultivated at all. But the Jews possessed an extensive literature, which in Egypt and the East generally had assumed the form

16

of "most philosophic" treatises. Indeed, it is quite clear that the Wisdom of Solomon could be enjoyed by none but cultured men.[8] Books of this sort, as well as the Bible, were accessible, and were read by some. The synagogue service was an exposition of Jewish doctrine upon topics that ranked as philosophic. While therefore it was mainly from among the masses that Jewish converts came, here and there men of education must have found the Jewish preachers as convincing as the philosophic revivalists, who boasted of no more respectable credentials.

The Roman state had found itself obliged to take cognizance of the foreign religious movements at an early date. The official acceptance of Cybele had promptly been surrounded by restrictions. Cybele was always to remain a foreign goddess. Romans were stringently forbidden to take part in her ceremonies.[9] Toward the forms of worship themselves, the Roman attitude was tolerant enough. As long as they were confined to Egyptians, Syrians, Cappadocians, the participants would be secure from molestation. But that the foreign rites might displace the ancestral forms was a well-grounded fear, and drastic precautions were taken against that. The Bacchanalian incident of 186 B. C. E. is the first of these instances.

In the same way the Roman police found it necessary at various times to proceed against astrologers, Isis-worshipers, and philosophers. The statement frequently occurring, that these groups were banished, is constantly misunderstood. It can apply only to foreigners in these classes, not to Roman citizens affected by these strange beliefs; but it implies that the Roman citizens so affected were sufficiently numerous to make the desertion of the national religion a probable contingency. Of course Roman citizens could not violate the laws that regulated religious observances with impunity. These laws, however, were ostensibly never directed against the religious observances, but against abuses and acts that were connected with them. That was true even in the case of the Bacchanalia, when the decree of the senate expressly permitted the celebration of the rites under proper restrictions.

Whether honestly or not, the Roman government aimed its measures solely at certain indubitably criminal acts, which, it was alleged, were associated with the practice of the foreign cults. These acts were often offenses against public morality. Conditions of high religious excitement often sought a physical outlet in dancing or shouting, and no doubt often enough, when the stimulation of wine or drugs or flagellation was added, in sexual excesses. Instances that were perhaps isolated and exceptional were treated as characteristic, and made the basis for repressive legislation.[10]

Another and better founded objection to many of the forms of foreign religion was the opportunities they offered for swindlers. As early as 139 B. C. E. the astrologers were banished from Rome, not because of the feeling that the astrological system was baseless, but because of the readiness with which professed astrologers defrauded the simple by portentous horoscopes, which they alone could interpret or avert.[11] The "Chaldeans" or *mathematici* included many men who were neither the one nor the other. It was obviously easier for a Syrian or Oriental generally to make these claims than for either Greek or Italian. Syrians in the city accordingly found the profession of quack tempting and profitable, and doubtless many Jews as well entered it.

We have evidence too that many of the mushroom political associations were grouped about some of these foreign deities. The possession of common *sacra* was, in a sense, the distinguishing mark of any organized body of men, and organization of the masses in all forms was the commonest device of the agitators of the revolutionary period. Clodius had his mobs grouped in *decuries* and *curiae*.[12] It is likely enough that in some of these groups, consisting largely of freedmen of foreign birth, various foreign deities were worshiped in the communal *sacra,* so that the various police measures restricting or forbidding these rites may have had strong political motives as well.

When Caesar reconstituted the state after Pharsalia, he knew from direct experience the danger that lay in unrestricted association ostensibly for religious purposes. The θίασοι, "cult-associations," which he dissolved were undoubtedly grouped about some Greek or Oriental deity. The Jews were specially exempted, for reasons easy to guess at, but which we cannot exactly determine.[13] This striking favor cannot but have immensely increased their influence. We need not sup-

pose that Caesar's orders were any more effective than
previous decrees of this character had been. But even
a temporary clearing of the field gave the active prop-
agandists among the Jews an opportunity which they
fully utilized.

We have sketches of Jewish activities in Rome during the following years drawn by master hands. In
every instance, of course, the picture is drawn with
distinct lack of sympathy, but it is none the less valuable
on that account. Easily of first importance is the information furnished us by the cleverest of Roman poets,
Horace.

Quintus Horatius Flaccus was the son of a former
slave. His racial origin accordingly may have been
found in any corner of the Mediterranean in which we
choose to look for it. That fact, however, is of little
importance, except that the consciousness of servile
ancestry must have largely influenced his personal intercourse, and his patriotism must have been somewhat
qualified, despite some vigorously Roman sentiments.
Suave, obese, witty, a thoroughly polished gentlemen
of wide reading and perfect manners, both sensual and
shrewdly practical, Horace had early reached the point
at which one descants on the merits of frugality and
simplicity at the end of a seven-course dinner. His star
was in the ascendant. His patron Maecenas was the
trusted minister of Augustus; and to Augustus, and not
Antony, fell the task of rebuilding the shattered frame-
work of the state. Secure in the possession of every
creature comfort, the freedman's son could loaf and
invite his soul.

That he did so in exquisite verses is our good fortune, and that he chose to put his shrewd philosophy and criticism of life into the form of sketches that are medleys of scenes, lively chat, satirical attacks, and portraits of types and individuals, makes the period in which he lived and the society in which he moved almost as vivid to us as that depicted in the letters of Cicero.

In one of his Satires—" Chats," as he called them— he tells the story of his encounter with a pushing gentleman, of a type familiar to every age. Horace cannot escape from the infliction of his presence, and miserably succumbing to the inane chatter of the bore, he comes upon his friend Titus Aristius Fuscus. But his hopes in that quarter are doomed to disappointment.

" Surely," says Horace, nudging Fuscus, " you said you had something you wanted to speak to me about in private."

"Yes, yes, I remember," answers Fuscus, " but we'll let that go for some more suitable time. To-day's the thirtieth Sabbath. Why, man, would you want to offend the circumcised Jews?"

" I can't say that I feel any scruples on that score."

"But I do. I haven't your strength of mind. I'm only a humble citizen. You'll excuse me. I shall talk over our business at some other time."

The little scene is so significant that we shall have to dwell on it. One unescapable inference is that the Jews in Rome were numerous, and that a great many non-Jews participated wholly or partially in their observances. Fuscus need not be taken seriously about his

own beliefs, but his excuse would be extravagant in the
highest degree if the situation of the Jews were not
such as has been suggested. Indeed, the terms of inten-
tional offensiveness which Fuscus uses indicate the
serious annoyance of either himself or Horace that that
should be the case.

The "thirtieth Sabbath" will probably remain an
unsolved riddle.[14] And whatever the day was, the
extreme veneration expressed by Fuscus in declining
even to discuss profane affairs is of course absurdly out
of keeping with the words he uses. Fuscus is simply
assuming the tone of a demi-proselyte, a *metuens Sabbata,* whose superstitious dread of the rites he has half
embraced would make him carry his devotion to an
excess. Horace thus obtains an opportunity of sketch-
ing a new type of absurdity, in the very act of girding
at the one which is the subject of the *sermo.*

And Horace makes still another reference to the
proselytizing activities of the Jews. "You must allow
me my scribbling," he writes to Maecenas in another
Satire. "If you don't, a great crowd of poets will come
to help me. We far outnumber you, and, like the Jews,
will compel you to join our rout."[15]

This is explicit enough in all conscience, and gives a
very vivid picture of the public preaching that must
have brought the Jews to the unwelcome notice of every
saunterer in the Roman streets. Horace, despite his
slave grandfather, is a gentleman, the associate of
Rome's aristocracy, a member of the most select circle
of the city's society. The Jewish proselytes, whether

fully converted or "righteous strangers," must have been very numerous indeed, if he was forced to take such relatively frequent notice of them. Horace has no pictures, like those of Juvenal, of presumptuous Syrians, Egyptians, or Greeks swaggering about the city. It is only these Syrian *Iudaei* whom he finds irritating, and wholly because of their successful hunt for souls.

It is true that all this may be due to personal circumstances in his own surroundings. Some of his acquaintances, or men whom he occasionally encountered, may have been proselytes; others may have been impressed by certain Jewish forms or ideas. Horace is taking his fling at them in his usual light manner. There is something ludicrous to a detached philosopher in the eager striving to save one's soul, and still more absurd in the earnest attempt to gain adherents for an association that promises salvation.

Once he takes a more serious tone. In the famous journey he made with Maecenas to Brundisium Horace is told of an altar-miracle at Egnatia. The incense melts of itself, it seems, in the local temple. "Tell it to the Jew Apella," says Horace, "not to me. I have always been taught that the gods live free from every care, and if anything wonderful occurs in nature, it is not because it has been sent down from heaven by meddlesome divinities." [16]

This Jew Apella—a dialect-form of Apollas or Apollonius [17]—is no doubt a real person, who may perhaps have recounted to Horace some of the miracles of the Bible. Horace's raillery is directed plainly enough at the credulity that will accept these stories, and equally at the troublesome theology which makes the god a factor in daily life. Life was much simpler if no such incalculable quantity were injected into it. And to keep life free from harassing and unnecessary complications was the essence of his philosophy.[18]

At about the same time another writer, the geographer Strabo, of Amasea in Cappadocia, makes a statement of special interest. As quoted by Josephus (Ant. XIV. vii. 2) he says: "These people have already reached every city, and it would be difficult to find a place in the whole world that has not received this tribe and succumbed to it."

Obviously the statement is a gross exaggeration, and at most applicable to the cities of Egypt and Cyrene, in connection with which it is made. But that such a statement could be made at all is excellent evidence that it was at least partially true, and that there were Jewish communities practically everywhere, although it can hardly be the case that they were everywhere dominant. However, the sketches by Horace are an eloquent commentary upon the statement of Strabo. Not merely the East or Africa, but the capital itself, was overrun with Jews, and their number was constantly increasing.

Horace, it has been said, wrote of and for a cultured aristocracy. So did the other poets of the age, Propertius, Tibullus, Ovid. But all of them were more than ordinarily familiar with the *bas-lieux* where disreputable passions might be gratified. The voluptuary

Ovid was especially prone to go down into the sewer for new sensations, and just as Horace met Jews in the boulevards, so Ovid knew them in the slums.

In his salad-days Ovid had written a manual of debauchery, which he called the "Art of Love." He was destined to regret bitterly the facility of verse and of conscience that gave birth to this bold composition. But written it was, and in his advice to the dissolute young Romans he enumerates the time and place for their amours.

> Rome [he says in *Ars Amatoria,* i. 55 seq.] is the place for beauties. Venus has her fixed abode in the city of her Aeneas. Whatever you desire you may find. All you have to do is to take a walk in the Porticus of Pompey or of Livia, ... Do not pass by the place where Venus mourns Adonis, or where the Syrian Jew performs his rites each seventh day. Nor overlook the temples of the linen-clad heifer from Memphis. She makes many what Jove made her. Even the fora favor Love, ... those where the Appian aqueduct gushes forth near the marble temple of Venus. . . . . But above all stalk your game in the theaters.

In these instances Ovid refers to place, not to time, and it is only as part of the passages as a whole that the individual references can be understood. It will be seen that all the localities, beginning with the Porticus of Pompey in the Campus Martius, are merely casual. It is at the theater and circus where Ovid's pupils are chiefly to pick out the ladies of their light loves. For that reason the other places specified are also, to a certain extent, show places. The mention of the law-courts is especially noteworthy in this connection.

We must therefore assume that in the Jewish proseucha and in the temple of the Egyptian Isis there were
to be found a certain number of curious onlookers,
particularly women, and while many of them became
ardent converts, a certain number were innocent of any
intentions except to while away an idle hour, and were
easy game for the professional ' mashers " for whom
Ovid writes. Isis and Judaism were the two Oriental
cults which at this time had the greatest success in
Rome. And we can easily imagine how the unoccupied
of all classes thronged to every new fashion in religious
stimulation as in others.

Ovid is as explicit in the selection of time as of place.

Do not disregard time, ... Avoid the first of April. Then
the rainy season begins, and storms are frequent. But begin
the day of the defeat at the Allia, or the day on which the
Sabbath feast comes again, which the Syrian from Palestine
celebrates. That's a day on which other business ought not to
be done. (Ars. Am. i. 413 seq.)

Again, in his palinode, with which he vainly hoped to
regain his shattered reputation, " The Cure for Love "
(vv. 214 seq.), he brings the same things together:

Off with you; take a long journey to some distant land. . . . .
The less you want to go, the more you must; remember that!
Be firm and make your unwilling feet run. Do not pray for
rain. Let no imported Sabbaths hinder you, nor the day on
which we remember the disaster on the Allia.[12]

As far as Ovid is concerned, and we must assume he
is speaking for Fuscus' *multi,* a certain Jewish feast,
whether it is the Sabbath or some special holiday, such
as the Day of Atonement, is marked with the Dies

Alliensis, the fifteenth of July, the day on which, in 390 B. C. E., the Romans suffered their great defeat at the hands of the Gauls, and which was in consequence an ill-omened day from that time forth. Again, the Sabbath is classed with the rainy season as a day that might ordinarily incline a man to put off serious business.

As stated in the Notes, it is a common error to suppose that the generally ill-omened character of these days makes them eminently proper for flirtation. No Roman, however cynical, could flout superstition to that extent. The advice is given for purely practical considerations. The rainy season at the time of the equinoxes is an inauspicious time to begin a courtship, which, as we have seen in the previous passage, must be carried on almost wholly in the open air. Social gatherings in the houses of friends in the society of ladies were not common. There was nothing among the Romans to correspond to modern five-o'clock's or receptions, at which court might be paid to anyone who had caught the fancy of the Roman man about town. It is in the porticoes, in the idle crowds at the theater or circus, where the steps of ingratiating are to be carried out, and for these the rising of the Pleiades (Ars. Am. i. 409) is distinctly unpromising.

This is especially borne out by the passage immediately following the one quoted from the "Art of Love" (Ars. Am. i. 417 seq.). The most inauspicious day to attempt the beginning of an intrigue is the lady's birthday. Gifts are in order then, and they undoubtedly deplete one's pocket-book. Ovid is jocose here, but the

point is the same throughout. The hints and suggestions are as practical and direct as the formula of Ovid's
face-powder, which he also sets forth in the unfinished
verses called *Medicamina Faciei Femineae.*

That which makes the Dies Alliensis and the Jewish
Sabbath desirable is the fact that the former is in mid-
July and the latter in the early fall, the most delight-
ful of Italian seasons. Then an unbroken series of cloud-
less skies is almost assured; and the Roman fop could
count on meeting his fair one day after day in one of
the places of assignation so conveniently enumerated by
Ovid.

The phrase *rebus minus apta gerendis,* "unsuitable
for transacting business," is best taken as given in the
translation (above, p. 251). Ovid knows that under-
takings are rare on that day, and that causes its insertion. If it were merely that cessation of ordinary
business made it easier for idlers to pursue their amours,
it must be remembered that the *jeunesse dorée* had no
other ordinary business than falling in love.

The reference in the "Cure for Love" (above, p.
251) is of quite a different character. It will be noted
that *pluviae,* "the rainy season," which in the first case
is particularly contrasted with the Sabbath and the
Allia day, is here associated with them. "Let nothing
hinder you," says Ovid, "neither a good excuse nor a
bad one; neither the weather nor superstition." The
point of the reference in the two cases is accordingly
not at all the same. In the first instance the accidental
fact that the Allia day and a certain Jewish festival

occur during pleasant weather singles them out for mention. In the second it is the religious association of the day that Ovid has in mind.

As far as Ovid is personally concerned, there is no more than in Horace a trace of sympathy for the Jewish cult. We have seen that in every instance this cult is only one of several illustrations. The adjective *peregrina,* " foreign," applied to the Sabbath, gives the tone of all the passages. Ovid is a collector of light emotions. Of serious beliefs he has no vestige. But the presence of these Syrians in the city interests him as anything else picturesque would. He takes cognizance of the part they play in the life of the city, and is a valuable witness on that point.

The same inference may be drawn from the letter of Augustus to Tiberius (Suet. Aug. 76) : " There is no Jew, my dear Tiberius, who keeps his fast on the Sabbath as I kept it to-day." If the considerations advanced in Note 19 are valid, the Sabbath here is the Day of Atonement. But the significant fact is the use of the illustration at all. It confirms Strabo's statement of the extent and success of the propaganda of the Jews that all these writers in some way mention their presence.

That the preaching of the Jews was vigorous and aggressive is almost a necessary inference. We know no less than three of their synagogues by name, Augustenses, Volumnienses, Agrippenses,[20] and we have no reason to assume that these three exhausted the list. To many Romans the ardor of their proselytizing was offensive. It seemed a systematic attempt to transform the ancestral faith of the state. A casual reference in Valerius Maximus, a contemporary of Tiberius, charges the Jews with having attempted " to contaminate Roman beliefs by foisting upon them the worship of Jupiter Sabazios."[21] Valerius goes on to say that the praetor Hispalus expelled the Jews for that reason as early as 139 B. C. E. If such a thing took place, it was undoubtedly an act similar to an expulsion under Tiberius (below, p. 306), and was based on definite infractions of law, perhaps the law against unlicensed fortune-telling. The Jews in both cases were associated with the Chaldeans, a fact that makes the supposition more likely. But Valerius has in mind the conditions of his own day, when the success of the Jewish propaganda was bitterly resented, as we have seen, by Horace and Fuscus, and, as we shall later see, by Seneca and his associates generally.

If we try to imagine what the Jewish Roman communities of that day were like, we shall have to think of them as a proletariat. Freedmen in the second or third generation must have constituted a large part of them, and later references make it likely that many earned their livelihood by the proscribed arts of divination and fortune-telling. As in Alexandria, the bulk were probably artisans. Some were physicians, a profession then ranking in social degree with the manual trades, and usually exercised by slaves or freedmen.[22] The Roman encyclopedist Celsus mentions two Jewish medical authorities (De Med. V. xix. 11; xxii. 4). But the majority must have formed part of the pauperized city mob, turbulent and ignorant, and no doubt only moderately acquainted with their own laws and literature, so that we cannot be surprised to find indications of many things among them that were regarded as sacrilege in Jerusalem, such as carved animal figures on tombstones.[23]

However, there must at least have been some of a different type, whose command of their controversial literature enabled them to meet the competing philosophies upon their own ground and impress themselves upon some of the men of Augustus' own circle.

CHAPTER XVII
THE JEWS OF THE EMPIRE TILL THE REVOLT

One of the great determining events in ancient and modern history took place on January 1, 27 B. C. E., when Gaius Caesar Octavianus, returned from his successful campaigns in the East, was solemnly invested with the civil and military primacy of the Roman world. The importance of that particular historic moment is due of course not to anything in itself, but to the fact that it was the external and overt stamp put upon the development of centuries. The basic governmental scheme of ancient society—the city-state—was bankrupt. Its affairs were being wound up, and the receiver was in possession.

The reconstitution by Augustus appeared to the men of his day as the inauguration of an epoch. Poets hailed the dawn of a new day, and unqualifiedly saluted its great figure as a living god.[1] But we shall receive a false impression of the time and its condition, if we assume it to resemble an empire of modern type.

The Roman empire as founded by Augustus was simply the expression of the fact that between the Euphrates and the Ocean, between the Danube and the great African Desert, all the various forms of constituted authority were subject to revision by the will of the Roman people, i. e. those who actually lived, or had

17

an indefeasible right to live, within the walls of the Roman city. The *populus Romanus* had chosen to delegate functions of great extent and importance to a single man, to Augustus; but the power wielded by Augustus was not in any sense the power of an unrestrained master, nor was the rule of the Roman people the actual and direct government of the nations subject to it.

It would be quite impossible to enumerate the various communities which, under Augustus, as they had before, maintained their customs as the unbroken tradition of many centuries. In the mountains of Asia Minor it is likely that such a people as the Carduchi, whom Xenophon encountered there, were still under Augustus determining their mutual rights and obligations by rules that were either the same as those of Xenophon's time or directly derived from those rules.[2] So the cartouches on the Egyptian monuments might have been read by the clerks of Amen-hem-et, and would have excited no queries from them. The communities of the Mediterranean enforced their law— that is, the rules which constrained the individual member to respect the claims of his fellows—without noticeable break. The difference was that there was a limit to which it might be enforced, and that limit was set by the caprice of another and a paramount people.

Although the sovereignty of the Roman people was limitless, it was not, as a matter of fact, capriciously exercised. During the republic the theory of provincial organization had been somewhat of the following nature. Within any given territory contained in the limits of the province, there existed a certain number of individual civic units, which might take the form of city-states, territorial states of varying extent, leagues of communities, kingdoms tetrarchies, or hieratic religious communes. Any or all of these might be gathered within a single province, a word which is essentially abstract, and denoted a magisterial function rather than a territory. Into the midst of these *civitates,* this jumble of conflicting civic interests, there was sent a representative of the sovereign Roman people, invested with *imperium,* or supreme power, a term in which for Romans was the essence of the higher magistracies. Since the provincial magistrate had no colleagues, and since the tribunician check upon him was inoperative beyond the first milestone from the city, the wielder of the *imperium* outside of Italy was at law and often in fact an absolute despot for the period of his office.

However, in theory his functions were divided as follows: first, he was the only officer with jurisdiction over the Roman citizens temporarily resident in the province; secondly, he kept the peace; thirdly, he guaranteed the treaty rights of those communities that had treaties with Rome; and fourthly, he enforced and maintained the local customary law of all these communities. His judicial functions might include cases of all these kinds, so that in rapid succession the praetor or propraetor might be called upon to enforce the Twelve Tables and an ancient tribal usage of the Galatian Tectosages.

The checks upon the holder of *imperium* at Rome consisted in the peculiar Roman theory of magistracy, one of the corollaries of which was the right of any other equal or superior magistrate, or of any tribune, to veto any administrative act. A second check lay in the right of appeal in capital cases to the people. A third was found in the accountability for every illegal or oppressive action. This accountability however existed only after the magistracy had expired.

Outside of Rome only the last check existed. For everything done beyond the functions enumerated above, it was possible, even usual, to attempt to make the governor responsible after his term of office was over. We know how frequently that attempt was futile, and how constantly and flagrantly corrupt juries acquitted equally corrupt governors. "Catiline will be acquitted of extortion," writes Cicero in 65 B. C. E., "if the jury believes that the sun does not shine at noon." [3] The jury evidently thought so, since he was acquitted. But upon occasion, and generally when there were personal and political motives at work as well, these governors were convicted, so that there was always a certain risk attached to any attempt at playing the tyrant for the brief period of a governor's authority. [4]

The Augustan monarchy brought no real change into the theory of provincial organization, except as to relatively unimportant details. But one great reform was instituted. The responsibility of the governor became a real one, and was sharply presented to those officials. For the provinces, accordingly, the advent of Augustus

was an unmixed blessing, since, except for a few senti-
mentalists, the presence of the Roman representative as
the final court of appeal was not at all resented. We
can accordingly understand the extravagance with
which the rich and populous East, always the center of
wealth and civilization, received the Reformer, and the
unanimity and perhaps sincerity with which he was
hailed as living god.[5]

We cannot be certain that this was encouraged by
Augustus himself. There is nothing in his character
that indicates any special sympathy with the point of
view demanded by it; nothing of that daemonic strain
noticeable in Alexander, which makes it easy to believe
that the latter was one of the first to be convinced by the
salutation of the priests of Ammon. But Augustus
recognized at once the value for unity that the tendency
to deify the monarch possessed. The reverence for the
living monarch, to be transformed into an undisguised
worship at his death, was, however, to be superimposed
upon existing forms. Nothing was more characteristically Roman than Augustus' eagerness to make it clear
that the vast domain of the empire was to remain, as
before, a mass of disparate communities of which the
populus Romanus was only one, although a paramount
one, and that in each of these communities every effort
was to be made to maintain the ancestral ritual in
government and worship. What he added was simply
the principle that to keep the community together, to
prevent the chaos and anarchy of a dissolution of the
empire, it was necessary to bestow on the *princeps,* on

the First Citizen of the paramount Roman people, such powers and functions as would assure the coherence of the whole. These powers he selected himself. Such a step as that taken by the Constitution of Caracalla, which attempted to enforce a legal merging of all the communities into a single state, would have been nothing else than abhorrent to Augustus.[6] And, indeed, it was a distinctly un-Roman idea.

In Rome Augustus was chiefly intent upon a restoration of everything that could well be restored in the social, religious, and political life of the people. Certain of the political elements, such as the actual sovereignty of the *populus,* as far as it could be physically assembled in the Campus Martius, had to be abandoned, as demonstrably inconsistent with the larger purpose which Augustus had set himself. But in every other respect, he did not, as Julius Caesar had done, compel the Romans to face the unpleasant fact that a revolution had taken place, but professed to be simply a restorer of the ancient polity. Perhaps he did not face the facts himself. At any rate he seems sincerely to have believed that morality and sobriety could be reconstituted by statute, and that one, by dint of willing, might live under Caesar as men lived under Numa —barring such un-Sabine additions as marble palaces and purple togas.

With his mind full of these views, Augustus could hardly be expected to regard favorably those tendencies in his own time which inevitably made for real unity of the empire in speech, blood, and religion. He was quite

aware that this unity would not be produced by a
coalescing of everything into new forms, but by the
conquest of all or most of the existing elements by the
one most powerful or most aggressive. Unchecked,
it was likely that Greek speech would drive out Latin,
Syrian blood dominate Roman, or any one of the various Oriental worships dislodge the Capitoline Triad.

On the last point he had even a definite policy of
opposition. His sagacious adviser Maecenas had laid
great stress upon the ease with which foreign religions
introduce a modification of habits of life, in his last
words:[7]

Take active part in divine worship, in every way established by our ancestral customs, and compel others to respect
religion, but avoid and punish those who attempt to introduce
foreign elements into it. Do so not merely as a mark of honor
to the gods—although you may be sure that anyone who
despises them, sets little value upon anything—but because
those who introduce new deities are by that very act persuad-
ing the masses to observe laws foreign to our own. Hence
we have secret gatherings and assemblies of different sort,
all of which are inconsistent with the monarchical principle.

His commendation of Gaius' avoidance of sacrifice
at Jerusalem was of a piece with this policy.[8]

The Jews in Rome, who had been directly favored
by Caesar, had to be contented, as far as Augustus was
concerned, with freedom from molestation. However,
this freedom was real enough to enable their situation
in Rome to reach the development hinted at in the
Augustan poets, although their activities militated
strongly against the most cherished plans of Augustus.

In the rest of the empire the Jews of the various

communities found their situation unchanged. Even the obnoxious privileges which they had in several cities of Asia continued unimpaired,[9] and here the orthodox Jewish propaganda and a few generations later the heterodox Jewish propaganda made rapid strides.[10]

Judea belonged, in spite of the quasi-independence of Herod, to the province of Syria, which meant that such dues as Herod, the Jewish king, owed Rome would be enforced, if he were recalcitrant, by the Roman legate at Antioch. Herod's name throughout the empire was as much a synonym for wealth as it is now for cruelty. And his wealth and power advertised the Jews notably, a fact which their propaganda could scarcely help turning to account.[11]

The attitude of the various Jewish synagogues and communes toward Judea was one that appeared to the men of the day as that which bound various colonies of a city to the mother-city. Indeed the Jewish communities outside of Palestine were styled explicitly colonies, ἀποικία. Such a tie, however, was conceived in the Greek fashion and not in the Roman. The Greek colony was bound to its mother-city by sentiment only, not, as in the case of the Romans, by law. That sentiment might be powerful enough at times, but it was not inconsistent with the bitterest warfare. Consequently such movements as appear in Palestine need not at all have been reflected in the synagogues of the East and West, and there is nothing to indicate that the active and successful proselytizing of the Asiatic and Roman

synagogues was either directed or systematically encouraged by the Pharisaic majority in the Sanhedrin
at Jerusalem. It will at all times create a wholly false
impression to speak of the Jews of that period as of a
single community bound by common interests and open
to identical influences. The independence of the Jewish
congregations of one another was quite real, and was
even insisted upon. Neither the high priest nor the
Nasi of the Sanhedrin pretended to any authority
except over those legally resident in Judea; and often,
when the reverence for the temple and the holy city was
most strongly emphasized, intense contempt might be
manifested for those who were at the moment the
holders of the supreme authority in the mother-country.

Another matter that is apt to be lost sight of in this
connection is the fact that not all Jews of the time
lived within the Roman empire. The Persian kingdom, which Alexander had conquered, and which the
Seleucidae had with varying success attempted to maintain, had fallen to pieces long before the Roman occupation of Syria. Media, Babylonia, Bactria resumed a
quasi-independence, which however was soon lost when
the obscure province of Parthia—as Persis had done
five centuries before—assumed a dominance that ended
in direct supremacy. The Roman limits were set at the
river Euphrates, leaving Armenia a bloody, debatable
ground. The one great moment in the history of this
new Parthian empire was the decisive defeat of Crassus
at Carrhae in 58 B. C. E., a victory that gave the
Parthians sufficient prestige to maintain themselves

under conditions of domestic disorder that would ordinarily have been fatal. The Augustan poets and courtiers might magnify the return of the Roman standards by King Phraates to their hearts' content. They might, as they did, exultantly proclaim that the Crassi were avenged, that the known world to the shadowy confines of the Indus bowed to the will of the living god Augustus. The fact remained that, after Carrhae, the conquest of the country beyond the Euphrates ceased to be a part of the Roman programme, and, except for the transient successes of Trajan, was never seriously attempted.

In this Parthian kingdom, of which the capital was the ancient and indestructible city of Babylon, Jews had dwelt since the time of Nebuchadnezzar. There is even every reason to believe that those who remained at Babylon were decidedly not the least notable of the people in birth or culture. And between Babylon and Judea there was constant communication. When Babylon became the seat of the only power still existing that seemed formidable to Rome, it is obvious that the uninterrupted communication between the Jews of that section and the mother-country would create political situations of no slight delicacy, and may have played a much more important part in determining the relations of the governing Romans to the Jews than our sources show.

That there was at all times a Parthian party among the Palestinian Jews there can be no doubt. We know too little of the history of Parthia to speak confidently

on the subject, but Parthian rulers seem to have brought
to the Jewish religious philosophy a larger measure of
sympathy and comprehension than most Roman representatives. While the existence of Parthian sympathizers may date almost from the beginning of
Parthian supremacy, their presence was very concretely manifested when Jannai's son, Aristobulus,
appealed to Parthia as Hyrcanus had appealed to Rome.
Indeed a Parthian army invaded and captured Palestine, and gave Aristobulus' son, Mattathiah-Antigonus,
a brief lease of royal dignity. Every instance of dis-
satisfaction with the Roman government was the occasion for the rise of Parthian sympathies.

It may further be recalled that Parthia was the continuation of Persia. Of all foreign dominations the
Persian rule was the one most regretted by the Jews,
and the Persian king's claim to reverence never died
out in the regions once subject to him. We may remember with what humility, some years later, Izates of
Adiabene dismounted and walked on foot before the
exiled Parthian king, although the latter had gone to
him as a suppliant, and had been prostrate in the dust
before him. The prestige of the Great King, diminished
considerably to be sure, had still not completely faded.[12]

The one general term that covered all the Jews of
various types was "race of the Jews," *gens Iudaeorum,*
γένος Ἰουδαίων. It was meant to be a racial descriptive
appellation, and was constantly combined with other
adjectives denoting nationality or citizenship. The
temptation to make an actual unit of any group that
can be covered by a single term is well-nigh irresistible,

and it is strengthened for us by the century-old associations that have made Palestine the embodiment of an ideal. Varying as the Jews of that time were in temperament, character, occupations, position, and mental endowments, the fate and vicissitudes of the mother-country, and particularly of the holy metropolis Jerusalem, went home vividly to all of them, scattered as they were between the shores of the Caspian Sea and Spain. In this respect the *gens Iudaeorum* was a real unit. Their hearts were turned to the Zion Hill.

Not all Palestine, however, formed this mother-country. The mere fact that the Hasmoneans had brought a great deal of the surrounding territory under subjection, and made the boundaries of their power almost as extensive as those of David and Solomon, did not make a single country of their dominions. The real metropolis was Jerusalem and its supporting territory of Judea. In this predominance of the city in post-Exilic Judaism, we may see either Greek influence or the continuance of the ancient city-state idea, as much a general characteristic of Eastern civilization as it is specifically of Greek. Not even undoubted Jewish descent, or loyalty to the Jewish Law, made of the adjacent lands an integral part of Judea. The Jews of Gaulonitis, Galilee, Ituraea, Peraea, Trachonitis, Idumaea, were, like the Jews of Rome, of Alexandria, or of Babylon, Jews of foreign nationality to inhabitants of Jerusalem, although the association was notably closer and the occasion of common performance of Jewish rites much more frequent than was the case with the more distant Jews.

Tombs of the Judges.

TOMBS OF THE KINGS, VALLEY OF KEDRON, JERUSALEM

(From Wilson's "Jerusalem")

The Idumean Herod had been confirmed by Rome in the sovereignty of a wide and miscellaneous territory, which included Greek cities, as well as these territorial units enumerated above. The favor he enjoyed granted him practically all the privileges that an independent sovereign could hold, except that of issuing gold coins.[13] Further, the authority was only for his life. The right of disposing of his dominions was no part of his power. His will was merely suggestive, and carried no weight beyond that.

His favor in the eyes of the Romans was based upon his scarcely disguised Hellenic sympathies and his proven loyalty to his masters. The Parthian invasion of 40 B. C. E. and the existence of Parthian sympathizers made the maintenance of order in Palestine a matter of the highest importance. The significance of these Eastern marches for the stability and safety of Rome was even greater than those of the North along the Rhine, where also constant turbulence was to be feared, and eternal vigilance was demanded. In the East, however, there was not merely a horde of plundering savages to be repelled, but the aggression of an ancient and civilized power, bearing a title to prestige compared with which that of Macedonian and Roman was of recent growth. And Parthian successes here immediately jeopardized Egypt, already rapidly becoming the granary of the Empire.

Quite in accordance with Roman policy, indeed with ancient policy in general, Augustus vastly preferred to have the peace of this region assured by means of a reliable native government than directly by Roman administration. The Romans did not covet responsibility. If a native prince was trustworthy, it was a matter of common sense to permit him to undertake the arduous duty of policing the country rather than assume it themselves. The difficulty was to discover such a man or government. Experience and the suspiciousness that was almost a national trait convinced the Romans that only very few were to be trusted, and these not for long. In Herod, however, they seemed to have discovered a trustworthy instrument, and while it is not strictly true that the powers conferred upon him were of unexampled extent, they were undoubtedly unusual and amply justified the regal splendor Herod assumed. The readiness with which Herod's loyalty to Antony was pardoned demonstrated the clear perception on the part of Augustus of how admirably Herod could serve Roman purposes here.

One of the motives that generally impelled Romans to permit native autonomy was no doubt to gain credit for generosity with their subjects. They might be forgiven for supposing that Roman rule would be more acceptable if it came indirectly through the medium of a king that was himself of Jewish stock. The distinction between Idumean and Jew proper would hardly be recognized by a Roman, although the distinction between the geographical entities of Idumaea and Judea was familiar enough.

But the Romans likewise knew and consciously exploited Herod's unpopularity. Strabo states that the humiliating execution of Antigonus was intended

to decrease the prestige of the latter and increase that
of Herod.[14] Josephus and the Talmud would be ample
evidences themselves of the hatred and the bitter antagonism with which Herod was regarded.[15] None the
less it may well be that the unpopularity was largely
personal, and produced by the violence and cruelties of
which Herod was guilty. It appears so in Strabo's
account. Idumean descent cannot have been the principal reproach directed against Herod by his subjects.
On more than one occasion the Idumeans had evinced
their attachment to the Jewish Law.[16] Nor was Herod
wholly without ardent supporters. In the cities which
he had founded there were many men devoted to him.
Even—or perhaps especially—among the priests, there
was a distinctly Herodian faction.[17] It is highly likely
that hatred of Herod was especially strong in those who
hated Rome as well, either through Parthian proclivities or because Rome seemed to present a danger
to the maintenance of their institutions. And among
these men were, it appears, most of those whose teachings have come down to us in the course of later
tradition.

To the Romans this devotion of the Palestinian Jews
to their Law seemed an excessive and even reprehensi-
ble thing. As we have seen, the Jews were qualified as
superstitiosi, " superstitious " (above, p. 177). In general, to be sure, zeal for ancestral institutions was supported by the Romans, and they were not particularly
concerned that foreign institutions should resemble
theirs. However, if there were any from which a

breach of the peace was to be apprehended, they might be regarded as practices to be suppressed.

The Romans had shown for certain Jewish customs a very marked respect. The intense Jewish repugnance to images was at first difficult for Romans to realize, since they had been training themselves for generations to test the degree of civilization by the interest in the plastic arts. That there might be among barbarians no statues was natural enough: that the barbarians would refuse to take them when offered, was incomprehensible. But, hard though it was to realize, the Romans quickly enough did realize it. The capital concession of issuing no Roman coins for Judea with anything but the traditional symbols on them, of carefully eliminating those which bore the emperor's effigy, undoubtedly showed their good-will in the matter.[18] And the fact may be noted that after the coins celebrating the triumph of Vespasian and Titus, with the Latin and Greek legends Ἰουδαίας Ἑαλωκυίας, *Iudaea capta,* "For the Conquest of Judea," no Roman coins with imperial effigies appear till the radical reorganization by Hadrian. That indicated clearly enough the extent to which the Romans were willing to respect what was to them a purely irrational prejudice.

One other matter was easier for Romans to comprehend, and that was the inviolable sanctity of certain things and places. It was a common enough conception that certain places were unapproachable to all but a few, ἄδυτα; and that certain things, like the Palladium, suffered profanation from the slightest touch. They sub-

mitted accordingly with a good grace to exclusion from
most of the temple precincts, and Nero [20] readily gave
his consent to the building of the wall that prevented
Agrippa II from turning the temple ceremonies into a
show for his courtiers. The punishment of a Roman
soldier, who tore a scroll of the Pentateuch, is another
case in point. The soldier may have been a Syrian
enrolled from the section in which he served, and
not properly a Roman at all. None the less an arbitrary
and distinctly unsympathetic procurator felt his responsibility for threatened disorders keenly enough to make
this drastic example. [20]

Herod had kept order. He had done so with a high
hand, and had met with frequent rebellions. Himself
wholly inclined to complete Hellenization, he had made
many efforts to conciliate his Jewish subjects. His
lust for building he gratified only in the pagan cities
subject to him. His coins bear no device except the
inanimate objects and vegetable forms allowed by law
and tradition. With cautious regard to certain openly
expressed fears on the part of the Jews he rebuilt the
temple on a magnificent scale. He spoke of the Israelites as "our ancestors." [21] As has been said, he did not
wholly want adherents among priests and people. That
he died as an embittered and vindictive despot, conscious of being generally detested, and contriving
fiendish plots to make his death deplored, is probable
enough, and is amply explained by the domestic difficulties with which he had to contend all his life. [22]

18

In some cases at least, it was his zeal for orderly administration that caused friction with the people. His law sentencing burglars to foreign slavery is an instance (Jos. Ant. XVI. i. 1). In general, however, the mere suppression of more or less organized brigandage was a task that took all his attention, but this " brigandage " was often a real attempt at revolution, in which popular teachers were suspected of being implicated, and every such suppression carried with it in its train a series of executions that did not increase the king's popularity.

These "robbers" or "brigands" were of different types. The distinction which Roman lawyers made between war proper, *iustum bellum,* and brigandage, *latrocinium,* was in Syria and the surrounding regions rather quantitative than qualitative. So, after Herod's first defeat by the Arabians, " he engaged in robberies," τοὐντεῦθεν ὁ μὲν Ἡρώδης λῃστείαις ἐχρῆτο (Jos. Ant. XV. v. 1), which meant only that he made short incursions into the enemy's country, until he had the strength to attempt another pitched battle. So also of the Trachonitians (*ibid.* XVI. ix. 3). Every one of the expeditions in which the Hasmonean rulers had increased their dominions had been in the eyes of the Syrian historians "robberies." Itureans and other Syrians had been guilty of them under the last Seleucids.[23] In the prologue to Pompeius Trogus' Thirty-ninth Book, as contained in Justin's epitome,[24] we hear the conquests of John Hyrcanus and Alexander Jannai described as *latrocinia*. And again (xl. 2) we read that Pompey refused the petition of Antiochus, son of Cyzicenus, to be called king of Syria, on the ground that Antiochus had miserably shirked his responsibilities for eleven years, and he, Pompey, would not give him what he could not maintain, "lest he should again expose Syria to Jewish and Arabian brigands," *ne rursus Syriam Iudaeorum et Arabum latrociniis infestam reddat.*

Herod had kept these robbers in check, and had effectually fulfilled his tacit engagement to the *populus Romanus.* His death immediately removed the strong hand. His son Archelaus found an insurrection on his hands almost at once, which he suppressed with great bloodshed. The moment he left for Rome to maintain his claims to a part of this inheritance, the governor of Syria suppressed another revolt; and hardly had he turned his back, when his procurator Sabinus found himself surrounded by a determined band of rebels recruited principally from Galilee, Idumaea, Jericho, and the trans-Jordan territory. In spite of a successful sortie by the Romans, Sabinus was nothing less than besieged in the Tower of Phasael.

Innumerable (μύριοι) disorders, Josephus tells us (Ant. XVII. x. 4), occurred at about the same time. Some two thousand of Herod's soldiers engaged, as was so often the case, in plunder on their own account. Sepphoris in Galilee was seized and plundered by Jucah, son of the highwayman (ἀρχιλῃστής) Hezekiah, who made the neighboring country dangerous with his band of "madmen" (ἀπονενοημένοι). At Jericho Simon, a former slave of Herod, had himself proclaimed king and sacked the palace there. But more serious than these was the band of outlaws commanded by four brothers, of whom only Athronges is mentioned. These attacked both the local troops and even Roman detachments and were not suppressed till much later.[25]

All these disorders required the presence of Varus [26] once more. He marched on Jerusalem at the head of an army, turning over the various towns on his route to be sacked by his Arabian allies, precisely as both British and French used their Indian allies during the colonial wars in America.

The effect of such conditions in so critical a place as Judea, was to call Roman attention to the country to a much greater extent than was advantageous to the Jews. The region very naturally appeared to them as a turbulent and seditious section, much as Gaul did to Julius Caesar and largely for the same reason, the instinctive love of liberty and the presence of "innovators," νεωτερισταί, *cupidi rerum novarum,* restless and ambitious instigators of rebellion.[27] The Jerusalem Jews are, to be sure, very eager to escape the reproach of disloyalty. The rebellion was the work of outsiders (ἐπήλυδες), to wit, the Galileans and Gileadites above-mentioned.[28]

Varus crucified two thousand men, and then disbanded his auxiliary army. The latter, composed obviously of natives of the country, proceeded to plunder on their own account. Varus' prompt action brought them to terms. The officers were seized and sent to Rome, where, however, only the relatives of Herod, who had added impiety to treason, were punished.

But the reproach of being a seditious people was resented by other Jews than those of Jerusalem. The Jews in Rome were largely descended from those who had left the country before even Antipater, Herod's father, had become powerful there. On them, of course, the house of Herod could make no claim, and for obvious reasons closer relations with Rome seemed to them eminently desirable. The Jewish embassy which Varus had permitted the Judeans to send—how selected and led we have no information—was joined by an immense deputation from the Roman synagogues. The substance of their plea was the petition that they be made an integral part of the province of Syria. " For it will thus become evident whether they really are a seditious people, generally impatient of all forms of authority for any length of time " (Jos. Ant. XVII. ii. 2; Wars, II. vi. 2).

This plea, to be joined to Syria, is particularly significant if we remember that the motive of the Jews in sending the embassy was, in the words of the Wars (II. vi. 1), to plead for the autonomy of their nation (cf. Ant. XVII. xi. 1). We see strikingly confirmed the theory of the Roman provincial system, in which the proconsul or propraetor was only an official added to, but not superseding, the local authorities.

The representative of Archelaus, Nicolaus of Damascus,[29] charged the former's accusers with "rebellion and lust for sedition," with lack of that culture which consists in observance of right and law. Nicolaus had in view primarily the Jewish accusers of his employer, but no doubt made his remarks general. In the earlier version of the embassy, as it appears in the Wars (II. vi. 2), it is the whole nation that Nicolaus charges directly with " a natural lack of submission and loyalty to royal power."

Augustus declined to continue the heterogeneous kingdom of Herod. A brief trial of Archelaus as ethnarch of Judea proper convinced him of the latter's worthlessness. The request of the Jewish envoys was now granted. Judea became a part of Syria—and the agent or *procurator* of the Syrian proconsul took up official residence at Caesarea. We find, however, that this step, which the Jews themselves had suggested, almost immediately provoked a serious rebellion in Galilee, led by one Judah of Gamala in Galilee and by a Pharisee named Zadok, who, if we may believe Josephus, were appreciably different from the various "robbers," λῃσταί, whom he had formerly enumerated, and, in his eyes, even more detestable than they were. They placed their opposition on the basis of a principle. This principle was that of the sinfulness of all mortal government and the consequent rejection of Roman authority as well. Accordingly they refused to pay tribute. These advocates of a pure theocracy had of course obvious Scriptural warrant for their position, but the relatively rapid spread of such a doctrine in the form of an actual programme of resistance can be accounted for only by the extremely unsettled state of the country and the still more unsettled state of men's minds.

That this Judah formed a fourth sect of the Jews in addition to the three, Pharisees, Sadducees, and Essenes, already in existence, as Josephus tells us, may not be quite true.[30] Men of his type are scarcely founders of sects. But there can be no doubt that the doctrines which these zealots espoused were those which Josephus has described. The later history of Europe has abundant examples of such groups of fanatic warriors maintaining one of many current religious dogmas, especially in times of economic and political disorder. Of such incidents the Hussite bands of Ziska and the Anabaptist insurrection are examples. In this case the distress and uncertainty were largely spiritual. The economic conditions, while bad, had not become particularly worse. Indeed, if anything, more direct administration had somewhat lightened the burdens, by making them less arbitrary and by removing the heavy expense of a court and the need of footing the bill for Herod's building enterprises.

Josephus regards the great rebellion of 68 c. e. as the direct consequence of this insurrection of Judah. He is therefore very bitter against this " fourth philosophic system," which spread among the younger men and brought the country to ruin. It is at least curious that in his earlier work, the Wars, in which the recollection of Jewish disaster would be, one would suppose, vastly more vivid, he does not ascribe to this rebellion any such far-reaching effects (Wars, II. viii. 1) ; nor is it in any degree likely that this insurrection was after all more than what it appears to be there, a sporadic outburst in that hotbed of unrest, the Galilean ·hills, noteworthy only for the special zeal with which the theocratic principles were announced.

No riots or disturbances are mentioned in Judea till the famous image-riots of the time of Pontius Pilate. However we may wish to discount the highly colored narrative preserved in Josephus, there can be no doubt that these riots did take place. It may even be that the representation of influential Jews induced the much desired concession on Pilate's part of removing the "images." But what these images were does not appear with any clearness from Josephus' account, and of course we are under no obligation to take literally the "five days and five nights" during which the ambassadors lay prostrate, with bare necks, at Pilate's feet.

Josephus speaks of the "images of Caesar which are called standards" (Wars, II. ix. 2; Ant. XVIII. iii. 1). The Roman standards, *signa, σημαίαι*, often contained representations of the emperor. But these were in the form of medallions in flat relief, hung upon the standard. They would have been noticed only upon relatively close inspection. There were also statues in the camp. But it is quite unlikely that if the Roman provincial administrators were instructed to issue no coins with the imperial effigy, they would be allowed to carry into the city actual statues of the emperor. They may well have forgotten that the military standards would be themselves offensive, if they bore, as they always did, the representation of animal forms. All legions at this time carried the eagle, and most of them had other heraldic animals as well.[31]

Now it may be remembered that the chief legion permanently encamped in Syria, of which detachments must have accompanied Pilate upon his transference of the praetorium from Caesarea to Jerusalem, was the Tenth Legion, called Fretensis (Leg. X Fretensis), and that its standards were a bull and a pig.[32] To the mass of the Jews the carrying, as though in triumph, of the gilded image of an unclean animal must have seemed nothing less than derision, and can easily explain the fury of the populace.

Another of the Syrian legions, of which certain divisions may have been with Pilate, was the Third Gallic Legion (Leg. III Gallica). This legion, like the X Fretensis, bore a bull as a standard, which, while less stimulating to the mass of the population, must have seemed even more than the pig the emblem of idolatry to those who had the history of their people in mind.[33]

If this was the occasion of the disturbance, Pilate may well have been innocent of any provocative intention. That can scarcely have been altogether the case in the riots provoked by the aqueducts. Pilate seized certain sacred funds for that purpose, and in this case no official, Roman or Greek, could have failed to understand the nature of the funds or the offense involved in using them for secular purposes.

A certain significance is attached to the Samaritan episode mentioned by Josephus (Ant. XVIII. iv. 1). It is one of the incidents that become more and more fre-

quent.   The promises of a plausible thaumaturg cause
an enormous throng to gather.   It does not appear that
he had any other purpose than that of obtaining credit
as a prophet or magician.   But Pilate, as most Roman
governors would no doubt have done, held the unlicensed assemblage of armed men to be sedition, and
suppressed it as such.

Shortly afterwards Palestine and the closely connected Egyptian communities were thrown into a
frenzy of excitement by the widely advertised attempt
of Gaius to set up his statue in the temple at Jerusalem.
The imperial legate at Antioch had no desire whatever
to arouse a rebellion in which all the forces of religious
hatred would be let loose upon him.   He therefore tem-
porized and postponed at his own imminent peril.   In
view of the constantly threatening attitude of Parthia,
Petronius [34] may well have felt his responsibility with
especial force.   Only a few years before, an invasion
on the part of the Parthian king Artabanus had been
generally feared.   Agrippa had even been accused of
complicity with the Parthians.[35]   The governor of Syria
had every reason to hesitate to gratify the caprice of
an obviously insane emperor at so great a risk to the
state.   Luckily for him, the assassination of Gaius
saved him from the consequences of his hesitation.
His subsequent procedure against the people of Doris [36]
indicated a lively comprehension on his part of the
inflammable character of the people he had to govern
and the particular importance to be attached to this
question of images.

To the Roman historian, the incident of Gaius' attempted erection of his statue in the temple is only an illustration of the readiness with which this nation rebelled. Tacitus[37] treats the period between insurrections as one of smouldering revolt. The incident of Gaius precipitated an outbreak (Hist. v. 9), which his death calmed, and enabled the Jews to suppress their inclinations a few years longer. *Duravit tamen patientia Iudaeis,* he tells us, *usque ad Gessium Florum procuratorem,* "The submission of the Jews lasted till the procuratorship of Gessius Florus."

The short reign of Herod's popular grandson, Agrippa, "the great king Agrippa, friend of Caesar and the Romans," as he calls himself on his coins and inscriptions,[38] rather confirmed Roman anxiety about the loyalty of their Jewish subjects than lightened it. It was by a complete adoption of Jewish customs— an adoption that can hardly have been sincere—that Agrippa secured and maintained his hold on their affections.[39] His deference to the religious leaders of the people was unqualified. His dealing with the Pharisee Simon, who publicly challenged his right to enter the temple precincts at all, is an illustration.[40] The Pharisaic tradition of his reign as preserved in the Talmud is that he was a pious and scrupulously observant Jew, painfully conscious that his Idumean origin made him half a stranger in Israel.

But to Rome Agrippa's methods, in spite of their success, indicated only that no real progress had been made in the subjugation of Palestine. Rome was not without experience of lands difficult to subdue. Gaul, Belgium, Germany, Britain, were all lands where insurrections might at any time be feared through the devotion of an influential minority to their ancestral customs. But in Palestine there was even less appreciable increase in Romanization or Hellenization of customs than in the countries mentioned. To an antiquary and scholar like the emperor Claudius there might be something interesting and admirable in the maintenance of an historic culture, but to the Roman administrative official, accountable for the security of the East, there was little that was admirable about it.

A quarrel between the Jews of Peraea and the neighboring city of Philadelphia may have had only local significance. And the Ptolemy executed by Fadus may have been only a common highwayman.[41] But a very little later the success of a certain Theudas, an "impostor," γόης τις ἀνήρ, Josephus calls him, in gaining adherents as a prophet is highly significant.[42] This Theudas undertook to divide the Jordan, and pass across it with his followers. It is noteworthy that every such claim to miraculous power immediately elicited drastic action on the part of the Romans. Theudas' followers were cut down in a cavalry raid, and he himself was captured and beheaded. Roman officials apprehended danger chiefly from this source, and were particularly on their guard against it.

Such incidents as the riots provoked by individual soldiers cannot have been frequent. As has been said in one case, the Roman commander executed a soldier

whose outrage had stirred up a revolt. But a garrison
of foreign soldiers in a warlike country furnishes constant incentives to friction, which may at any time burst
out into a general war. In Samaria and Galilee there
were abundant pretexts for mutual attacks, the net
result of which was that the land was full of brigandage, which indicates that the Roman police here were
strikingly ineffective. And in all cases the suspicion
that attached to every armed leader was that his motives
were treasonable as well as criminal. So Dortus of
Lydda was accused by the Samaritans of directly
preaching rebellion.

Under Nero, says Josephus, the country went from
bad to worse, and was filled with brigands and impostors." How little it was possible to distinguish between
these two classes appears from the fact that Josephus
continually mentions them in couples. Those whom
he calls Assassins, or Sicarii, can be placed in neither
category. One thing is evident. Their apparently
wanton murders must have had other incentives than
pillage, for even Josephus does not charge them with
that; they were obviously animated by a purpose that
may be called either patriotism or fanatic zeal, depend-
ing upon one's bias. That is shown plainly enough in
a casual statement of Josephus that these brigands were
attempting to foment by force a war on Rome, τὸν δῆμον
εἰς τὸν πρὸς Ῥωμαίοις πόλεμον ἠρέθιζον.

The usual "prophet," in this case an unnamed Egyptian, appears with his promise to make the walls of
Jerusalem fall at his command, and the usual attack

of armed soldiers on a helpless group of unarmed
fanatics. In the Wars, Josephus speaks of a great number of these self-styled prophets (II. xiii. 4) : " Cheats
and vagabonds caused rebellion and total subversion of
society, under the pretense of being divinely inspired.
They infected the common people with madness, and
led them into the desert with the promise that God
would there show them how to gain freedom." The
procurator Felix took the customary measures of treat-
ing these expeditions as open sedition and crushing
them with all the power at his command—acts which
can only have inflamed the prevailing disorders.

The picture drawn by Josephus of the Judea of those
days represents a condition nothing short of anarchy.
Such a situation could have existed only under an
incompetent Roman governor. Whether the procurator Gessius Florus was or was not quite the monster he is depicted as being in the Wars, he can
scarcely have been an efficient administrator. It is
very likely that the various acts of cruelty imputed to
him by Josephus were examples of the intemperate
violence of a weak man exasperated by his own failure
to control the situation. However this may be, it certainly was not the excesses of an individual governor
that provoked the rebellion of 68 c. e., even if we accept
Josephus' account of him in full, and assume him to
have been a second and worse Verres. The outbreak
of that year was the result of causes lying far deeper
in the condition of the time and the character of the
people.

The Jews were not the only nation that fought with
desperate fury against complete submergence in the
floods of Roman dominance. The spread of the Roman
arms had encountered, from the beginning, seemingly
small obstacles that proved more serious checks than
the greater ones. Thus, after the Second Punic War,
when Rome was already in the ascendant in the world,
the relatively fresh strength of a conquering people
was all but exhausted in the attempt to subdue and
render thoroughly Roman the mountain tribes of the
Ligurians in the northern part of the peninsula.[1] In
later times, after Caesar's conquest, the subjugation
of Belgium was a weary succession of revolts and
massacres and punitive expeditions that stretched over
several generations. Similarly in Numidia it was
found that formal submission of the tribes that filled
this region insured no permanence of control.[2]

In the last cases, however, the danger that was
warded off seemed in Roman eyes to be remote. In the
case of Judea the very existence of the eastern empire
was threatened. On the other side of the Syrian desert
there was a watchful and ready enemy, who might
appear in force at any time and with whose arrival
there might break out into open conflagration the

smouldering disloyalty that still was present in the Asiatic provinces.

The Jewish rebellion of 68 c. e. was not an isolated phenomenon. For the Jews it formed the beginning of a series of insurrections that did not end till the founding of Aelia Capitolina put a visible seal on the futility of all such attempts. To us the outcome seems so inevitable that the heroism of the Zealots has stood for centuries as a striking example of unrestrained fanaticism. To take a modern instance, if the single island of Cyprus were to attempt, by its unaided strength, to cast off the British rule, it would not seem to be engaged in a more completely forlorn enterprise than were the Jews who undertook to defy the power of the legions. And yet those who began and conducted the revolt were neither fools nor madmen, and the hopes that buoyed them must have been very real when they attempted the impossible.

We must first of all remember that a foreign suzerainty was not necessarily incompatible with Jewish theocratic ideals. Tradition had accustomed the Jews to Assyrian and Persian dominance, and their most sacred recollections contained ample warrant for those who would bear the rule of Caesar with complete equanimity. But it had been axiomatic that the rule of a foreign master was a divinely imposed penalty, a trial, a test of submission. At some time the period of trials would cease, and the normal condition of complete freedom from outside control under the sway of God would be restored. The Messianic hope made that situation more and more vividly present to the hearts of men.

Nor did actual experience of recorded history make this possibility a vain dream. The vicissitudes of fortune, the sudden rise of obscure nations to supremacy, and their quick destruction, were rhetorical commonplaces. The East knew abundant cases of the kind. Empires had risen and crumbled almost within the recollection of living men. That was particularly so after Alexander, when sudden glories and eclipses were too common to be noteworthy.

And we must further reckon with the fact that a potent incentive was the living faith in an actual God, who could and did hurl the mighty from their seat. To these men the destruction of Senracherib or the triumph of Gideon was no legend, but a real event, which might occur in their days as in the days of their fathers. The attempt, accordingly, to secure the independence of a small portion of the empire need not have seemed to the men that undertook it quite as insensate a proceeding as it does to us.

Our most complete source for the period is discredited by the *parti pris* of the author, the disloyal Josephus. The Roman sources indicate that in the Jewish revolt there was nothing different from the revolts in other parts of the world, revolts to which Romans were accustomed. There was no direct external provocation. There was no one event that seemed to account adequately for an outburst just then. But we find no indication that Romans felt it to be a strange

19

or inexplicable fact for men to rise in order to recover their freedom. The imperial interests demanded that the hopelessness of such rising should be made apparent. It was therefore to the leaders of the community, the aristocracy, that Romans looked to keep in check the ignorant multitude to whom the superiority of Romans in war or civilization might not at all be apparent.

The contemptible young rake who, as Agrippa II, continued for some years the empty title of "king of the Jews," was no doubt at one with the smug Josephus in his sincere conviction of the overwhelming might of the Romans and the folly of attacking it. We cannot sufficiently admire the successful way in which the king concealed his heartfelt pity for the sufferings of the Jews, "since he wished to humble the exalted thoughts they were indulging," as Josephus naïvely tells us (Wars, II. xvi. 2). However, not mere truckling to the Romans, but sober conviction, would sufficiently account for the pro-Roman leanings of men like Agrippa and Josephus. The long speech put in the king's mouth (*ibid*. II. xvi. 4) was perhaps never delivered, but it states the feeling of the pro-Roman party and of the Romans themselves eminently well.

Both Josephus and Agrippa could hold no other view than that it was some single act or series of acts of the procurator Florus that animated the leaders of the revolt. It seemed to them a "small reason" for engaging in what was conceded even by the most hopeful to be a desperate and frightful war. The burden of the

king's supposed speech, however, in which we are justified in seeing the sentiment of the historian, is this:
"Who and what are these Jews that they can refuse to
submit to that nation to which all others have submitted?"[3] We find enumerated for us the extent and
wealth of the Roman possessions with a fervor of
patriotism that might have shamed many a Roman.
"Are you richer than the Gauls, more powerful in
body than the Germans, wiser than the Greeks, more
numerous than all the inhabitants of the earth put
together?" he asks, and enforces his question with a
detailed account of the enormous numbers of people
who in the several provinces are kept in check by a
handful of legionaries.

As an appeal to common sense, the speech, in spite of
its obvious exaggerations, ought to have been successful. But what the Romans and the Romanized Jews
chose to overlook was that common sense was scarcely
a factor in producing the "exalted opinions" which
Agrippa sought to abase. The glowing assurance of
direct divine interposition was of course lacking to the
speaker, and the wilder and more exuberant fancies
that made the present time big with great upheavals and
opened vistas of strange and sweeping changes, could
not be answered by a statistical enumeration of the
forces at the disposal of Romans and Jews respectively.

In the previous chapter one fact has been frequently
mentioned which Josephus states quite casually as an
ordinary incident of the events he is describing. That
fact is the readiness with which the Romans took

alarm, not only at the armed "brigands," who were really at all times in open revolt, but at anyone who, posing as preacher or prophet, gathered a crowd about him for thoroughly unwarlike purposes. We do not find elsewhere in the empire this quickness of animadversion on the part of the authorities to such acts. The Armenian Peregrinus was quite unmolested by the Roman officials when he undertook to perform before the eyes of the assembled crowd the miracle of Hercules on Mount Oeta.⁴ Nor is there any evidence, however large the multitude was that surrounded the itinerant magician elsewhere, that riot and subversion were apprehended from that fact. Yet when the Egyptian promised to divide the walls of Jerusalem (above, p. 285), or Theudas to pass dryshod over the Jordan, or another man to discover the hidden treasures on the Gerizim (above, p. 284), a troop was sent at once to crush with bloody effectiveness an incipient rebellion. Obviously, in Judea, and not elsewhere, the assertion of divine inspiration carried with it a claim to certain political rights, or was deemed to do so, which was incompatible with Roman sovereignty.

It is easy enough to understand what that claim was, and easy enough to understand why it does not stand forth more clearly in Josephus' narrative. The coming of the Messianic kingdom had been looked for by previous generations as well, but in the generation that preceded 68 C. E. it became more and more strongly believed to be immediately at hand and to demand from those who would share in it a more than passive reception.

We are not to suppose that every one of these impostors or thaumaturgs claimed Messiaric rank. That it is not expressly stated by Josephus proves little, since he actively strove to suppress any indication that there were rebellious incentives among his people other than the brutal oppressions of Florus. But to claim to be Messiah was a serious matter both to the people and to the Roman officials, and we assume that these rather vulgar swindlers hardly dared to go so far. However, whether individuals did or did not make these pretensions, it is clear that during the reign of Nero the sense of an impending cataclysm was growing, and the most fondly held dreams of the Jews, which clustered about the Messianic idea, seemed to come near to realization.

Besides the cumulative force which the Jewish eschatology and Messianic hope acquired by the mere tradition from generation to generation, there was another and more general factor. The constitution established by Augustus might strive as it would to resemble with only slight modifications the republican forms it displaced. The East, for its part, had never been deceived into regarding it otherwise than a monarchy. And as such it was an unmistakable notch in the course of events. At a specific moment, whether it was Caesar's entry into Rome or Augustus' investiture with the principate, living men had seen and noted a page turned in the history of the world.

In this new monarchical constitution, the weak point was the succession. The glamour of acknowledged

divinity rested upon Julius Caesar and Augustus, and
in their blood there seemed to be an assurance of title to
the lordship of the world. What would happen if this
blood should fail ? No machinery existed that would
automatically indicate who the successor would be.
Changes of dynasty, whether regular or violent, were
of course no new thing to the East, but this was
not the same. The Roman empire was unique. The
imperator, or αὐτοκράτωρ, was as new in conception
as in title. Divinely established, the imperial dignity
would be divinely maintained in those who by their
origin could claim an unbroken chain of divine descent.
He whom we know as Nero was on the monuments
"Nero Claudius Cæsar, son of the god Claudius and
great-great-grandson of the god Augustus"; and the
last was at all times officially styled *Divi filius,* " son
of the God."[5]

But Nero's childlessness made it plain that the divine
maintenance would be wanting. With Nero, the line of
Augustus would become extinct. For Rome that pre-
saged confusion and civil war. For the little stretch of
country between the Lebanon and the River of Egypt,
it loosed all the hopes and fears and expectations to
which each generation had added a little, and which
were to be realized in the dissolution that was hurrying
on.

Nor must we forget that the reign of Nero had been
marked by frequent rebellions. Armenia had revolted
and been subdued. At the other end of the Roman
world, the Britons had risen in a bloody insurrection.

And in the very midst of the Jewish war, the inevitable
Gallic rebellion broke out, ostensibly against Nero personally, but doubtless impelled by motives of national
feeling as well.   Perhaps, if we had as detailed a narrative of the British, Armenian, and Gallic insurrections
as we have of the Jewish, we should find many prelimi-
nary conditions the same.   Perhaps in those countries
too " brigands " and " impostors " stirred the people to
revolt by playing upon their sacred traditions and
appealing to their hopes of a national restoration.'

One very curious circumstance is the association of
this last emperor of the Julian house with the Jews
generally and the Messiahship particularly.   How far
it is possible to discover the real Nero under the mass
of slanderous gossip and poisonous rhetoric which
Suetonius and Tacitus have heaped upon him, is not
easy to determine, nor is it necessary to do so at this
point.   One thing may, however, be insisted upon.   He
courted and achieved a high degree of popularity.   This
is hinted at, not only in the fact noted in Suetonius
(Nero, 37), that in a public prayer he ostentatiously
referred only to himself and the people, and omitted
any mention of the senate, but is expressly referred to
in the same writer (*ibid.* 53) : *Maxime autem popu-*
laritate efferebatur, omnium aemulus qui quoquo modo
animum vulgi moverent, "Above all, his chief desire
was for popularity, and, to gain this, he imitated all who
in any way had caught the fancy of the mob."   To this
may be added the confirmatory evidence of the lasting
veneration felt for his memory by the populace (*ibid.*

57) and the assumption of his name by Otho when the latter desired to court popular favor (Suetonius, Otho, 7).[7]

This favor among the masses in the city would of itself indicate a hold on the Oriental part of his subjects, which Nero's personal traits make especially likely. And of these Oriental or half-Oriental Romans a very considerable fraction were Jews. The all-powerful Poppaea Sabina, Nero's mistress and afterwards his wife, is on good grounds believed to have been a semi-proselyte, a *metuens*.[8] Josephus ascribes Nero's interference to her influence when Agrippa II attempted to make a display of the temple ceremonies. It is also not unlikely that the change of attitude on the part of Josephus toward Nero was due to the general feeling of the Roman Jewry toward his memory—a feeling of which Josephus had no cognizance in writing the Wars, but which had come to his attention when the Antiquities was composed. In the Wars (IV. ix. 2) we hear " how he abused his power and intrusted the control of affairs to unworthy freedmen, those wicked men, Nymphidius and Tigellinus." In the Antiquities (XX. viii. 3) we find a temperate paragraph warning readers that the extant accounts of Nero are thoroughly unreliable, especially the accounts of those " who have impudently and senselessly lied about him."[9]

That among the Roman populace there were some who believed that Nero was not dead, but still alive, and would return to be avenged upon his foes, is not strange. But it is particularly strange that in the extreme East the hereditary rivals of Rome, the Parthians, cherished his memory, so that their king Vologaesus expressly asked for recognition of that fact when he strove to renew his alliance with Rome. It was among the Parthians that the man who claimed to be Nero found enthusiastic support about 88 c. e. (Suet. Nero, 57). The Parthians seem to have been ready to invade the Roman empire to re-establish this " Nero " (Tac. Hist. I. ii. 6). That, it is true, happened long afterward; but directly after Nero's death, in the very throes of the Jewish war, a similar belief spread like wildfire over Greece and Asia Minor, and a slave, by calling himself Nero, secured temporary control of the island of Cythnus (Tac. Hist. I. ii. 8).

One phrase of Suetonius is especially noteworthy. Long before Nero's death it had been prophesied that he would be deposed, and would return as lord of the East: *Nonnulli,* Suetonius goes on to say, *nominatim regnum Hierosolymorum* [*spoponderant*], " Some assured him specifically that he would be king of Jerusalem."

There is no direct confirmation in the Jewish sources of this association of Nero with a restored kingdom at Jerusalem. The very late Talmudic legend which states that Nero became a convert and was the ancestor of Rabbi Meïr[10] must, of course, be disregarded. No notable heathen sovereign escaped conversion in the Jewish legends. To the Christians, Nero was Belial or Antichrist for reasons obvious enough, and the Sibylline verses which so represent him are probably of Christian origin. But since the Messianic idea of the Jews was well-known throughout the Roman world (Suet. Vespasian, 4), the prediction made to Nero meant nothing less than that he was the promised Messiah, a conception startling enough, but perhaps less so to Nero's generation than to ours.

It may further be possible to find an association between Nero and the Jews in the words that Philostratus[1] (Life of Apollonius, v. 33) puts in the mouth of the Alexandrian Euphrates. The Jews, Euphrates says, are the enemies of the human race almost as much as Nero, but it is the latter against whom Vespasian should direct his arms, not the former.

Whether, however, it was Nero or someone else, the intense force of the Messianic idea of the time of the revolt is attested explicitly by Suetonius in the passage alluded to above. *Percrebuerat Oriente toto vetus et constans opinio esse in fatis ut eo tempore Iudaea profecti rerum potirentur,* "Throughout the length and breadth of the East there was current an old and unvarying belief to the effect that it was decreed by fate that supreme power would fall into the hands of men coming from Judea." If to Tacitus the insurrection was merely the expected outbreak of a turbulent province, repressed with difficulty in previous generations, and inevitable under all circumstances; if, to Josephus, the revolt was the foolish attempt of deluded but unfortunate men, driven mad by the oppressions of officials and led by selfish rascals, Suetonius, who retailed the gossip of the seven seas, had clearer insight

when he referred the actual outbreak of hostilities to
the general conviction that the result of the war would
determine the fate of the empire.   The Law would go
out from Zion: *Iudaea profecti rerum potirentur.*

The war, which resulted in the fall of Jerusalem,
was in the eyes of Josephus (Wars, Preface, § 1) the
greatest war in recorded history.   The words he uses
are very much like those of Livy when he is about to
describe the Second Punic War (Livy, XXI. i.), where,
it must be admitted, the statement seems somewhat
more fitting.   The Roman historians naturally enough
do not attach quite the same importance to a rebellion
in a border province, however dangerous or desperate.
But no one regarded it as an insignificant episode in
the maintenance of the imperial frontier.   There were
many accounts of it, most of them written "sophistic-
ally" (*ibid.* I. i. 1), *i. e.* with a definite purpose that
was quite apart from that of presenting a true version
of the facts.   These men, we are told by the author,
wrote from hate or for favor.   They desired to flatter
the Romans or to vent their spleen on the Jews.   The
accurate truth was, of course, to be found only in the
austerely veridical account written by Josephus in
Aramaic, and translated by him into Greek.

It is, accordingly, strange that in the one narrative
which we have from a source independent of Josephus,
there should appear details which suggest that flattery
of the Roman conqueror was not wholly absent from
Josephus' own narrative.   In the Roman History of
Cassius Dio (known principally by the Greek form of

his name, Dion Cassius), who wrote about 225 C. E., we find a version of the siege of Jerusalem in which Titus is something less than a demi-god, and the Jews something different from the wretched and besotted fanatics Josephus makes of them. Dio has little sympathy for the Jews in general, and finds their institutions repellent on the whole, but his account is simpler and actually more favorable to the Jews than the one presented in the pages of the Wars.

Such details as the wound received by Titus (Dio, lxvi. 5), which Josephus omits or modifies (Wars, V. vi. 2), are of minor significance, although even they indicate the strain Josephus was put to in his attempt to make Titus move in the midst of dangers like a present divinity. But there are other matters that Josephus does not mention, *e. g.* the desertion of Roman soldiers to the Jews in the very midst of the siege, the awe of the Romans toward the temple, so that they had to be actually forced to enter upon the forbidden precinct even when the building was in flames. But especially it is the Asiatic Roman, and not the Jew, who lays stress upon the heroic pride which the Jews displayed in the moment of their utmost extremity. "All believed it was not destruction, but victory, safety, happiness, to die with their temple" (Dio, lxvi. 6).

That the conquest of the capital seemed no usual triumph is evidenced by the closing words of Dio (*ibid.* 7) and by the inscription which was carved on one of the arches erected to Titus. Several such arches were erected. One on the lower ridges of the Palatine, at the edge of the forum, contains the famous relief of the triumph of Titus. The other was in the Circus Maximus, and of this we have only the copy of the inscription (C. I. L. vi. 944). It runs as follows:[12]

The Senate and People of Rome have erected this arch to the first of their citizens, His Sacred Majesty, Titus Caesar Vespasian, son of the God Vespasian, High Priest, invested for the tenth time with tribunician power, hailed commander seventeen times, chosen consul eight times, Father of his Country, because, led by the guidance, wisdom, and divine favor of his father, he subdued the race of the Jews, and destroyed their city of Jerusalem, a city which all kings, commanders, and nations before him have either attacked in vain, or left wholly unassailed.

Dio notes that the title "Judaicus" was not assumed by either Vespasian or Titus. The inscription just quoted makes it clear that their motive in doing so was not any desire to minimize the importance of their victory. Relatively less important triumphs over such people as the Adiabeni or Carpi resulted in the assumption of the titles of Adiabenicus or Carpicus. It has been urged with considerable plausibility[13] that the term "Judaicus" would suggest to the general public a "convert to Judaism," and at a moment when the spread of Judaism was, if anything, greater and more successful than ever, despite the fall of the temple, that was an impression dangerous to convey, particularly since Titus was himself under a strong suspicion of Eastern proclivities (Suet. Titus, 5). As a matter of fact, however, Dio's surprise is due to the conditions of his own time, when the emperors freely assumed these gentile cognomina. So Septimius Severus is Parthicus, Arabicus, Adiabenicus, Britannicus. In Vespasian's time that was distinctly not customary. None of his predecessors assumed these titles. The name Germanicus, used by Gaius, Claudius, and Nero, is a hereditary cognomen, and its assumption by Vitellius is due to a desire on the latter's part to associate himself with the memory of a name at all times endeared to the people.

But that the conquest of Judea seemed at the time quite equal to those which justified the assumption of such honoring titles, may be seen in the epigram of Martial (ii. 2) :

> *Creta dedit magnum, maius dedit Africa nomen*
> *Scipio quod victor quodque Metellus habet,*
> *Nobilius domito tribuit Germania Rheno,*
> *Et puer hoc dignus nomine, Caesar, eras.*
> *Frater Idumaeos meruit cum patre triumphos,*
> *Quae datur ex Chattis laurea, tota tua est.*

Crete granted a great name; Africa, a greater; the former to Metellus, the latter to Scipio. Even more renowned a title was derived from Germany and the conquered Rhine. That title, Caesar, your boyhood valor also earned. The Idumean triumph [14] you must share with your brother and father. The laurel wreath inscribed with the name of the Chatti—that is all your own.

The destruction of the city and temple affected the imaginations of all men, Jew and non-Jew, very powerfully. A large number of the various apocryphal books are referred to this period, especially those which are filled with lamentations over the desolate condition of the former princess among provinces. But dramatic

and affecting as it was, the destruction of the temple
was not at the time the epochal event it seems to us now
It made only a slight change in the political condition
even of Palestinian Jews, and even in the spiritual condition of the Jews at large it played seemingly a subordinate part.

CHAPTER XIX

THE DEVELOPMENT OF THE ROMAN JEWISH COMMUNITY

The Jews in Rome at the time of Cicero formed, we have seen, an important and numerous class amidst the largely orientalized plebs of the city. With the other foreigners resident in the city they had a powerful patron in Caesar, as their grief at his death attested. Under his successor they found at least an indulgent, if somewhat contemptuous, toleration, which however was directed not toward them specially, but toward the other foreigners in the capital as well. And as we have seen, the religious reformation of Augustus, and his active disapproval of foreign cults, did not prevent the Jews from spreading rapidly in all classes of society.

Under Tiberius we hear of a general expulsion of the Jews, as afterward under Claudius. "Expulsion of Jews" is a term with which later European history has made us familiar. In the case of such expulsions as the Jews suffered in England, France, Spain, and Portugal, we know that the term is literally exact. Practically all Jews were in the instances cited compelled to leave the country and settle elsewhere. The expulsion ordered by Tiberius was unquestionably wholly ineffective in practice, since there were many Jews in Rome shortly after, although we have no record that the decree was repealed. But it may be questioned whether even in theory it resembled the expulsions of later times.

The facts are given fully by Suetonius (Tiberius, 36):

Externas caerimonias Aegyptios Iudaeosque ritus compescuit, coactis qui superstitione ea tenebantur religiosas vestes cum instrumento omni comburere. Iudaeorum iuventutem per speciem sacramenti in provincias gravioris caeli distribuit: reliquos gentis eiusdem vel similia sectantes urbe summovit sub poena perpetuae servitutis nisi obtemperassent.

He checked the spread of foreign rites, particularly the Egyptian and Jewish. He compelled those who followed the former superstition to burn their ritual vestments and all their religious utensils. The younger Jews he transferred to provinces of rigorous climate under the pretense of assigning them to military service. All the rest of that ration, and all who observed its rites, he ordered out of the city under the penalty of being permanently enslaved if they disobeyed.

Undoubtedly the same incident is mentioned by Tacitus in the Annals (ii. 85), where we hear that " action was taken about the eradication of Egyptian and Jewish rites. A senatusconsultum was passed, which transferred four thousand freedmen of military age who were affected by this superstition to Sardinia in order to crush brigandage there. . . . . The rest were to leave Italy unless they abandoned their impious rites before a certain day."

Between these two accounts there are discrepancies that cannot be cured by the simple process of amalgamating the two, as has generally been done. These divergences will be treated in detail later. For the present it will be well to compare an independent account, that of Josephus, with the two.

Josephus (Ant. XVIII. iii. 5) tells us of a Jew, " a thoroughly wicked man," who was forced to flee from Judea for some crime, and with three worthy associates supported himself by swindling in Rome. This man persuaded Fulvia, a proselyte of high rank, the wife of a certain Saturninus, to send rich gifts to the temple. The presents so received were used by the four men for themselves. Upon the complaint of Saturninus, " Tiberius ordered all the Jews [πᾶν τὸ Ἰουδαϊκόν] to be driven from Rome. The consuls enrolled four thousand of them, and sent them to the island of Sardinia. He punished very many who claimed that their ancestral customs prevented them from serving." Apart from the incident which, Josephus says, occasioned the expulsion, we have a version here which is not quite in accord with the one either of Tacitus or of Suetonius.

Of these men Josephus is probably the nearest in time to the events he is describing, but also the most remote in comprehension. Besides the story just told, Josephus tells another, in which it is a votary of Isis who is deceived, with the connivance of the priests of the Egyptian goddess. The two incidents which he relates are placed in juxtaposition rather than connection by him, but the mere fact that they are told in this way indicates that a connection did exist in the source, written or oral, from which he derived them. Josephus does not mention that the Egyptian worship was attacked as well as the Jewish, and indeed he takes pains to suggest that the two incidents were not really connected at all

From all these statements, and from the reference
that Philo makes in the *Legatio ad Gaium*,[1] there is
very little that we can gather with certainty. This
much, however, seems established: an attempt was
made to check the spread both of Judaism and of
Isis-worship. In this attempt a certain number of
Jews were expelled from the city or from Italy. Four
thousand soldiers—actual or reputed Jews—were
transferred to Sardinia for the same reason. There are
certain difficulties, however, in the way of supposing
that it really was a general expulsion of all Jews, as
Josephus and Suetonius, but not Tacitus, say.

Tacitus' omission to state it, if such a general expulsion took place, is itself a difficulty; but like every *argu-
mentum ex silentio*, it scarcely permits a valid inference. It seems strange, to be sure, that a severe and
deserved punishment of the *taeterrima gens*, "that dis-
gusting race," should be represented to be something
much milder than really was the case. But Tacitus is
neither here nor in other places taking pains to cite the
decree accurately, and the omission of even a significant
detail may be laid to inadvertence.

But what Tacitus does say cannot be lightly passed
over. Four thousand men, *libertini generis*, "of the
freedmen class," were transferred to Sardinia for military service. All these four thousand were *ea superstitione infecti*, "tainted with this superstition." Now,
the Jews who formed the community at Rome in the
time of Cicero may have been largely freedmen, but
their descendants were not classed as *libertini generis*.

The phrase is not used in Latin of those who were of
servile origin, but solely of those who were themselves
emancipated slaves. There is, however, scarcely a possibility that there could have been at Rome in 19 c. e. so
large a body of Jewish freed slaves of military age.
There had been no war in recent times from which these
slaves could have been derived. We may assume therefore that most, if not all, of these men were freedmen
of other nationalities who were converts to Judaism.

This is confirmed by the words *ea superstitione
infecti,* "tainted with this superstition." These words
are meaningless unless they refer to non-Jewish proselytes.[2] Men who were born Jews could not be so characterized. If Tacitus had meant those who were Jews
by birth, it is scarcely conceivable that he would have
used a phrase that would suggest just the opposite. The
words, further, imply that many of these four thousand were rather suspected of Jewish leanings than
definitely proselytes. Perhaps they were residents of
the districts largely inhabited by Jews, notably the
Transtiberine region.

Again, to suppose that all the Jews were banished by
Tiberius involves an assumption as to that emperor's
methods wholly at variance with what we know of him.
A very large number of Jewish residents in Rome were
Roman citizens (Philo, 569 M), and so far from being
a meaningless distinction in the early empire, that term
through the influence of the rising science of jurisprudence was, in fact, just beginning to have its meaning and implications defined. A wholesale expulsion of

Roman citizens by either an administrative act or a
senatusconsultum is unthinkable under Tiberius. Exile,
in the form of relegation or expulsion, was a well-
known penalty for crime after due trial and conviction,
which in every instance would have to be individual.
Even in the Tacitean caricature[2] we find evidence of
the strict legality with which Tiberius acted on all
occasions. No senatusconsultum could have decreed a
general banishment for all Jews, whether Roman citizens or not, without contravening the fundamental
principles of the Roman law.

How thoroughly confused the transmission of this
incident had become in the accounts we possess, is
indicated in the final sentence from Suetonius: ' He
ordered them out of the city, under the penalty of being
permanently enslaved if they disobeyed." The very
term *perpetua servitus*, as though there were a limited
slavery in Rome at the time, is an absurdity. It becomes
still more so when we recall that slavery, except in the
later form of compulsory service in the mines and
galleys, was not known as a penalty at Roman law.
The state had no machinery for turning a freeman into
a slave, except by his own will, and then it did so
reluctantly. We shall be able to see what lies behind
this confusion when we have considered one or two
other matters.

The alleged expulsion is not mentioned by Philo in
the extant fragments. The allusion to some oppressive
acts of Sejanus (In Flaccum, § 1. ii. p. 517 M ; and Leg.
ad Gaium, § 24. ii. p. 569 M) is not clear. But it is diffi-

cult to understand the highly eulogistic references to Tiberius, then long dead, if a general Jewish expulsion had been ordered by that emperor.

That the senatusconsultum in question was general, and was directed indiscriminately at all foreign religions, appears not merely from the direct statement of Suetonius and Tacitus, and the association of the two stories by Josephus, but also from a reference of Seneca. In his philosophic essays, written in the form of letters to his friend Lucilius (108, 22), he says: "I began [under the teaching of Sotion] to abstain from animal food. . . . . You ask me when I ceased to abstain. My youth was passed during the first years of Tiberius Caesar's rule. At that time foreign rites were expelled; but one of the proofs of adherence to such a superstition was held to be the abstinence from the flesh of certain animals. At the request of my father, who did not fear malicious prosecution, but hated philosophy, I returned to my former habits."

The words of Seneca, *sacra movebantur,* suggest the τῶν ἐν Ἰταλίᾳ παρακινηθέντων of Philo (*loc. cit.*), "when there was a general agitation [against the Jews?] in Italy." It is further noticeable that the *mathematici, i. e.* the soothsayers, against whom the Roman laws were at all times severe, were also included in this decree.ᵃ

It has been pointed out before (above, p. 242) that the observance of foreign religious rites was never forbidden as such by Roman laws. From the first of the instances, the Bacchanalian persecution of 186 B. C. E., it was always some definite crime, immorality or impos-

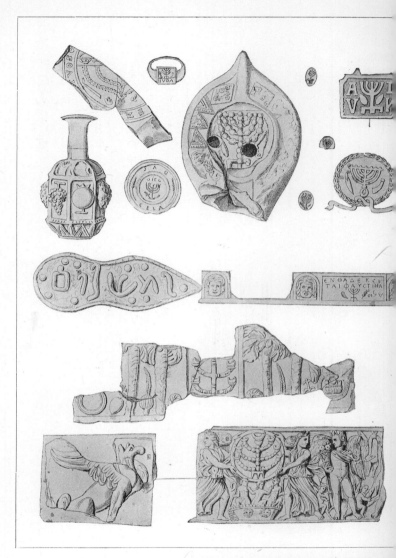

SYMBOLS AND INSCRIPTIONS FROM JE

(Fr

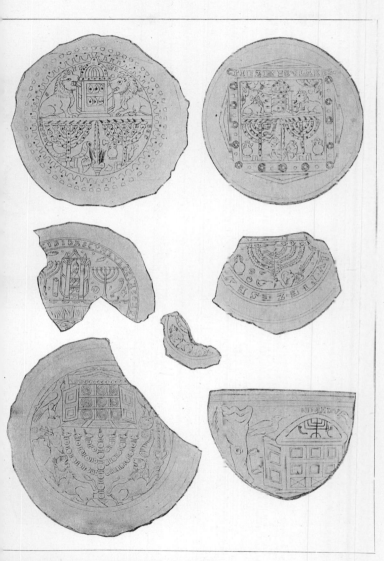

ture, that was attacked and of which the rites mentioned
were alleged to be the instruments. The "expulsion"
of the Isis-worshipers during the republic meant only
that certain foreigners were summarily ordered to
leave the city, something that the Lex Junia Penni in
83 B. C. E. and the Lex Papia of 65 B. C. E. attempted to
enforce, and which the Roman police might do at any
time when they thought the public interest demanded
it. Roman citizens practising these rites could never be
proceeded against, unless they were guilty of one of the
crimes these foreign practices were assumed to involve.

The two stories cited by Josephus, one concerning an
Isis-worshiper, the other a Jew, may not be true.
Whether true or not, the incidents they record surely did
not of themselves cause the expulsion of either group.
But these are fair samples of the stories that were probably told and believed in Rome, and similar incidents no
doubt did occur. The association of the *mathematici*
with the other two makes it probable that the senatusconsultum was directed against fraud the getting of
money under false pretenses, and that the Jewish, Isiac,
and other rites, as well as astrology, were mentioned
solely as types of devices to that end.

What actually happened was no doubt that in Rome
and in Italy overzealous officials undertook to treat the
observance of foreign rites as conclusive or at least pre-
sumptive evidence of guilt under this act. Perhaps, as
Philo says, it was one of the instances of Sejanus'
tyranny to do so. But there is no reason to doubt
Philo's express testimony that Tiberius promptly

checked this excess of zeal and enforced the decree as
it was intended (*loc. cit.*) : ὡς οὐκ ἐπὶ πάντας προβάσης τῆς
ἐπεξελεύσεως, ἀλλ᾽ ἐπὶ μόνους τοὺς αἰτίους—ὀλίγοι δὲ ἦσαν
—κινῆσαι δὲ μηδὲν ἐξ ἔθους ; *i. e.* " since the prosecution
was not directed against all, but only against the guilty,
who were very few. Otherwise there was to be no
departure from the customary attitude."

The transference of the four thousand recruits,
libertini generis, to Sardinia undoubtedly took place,
and was very likely the expression of alarm on the part
of Sejanus or Tiberius at the spread of Judaism in
Rome. It may well be that the removal of these men
was caused rather by the desire to withdraw them from
the range of proselytism than by the purpose of allowing them to die in the severe climate of Sardinia. There
is as a matter of fact no evidence that Sardinia had a
noticeably different climate from that of Italy. It was
one of the granaries of the empire.[5]

Perhaps we may reconstitute the decree as follows:
The penalty imposed was, for foreigners, expulsion ;
for Roman citizens, perhaps exile ; for freedmen, for-
feiture of their newly acquired liberty in favor of their
former masters or the latter's heirs. This last fact will
explain the statement of Suetonius. Many of the
people affected were no doubt freedmen, and several
instances where such a penalty was actually inflicted
would account quite adequately for the words *perpetua
servitus* of Suetonius. The " malicious prosecution,"
calumnia, which Seneca asserts his father did *not* fear,
would be based, as against Roman citizens, on the viola-

tion of this law against fraudulent practices, of which, as we have seen, the adoption of foreign rites would be taken as evidence.

The personal relations between Gaius and the Jewish king Agrippa seemed to guarantee an era of especial prosperity for the Roman Jews. However, the entire principate of that indubitable paranoiac was filled with the agitation that attended his attempt to set up his statue at Jerusalem. His death, which Josephus describes in gratifyingly minute detail, brought permanent relief on that point.

It is during the reign of his successor Claudius that we hear of another expulsion: *Iudaeos impulsore Chresto adsidue tumultuantis Roma expulit* (Suet. Claud. 25), "The Jews who engaged in constant riots by the machinations of a certain Chrestus, he expelled from Rome." It has constantly been stated that this refers to the agitation in the Roman Jewry which the preaching of Christianity aroused. For that, however, there is no sufficient evidence. Jesus, to be sure, is called Chrestus, Χρηστός, the Upright, in many Christian documents.[6] This play upon words is practically unavoidable. But Chrestus is a common name among all classes of society.[7] Jews would be especially likely to bear it, since it was a fairly good rendering of such a frequently occurring name as Zadok. The riot in question was no doubt a real enough event, and the expulsion equally real, even if it did not quite imply all that seems to be contained in it.

If it were a decree of general expulsion of all Jews, it would be strikingly at variance with the edicts in favor of the Jews which Claudius issued, and which are contained in Josephus (Ant. XIX. v.). As in the case of other documents cited here, there is no reason to question the substantial accuracy of their contents, although they are surely not verbatim transcriptions from the records. It is as clearly impossible in the case of Claudius as in that of Tiberius to suppose an arbitrary disregard of law on his part, so that a general ejection of all Jews from the city, including those who were Roman citizens, is not to be thought of.

Neither Tacitus nor Josephus mentions the expulsion. The silence of neither is conclusive, but it lends strong probability to the assumption that the decree cannot have been so radical a measure as a general expulsion of all Jews from the city would be. The passage from Suetonius is concerned wholly with acts of Claudius affecting foreigners—non-Romans, *i. e.* Lycians, Rhodians, Gauls, Germans—and if we keep in mind Suetonius' habits of composition, it is highly likely that he has put together here all that he found together in his source. We are to understand therefore by the *Iudaei* of this passage only foreign Jews, which implies that the majority of the Jews were not affected by it at all.

But were even all foreign Jews included? Is there anything in the passage that is not perfectly consistent with the assumption that some relatively small group of Jews led by a certain Chrestus was ejected from the city for disorderly conduct? The silence of the other writers, the total absence of effect on the growth of the Jewish population, would seem to make this after all the simplest meaning of Suetonius' words.

The fact of the expulsion is confirmed by that passage in the Acts of the Apostles in which the meeting of Paul and Aquila at Corinth is mentioned (Acts xviii. 1, 2): " [Paul] found a certain Jew born in Pontus, lately come from Italy with his wife Priscilla, (because that Claudius had commanded all Jews to depart from Rome)." The testimony is late,[3] but it will be noticed that Aquila is an Asiatic by birth, and so very likely had no legal right of residence at Rome in any circumstances.

Finally, expulsion " from Rome " may have meant only exclusion from the *pomoerium,* the sacral limit of the city that followed an imaginary line not at all coincident with its real walls. To escape from the operation of the decree, it would merely have been necessary to cross the Tiber, where as a matter of fact the Jews generally lived, since the Transtiberine region was not included in the *pomoerium.* In general, expulsion from the city specified that the expelled person might not come within the first milestone, but in view of the difficulties presented by the assumption of a real expulsion, this supposition may also be considered.

Mention has already been made of the special association of Claudius' successor, Nero, with the Jews. The success that attended their efforts at propaganda during that emperor's reign is evidenced by the fact that Poppaea Sabina became a semi-proselyte. And during Nero's reign occurs an event of special importance to the Jews of Rome, the first Christian persecution.

In the reign of Nero, possibly in that of Claudius, there was brought to the various Jewish congregations of the Roman world, seemingly not beyond that, the "good news," εὐαγγέλιον, that a certain Jesus, of Nazareth in Galilee, was the long-promised Messiah. To most, perhaps, the facts cited of his life indicated only that he was one of the "many swindlers," γόητες ἄνθρωποι, like those whom Felix captured and put to death (Jos. Ant. XX. viii. 5). But some believed. If we are to credit the Acts of the Apostles, this belief at once produced a bitter conflict between those who did so believe, afterwards called Christians, and those who did not.[9] But the Acts in the form in which it has come down to us represents a recension of much later date, made when the enmity between Jew and Christian was real and indubitable.

It may be that in certain places those Jews who accepted the evangel almost at once formed congregations of their own, synagogues or ecclesiae (the terms are practically synonymous),[10] different from the synagogues of those who rejected it. But there were from the beginning differences of degree in its acceptance, and even in the existing recension of the Acts there is good evidence that its acceptance or rejection did not immediately and everywhere produce a schism.

In the city of Rome a persecution of Christians, as distinct from Jews, took place under Nero. That fact is attested by both Suetonius and Tacitus and by the earliest of the Christian writers. Tertullian quotes the *commentarii,* the official records for it.

The record as it appears in Suetonius is characteristically different from that in Tacitus. In Suetonius we have a brief statement (Nero, 16) : *Afflicti suppliciis Christiani, genus hominum superstitionis novce ac maleficae,* "Punishment was inflicted upon the Christians, a class of men that maintained a new and harmful form of superstition." This statement is made as one item, apparently of minor importance, in the list of Nero's creditable actions, as Suetonius tells us later (*ibid.* 19) : *Haec partim nulla reprehensione, partim etiam non mediocri laude digna, in unum contuli,* "These acts, some of which are wholly blameless, while others deserve even considerable approbation, I have gathered together." Whether the punishment of the Christians is in the former or the latter class does not appear.

In Tacitus, on the other hand, we have the famous account that Nero sought to divert from himself the suspicion of having set Rome on fire, by fastening it upon those "whom the people hated for their wickedness, the so-called Christians" (Ann. xv. 44). These were torn by dogs, or crucified, or tied to stakes and burned in a coat of pitch to serve as lanterns to the bestially cruel emperor. The truth of these stories depends upon the reliability of Tacitus in general. They have been received with justifiable doubt, ever since the quite conscienceless methods of Tacitus' rhetorical style have been made evident. The last form of punishment, the *tunica molesta,* has made a particular impression on the ancient and modern world. It is referred to by Seneca, Juvenal, and Martial, but by none of them associated with the Christians. From the passage in Seneca (Epist. ad Lucil. xiv. 4) it is simply a standard form of cruelty, such as the rack, thumbscrew, and maiden of later times. The very fact that the courtier Seneca dares to mention it as a form of *saevitia* would indicate that it was not used by Seneca's master, Nero. But what is particularly striking is that Tertullian[11] in his Apology does not mention any cruelties, in the sense of savage tortures, inflicted upon the Christians. The context (Apologeticus, § 5) indicates that the punishment was banishment to some penal colony, *relegatio,* a punishment considered capital at law, but still different from the *tunica molesta.*

But a new element was introduced in the case of the Christians, which, except in the treatment of the Druidic brotherhoods among the Gauls, is unusual in Roman methods. It is scarcely possible to read the Apology of Tertullian without being convinced that the profession of Christianity was in and for itself an indictable offense at Roman law since the time of Nero, quite apart from the fantastic crimes of which the Christians were held to be guilty.[12] Tertullian undoubtedly had legal training, and his exposition of the logical absurdities into which the fact led Roman officials is convincing enough, but the fact remains. The *nomen Christianum,* "the profession of Christianity," was considered a form of *maiestas,* "treason," and punished capitally. In effect this was an attempt to stamp out a religion, just as Claudius had sought to stamp out the Druids (Suetonius, Claud. 25). (Comp. above, p. 122.)

When Tertullian wrote, perhaps even in the time of Tacitus and Suetonius, the gulf between Jew and Christian was wide and impassable. It can hardly have been so in Nero's time. The statement that Nero's measures were instigated by Jews is a later invention for which there is simply no evidence whatever.[13] The fact that the *nomen Christianum* was either actually considered treason or partook of the nature of treason, makes it probable that the Messianic idea, which was the very essence of the evangel, was the basis of the Roman statute. In Judea the special and drastic crushing of every "impostor" has been spoken of, and its significance indicated (above, p. 292). The preaching of Christianity in Rome itself could only have seemed to Nero, or his advisers, an attempt at propagating, under the guise of religion, what had long been considered in the East simple sedition. While therefore the spread of Judaism, Isis-worship, Mithraism, was offensive, and attempts were made to check it, the spread of Christianity was an increase in crime and was treated as such. Perhaps a partial analogy may be offered in the attitude of conservative Americans to doctrines they regard as mischievous, like Socialism, and to those which are directly criminal, like some forms of organized Anarchism.

The elaborate scheme of salvation prepared by the Cilician Jew Paul [14] gradually gained almost general acceptance among Christians, although in the mother ecclesia at Jerusalem it found determined and obstinate resistance long after Paul's death. [15] The fundamental doctrine, that the Law was not necessarily the way of salvation for any but born Jews, and even for them was of doubtful efficacy, was the direct negation of the Pharisaic doctrine that through the Law there was effected immediate communion of man with God in this world and the next.

As long as the Christians were merely a heretical Jewish sect, their fortunes affected the whole Jewish community. When their propaganda became, not a supplement to that of the Jews, but its rival, and soon its successful and triumphant rival, its history is wholly separated, and the measures that dealt with the Christians and those that concerned the Jews were no longer in danger of being confused. To the Jews the success of the propaganda of Paul seemed to depend on the fact that he had abolished the long and severe ritual of initiation; he had increased his numbers by decreasing the cost of admission. So we find, shortly after the destruction of the temple, R. Nehemiah ben ha-Kannah asserting (Ab. iii. 6) that to discard the yoke of the Law was to assume the yoke of the kingdom and of the world; *i.e.* so far from making the path to unworldliness easier, it laid insuperable obstacles in the way. The statement is applicable to Jews of lax observance, but it seems particularly applicable to the Pauline Christians, who had not merely lightened the load, but deliberately and *ex professo* wholly discarded it.

Outside of the references that give us certain data about the external history of the Roman Jewish community of the first century, we have other data of a wholly different sort, data that allow of a more intimate glimpse into its actual life. They are furnished us by the Roman satirists, whose literary labors have scarcely an analogue in our days. Satire itself was assumed to be a Roman genre.[16] Whether or not it was of Roman invention, the miscellanies that have given us so many and such vivid pictures of ancient life are known to us wholly in Latin. It is safe to say that if satirists such as Horace, Persius, Juvenal, and Martial had not come down to us, ancient history would be a vastly bleaker province than it is.

Of Horace and his representation of Jewish life we have already spoken. It will be remembered that the one aspect which earned for the Jews his none too respectful raillery was their eager proselytism. And it is excellent evidence of how important this proselytism was in the Jewish life of the time, that in the two generations that stretched from Nero to Nerva the same aspect is present to men of such diverse types as Persius and Juvenal.

With Persius we enter a wholly different stratum of society from that of Horace and, as we shall later see, of Juvenal. Persius was by birth and breeding an aristocrat. He was descended from an ancient Etruscan house, and could boast, accordingly, of a nobility of

21

lineage compared with which the Roman Valerii and Caecilii were the veriest mushrooms.[17] But he was almost wholly devoid of the vices that often mark his class. An austere Stoic, his short life was dedicated to the severe discipline that his contemporary and fellow-Stoic Seneca found it easier to preach than to practise.

Persius wrote little, and that little has all come down to us. His Latin, however, is so crabbed and difficult that he is easily the least read of Roman poets.[18] His productions are called Satires. They are less that than homilies, in which, of course, the virtues he inculcates are best illustrated by the vices he attacks.

One of these vices is superstition. The mental condition that is terrified by vain and monstrous imaginings of ignorant men is set forth in the Fifth Satire:[19]

But when the day of Herod comes and the lamps on the grimy sills, garlanded with violets, disgorge their unctuous smoke-clouds; when the tail of a tunny-fish fills its red dish and the white jar bursts with wine, you move your lips in silent dread and turn pale at the Sabbath of the circumcised.

As a picture of Jewish life on the eve of the Sabbath, this passage is invaluable. We can readily imagine how the activities of a squalid suburb inhabited by a brawling class of men, mostly of Oriental descent, must have impressed both the grandee and the Stoic.

But the passage is cited here, not merely as a genre-picture, but more especially because it is again the phase of Jewish life, so often neglected in histories, that has brought the Jews to Persius' attention. The ordinary Roman, not saved from carnal weakness by

Stoicism, is found to stand in particular dread of the strange and nameless God of the Jews, to whom he brings a reverence and awe that ought legitimately to be directed only to the gods of his ancestors.

Persius wrote while the temple was still standing. In 70 the temple was destroyed. A gaping mob saw the utensils of the inner shrine carried in triumph through the city, and could feast its eyes, if it chose, on the admirable portrayal of that procession, on the Arch of Titus near the Forum. It might be supposed that the God who in Roman eyes could not save His habitation from the flames, could hope for no adherents among His conquerors. But after the destruction of the temple, in the lifetime of the very men who cheered Titus when he returned from Palestine, we see the propaganda more vigorous, if anything, than before.

It is in the pages of Juvenal that we find evidence of that fact, and here again we are confronted with a sharply outlined personality. Decimus Junius Juvenalis was born near Aquinum in Southern Italy, where the Italic stock had probably suffered less admixture with foreign elements than was the case at Rome. What his intellectual training was we can only conjecture from its results, the turgid but sonorous and often brilliant eloquence of his Satires. Whether they are true pictures of Roman life and society or not may be doubted. But they indubitably reflect his own soul. We see there a soured *raté*, a man embittered by his failure to receive the rewards due to his merits. In the capital of the world, the city where he, the man of undoubted Roman stock, should have found a career open before him, he discovered himself to be a stranger. He was no match for the nimble-witted Greeks that thronged every profession and crawled into entrances too low to admit the scion of Cincinnatus and Fabricius. How much of this was the venom of defeated ambition, and how much was honest indignation at the indescribable meanness of the lives he depicted, we cannot now determine.

Throughout all his work one note may be heard, the note of rage at a Rome where everything characteristically Roman was pushed into the background, a Rome in the hands of Greeks, Egyptians, and Jews. And in the case of the last it is particularly the danger noted by Strabo and Seneca,[20] of an actual conquest of Rome by the Jewish faith, that rouses his savage indignation.

The lines in which he states his feeling are well-known (Juvenal, Sat. xiv. 96 seq.) :

Some whose lot it is to have a father that reveres the Sabbath, worship nothing but the clouds and the sky and think that the flesh of swine from which their father abstained is closely related to that of man. Soon they become circumcised. Trained to despise the laws of Rome they learn, maintain, and revere the Law of the Jews, which Moyses has transmitted in a mystic volume ;—laws that forbid them to show the way to any but members of their cult, and bid them guide to a spring none but their circumcised brethren.

We need be at no pains to correct Juvenal's estimate of Jewish beliefs or Jewish theology. As in the case of Persius, the interest of the passage lies in the fact that it gives additional testimony to the success with which the Jewish synagogues, despite official frowns and even repressive measures, despite the severe conditions they imposed upon initiates, were constantly gaining in membership.

Juvenal's other references to the Jews [21] show us certain unlovely aspects of their life. The hawkers and fortune-tellers whom he describes are certainly not the best representatives of the Roman community. It is no part of his purpose to give a complete picture of the community. But it is his purpose to denounce the degeneration which made the imperial city a disagreeable place for real Romans to sojourn in, and the Jewish peddler at the Grove of Egeria and the swindling hags who sell potent spells for cash give him the colors he requires.

One other writer must be mentioned, Martial. With him we are in the very heart of Grub Street. Marcus Valerius Martialis came from Spain to the capital. He had evidently no definite expectation of any career beyond that of a man of letters, and such a career involved at that time (as it continued to do until the nineteenth century) something of the life of a parasite. He had at least some of the characteristics of a parasite —a ready tongue, a strong stomach, and an easy conscience. But within his own field of poetry, the epigram, he was a real master. Subsequent centuries have rarely equaled the mordancy of his wit or the sting of his lampoon. At the foot of the banquet tables, jostled by hungry mountebanks and the very dregs of Roman society, he kept his mocking eyes open to the foibles of his host no less than to the disgustingly frank vices of his fellows.

And Martial meets Jews on his way through the teeming city. But if Horace, Persius, and Juvenal have their eyes upon Romans that were being Judaized, Martial presents to us the counterpart, Jews that actually were, or sought to be, as Greek or Roman as possible. In speech it is likely that most Roman Jews (and Roman Christians as well) were Greek.[22] But Greek was almost as well understood at Rome as Latin, and perhaps even better understood among the masses. Two of his Epigrams (vii. 30, and xi. 94) make it clear enough that the Jew at Rome did not live aloof from his fellow-citizens, and wealthy Jews did not scruple to purchase in the market the gratifications they were especially enjoined by their faith to forego. We can readily believe that Martial is recounting real experiences, but these cases must have been exceptional. As we shall see later, the Jewish community was certainly not a licentious one. That point appears specifically from the controversial literature. But it is equally well to remember that as individuals they were subject to human passions, and the excesses found in other classes of society might also be met with among them.

Grecized in speech and name, and no doubt in dress, the Jews accepted for their conduct the external forms and standards about them. One very interesting indication of the completeness with which they identified themselves with the city in which they lived is the expression " fatherland " that they used of it; *e. g.* in

Akmonia (Ramsay, Cities and Bishops of Phrygia, no.
561). Again, in Ostia a large and well-carved slab was
recently found in which a decree of the Jews at Ostia
was set forth. The corporation grants to its gerusiarch,
Gaius Julius Justus, a place for a sepulchre. The officers are Livius, Dionysius, Antonius, and another man
whose name is lost (Not. Scav. 1907, p. 479). Surely
but for the unambiguous statement of the inscription
itself one would not have looked for Jews in this assemblage of Julii, Livii, and Antonii.

CHAPTER XX
THE FINAL REVOLTS OF THE JEWS

In the generations that followed the fall of the temple, changes of great moment took place, which we can only partially follow from the sources at our disposal.

The Mishnah gives in considerable detail the laws that governed the life of the Jew at this period, and also those that regulated the intercourse of Jew and non-Jew. But the Mishnah may after all have been the expression of an ideal as often as it was the record of real occurrences, and the range of its influence during the time of its compilation may have been more limited than its necessarily general phraseology indicates. The Mishnah of Rabbi Judah became the standard text-book in the Jewish academies of Palestine and Babylonia, although not to the total exclusion of other sources of Halakah. That did not occur at once; and even when it was complete, the authority of the presidents of the schools over the Jews resident throughout the world is more or less problematic.

For that reason it is especially necessary to note the invaluable records of actual life that appear in the papyri and inscriptions, especially where they show that the intercourse between Jews and pagans was far from being as precisely limited as the Mishnah would compel us to suppose, and men who are at no pains to conceal their Jewish origin permitted themselves certain indulgences that would certainly not have met with the approval of the doctors at Jamnia and Tiberias.

The tractate of the Mishnah which is called Aboda Zara, "Idolatry" or "Foreign Worship," lays down the rules under which Jew and heathen may transact such business as common citizenship or residence made inevitable. The essential point throughout is that the Jew must not either directly or indirectly take part, or seem to take part, in the worship accorded the Abomination. Nor are the seemingly trivial regulations despicable for their anxious minuteness. In all probability they are decisions of actual cases, and derive their precision from that fact.[1]

Certain passages in Aboda Zara (ii. 1) would unquestionably have made intercourse between Jew and pagan practically impossible except in public or semipublic places. But in the very same treatise it is implied that a pagan might be a guest at the Jew's table (v. 5); and indeed much of the detail of the entire tractate would be unnecessary if the provision contained in ii. 1 were literally followed out.

The Epigrams of Martial (above, p. 326), if we believe them, indicate that so far from fleeing the society of pagans for its sexual vices, some Jews at least sought it for the sake of these vices, as was the case with the rival of the Syrian Greek Meleager, more than two centuries before Martial. But it will be noticed that the subject of the last Epigram (xi. 94) is a renegade, who swears strange oaths, and is taunted by

Martial with what he is obviously trying to conceal. Besides, as to the particular vice there mentioned, it rests on the malice of the satirist alone. The victim of his wit denies his guilt.

Indeed it is just this particular vice, so widely prevalent in the Greek and Roman world, that the Jewish antagonists of the pagans seized upon at all times. It unquestionably characterized continental Greece and Italy much more than the eastern portions of the empire. For the Jews it seemed to justify the application of the words " Sodom and Gomorrah," particularly to the general city life of the Greeks. Some Jew or Christian scratched those names on a house wall of Pompeii.[2]

It is quite untrue to say that unnatural sexual excesses were so prevalent as to pass without comment among Greeks and Romans generally. However large they loom in the writings of extant poets, we may remember that poets are emotionally privileged people. The sober Roman and Greek did not find any legal or moral offense in illicit love, but unnatural lust was generally offensive from both points of view, and, however widely practised, it was at no time countenanced. Still, Jews and Christians would be justified in comparing their own unmistakable and specific condemnations in this matter with the mere disapproval with which decent heathens regarded it. For the Greek legend that made the fate of Laius, father of Oedipus,[3] a punishment of his crime in first bringing pederasty into the world, the Jews had the much more drastic punishment of Sodom;

and, in many passages of the Apocrypha, the fact of
this vice's prevalence is dwelt upon as a characteristic
difference between Jewish and gentile life.'

In many other matters there are evidences that not
all the regulations of Aboda Zara were carried out
by all Jews. In the Tosefta' we meet the express
prohibition of theatrical representations to the Jews, a
prohibition which, in view of the fact that dramatic
performances were at all times theoretically and actually
festivals in honor of Dionysus, seems perfectly natural.
But in spite of that, in the great theater at Miletus,
some extremely desirable seats in the very front rows
are inscribed τόπος τῶν Εἰουδαίων φιλοσεβάστων, "Reserved for His Imperial Majesty's most loyal Jews."'
It will therefore not be safe to assume that the Halakic
provision which forbade Jews to attend the theater
actually meant that Jews as a class did not do so.

But we find even stronger evidences of the fact that
the amenities of social life in Greek cities seemed to
some Jews to override the decisions of the law schools
in Palestine. In Asia Minor a Jew leaves money not
merely for the usual purposes of maintaining his monument, but also for the astounding purpose of actually
assisting a heathen ceremonial.' The instance is a late
one, but perhaps more valuable for that reason, because
the spread of the schools' influence increased constantly
during the third century.

At the fall of the temple the voluntary tax of the
shekel or didrachm, which had formerly been paid to
the temple at Jerusalem, and which was a vital factor

in the very first instances of conflict between the Jews and the Roman authorities (comp. above, p. 226), was converted into an official tax for the support of the central sanctuary of the Roman state on the Capitoline Hill. Whether Roman citizens who were Jews paid it, does not appear. All others however did. The bureau that enforced it was known as the *fiscus Iudaicus,* the word *fiscus* indicating here, as always, that the sums so collected were considered as belonging to the treasury of the reigning prince during the time of his reign, rather than to the public treasury.

It does not seem that this tax, except for its destination, was believed by the Jews to be an act of notable oppression, nor was its enforcement more inquisitorial than that of other taxes; but it became an especial weapon of blackmail in Rome and in all Italy, and this blackmail grew into dimensions so formidable that action had to be taken to suppress it.

In Rome, we may remember, there was no officer at all resembling our public prosecutor or district-attorney. The prosecution of criminals was an individual task, whether of the person aggrieved or of a citizen acting from patriotic motives. Indeed it had at one time been considered a duty of the highest insistence, and innumerable Romans had won their first distinction in this way. The delators of the early empire were in theory no different, though the reward of their activity was not the glory or popularity achieved, but the substantial one of a lump sum, or a share in the fine imposed, a practice still in vogue in our own juris-

dictions. Plainly, under such circumstances, there were
temptations to a form of blackmail which the Greeks
knew as συκοφάντεια, and the Romans as *calumnia; i. e.*
the bringing of suits known to be unjustified, or with
reckless disregard of their justification, for the purpose
of sharing in some reward for doing this quasi-public
service. Private prosecutors at Roman law were
required to swear that they were not proceeding
calumniae causa, "with blackmailing intent."[8]

The opportunities presented to delators by the *fiscus
Iudaicus* consisted in the fact that anyone of Jewish
origin, with the possible exception noted above, was
liable to the tax, and that there must have been many
who attempted to conceal their Jewish origin in order
to evade it. In view of the wide extent of the spread
of the Jewish propaganda, the delation was plausible
from the beginning. Suetonius tells us at first-hand
recollection of a case in which the charge of evading
the tax was made and successfully established.[9] In a
very large number of cases, however, the charge was
not established, but in these cases it was often apparently the policy of prudence to buy off the accuser rather
than risk the uncertainties of a judicial decision. It is
upon people who act in just such a way that black-
mailers, συκοφάνται, *calumniatores,* grew fat. And the
charge of evading the Jewish tax was easily made,
and disproved with difficulty, since all who followed
Jewish customs were amenable to it, and many Jewish
customs so closely resembled the practices of certain
philosophic sects that confusion on the subject was per-

fectly natural. We have seen this in the case of Seneca some years before this (comp. above, p. 310).

The emperor Nerva, in 96-98 C. E., removed the occasion of this abuse. Coins are extant with the legend *Fisci Iudaici calumnia sublata,* "To commemorate the suppression of blackmail arising from the Jewish tax." The *fiscus Iudaicus* itself continued into much later times, but blackmail by means of it was ended. How this was done we are not told. But an obvious and natural method would be to abolish the money reward which the delator or prosecuting witness received for every conviction. Plainly there would be no blackmail if there was no incentive thereto.

But this reform of Nerva affected rather those who were not Jews than those who were, since in the case of actual Jews, whether by birth or conversion, the tax was enforceable and the accusation of evading it was not *calumnia,* but patriotic zeal. It is likely enough that the measure of Nerva discouraged prosecution, even where it was justified, but the losses which the imperial fiscus sustained by reason of the successful evasion of the tax on the part of some individuals cannot have been great, since the Jews not only publicly professed their faith, but openly and actively spread it.

In the epitome of the sixty-eighth book of Cassius Dio (i. 2), we read that this measure of Nerva was one of general amnesty for the specific crime of "impiety," or ἀσέβεια: "Nerva ordered the acquittal of those on trial for impiety, and recalled those exiled for that crime. . . . . He permitted no one to bring charges of impiety or of Jewish method of living."

Unfortunately this passage is extant only in the epitome made of this book by Xiphilinus, a Byzantine monk of the eleventh century. We have no means of knowing to what extent the epitomator is stating the impression he received from his reading, largely colored by his time and personality, and to what extent he is stating the actual substance of the book. If there really was in Rome an indictable offense which consisted in adopting Jewish customs as distinguished from the general charge of impiety, such an offense does not appear elsewhere in our records. We must remember that there is no indication that the men freed by Nerva had been suffering under the despotic caprice of Domitian, but on the contrary there is the specific statement that they were being duly prosecuted under recognized forms.

It is highly likely that the two accusations which Xiphilinus gives are really one: that Nerva discouraged prosecutions for impiety, and that among the instances of men acquitted, which Dio gave, were some who were converts to Judaism, or believed to be so. In one instance, a constantly cited one, that is precisely what is the case, and that is the condemnation, in the last year of Domitian's reign, of Flavius Clemens and Flavia Domitilla, both of them kinsmen of the emperor.[10]

In the case of these, we hear that Clemens was executed for "atheism," and that under this charge many others who had lapsed into the customs of the Jews were condemned, some of them to death, others to loss of their property, Domitilla to exile.

In Suetonius we have a wholly different version
(Dom. 15). Flavius Clemens, we read, was a man
contemptissimae inertiae, " of thoroughly contemptible
weakness of character," but enjoying till the very last
year of Domitian's life the latter's especial favor.
Clemens' two children were even designated for the
succession. The emperor was, during this year, a prey
to insane suspicions, which amounted to a real *mania
persecutoria,* and on a sudden fit had Clemens executed.
The context and general tone of the passage suggest
that the charge, real or trumped up, against Clemens
was one of treason, not impiety.

Clemens' relationship, his undoubted connection with
the palace conspiracy that ultimately resulted in the
assassination of Domitian, make this account the more
likely one, but the " many " mentioned in the epitome of
Xiphilinus require us to assume that at least some of
the men actually prosecuted for " impiety," or atheism,
were so charged upon the evidence of Jewish practices.

It has been stated, and it must be constantly re-
iterated, that impiety was a negative offense, that it
implied deliberate refusal to perform a religious act
of legal obligation, rather than the actual doing of some
other religious act. If "impiety" were really the
offense here, the "many" that were charged with it
under Domitian and Nerva must have been so charged
because they neglected certain ceremonies which the
laws made obligatory. In Greek communities ἀσέβεια
was a relatively common offense, and indictment for it
of frequent occurrence. But it is doubtful whether

there was such an indictment at Roman law. There
is no Latin term for ἀσέβεια. The word *impietas* is
generally used in a different sense. The Greek Dio or
his late Byzantine epitomator has evidently used that
term here to describe in his own words what seemed to
him to be the substance of the accusation rather than
to give a technically exact account of the charge against
these men.

In later law writers certain offenses are discussed
under which forms of impiety or ἀσέβεια might be
included. But these offenses are treated either as
sedition or as violations of the Sullan Lex Cornelia
de Sicariis et Veneficis, "Statute of Assassins and
Poisoners." The latter law seems to have been a
general statute containing a varied assortment of pro-
visions, but all of them relating to acts that tended to
the bodily injury of anyone, whatever the motive or
pretext of that injury.[11]

The "many," then, who, as Xiphilinus says, were
prosecuted for "impiety," because they lapsed into Jewish rites, may have been indicted under the Lex Cornelia
—no doubt as a pretext—or charged with treason upon
proof of Jewish proclivities. The Palestinian Jews,
we may remember, were until recently in arms against
Rome. In all these cases, the indictments were probably far-fetched pretexts devised by the morose and
suspicious Domitian during his last year of veri-
table terror in order to get rid of men whom he suspected (often justly) of plotting his assassination.
These are the men whom Nerva's act of amnesty freed.

22

The famous jurist Paul, who wrote in the first part of the third century, discusses the restrictions imposed upon the spread of Jewish rites, under the heading of " sedition " or " treason." The justification for that treatment lies in the series of insurrections of the Eastern Jews of which the rebellion of 68 C. E. was merely the beginning. Our sources for the events of these rebellions are remote and uncertain, and the transmission is more than usually troubled; but a chance fragment, as well as the kernel of the lurid account presented by Xiphilinus' epitome of Dio, leaves no doubt that the struggle was carried on with memorable ferocity, and left a lasting impression on the people whom it concerned.

If Dio is to be believed, the outbreak that took place in the reign of Trajan (115 C. E.) in Cyprus, Cyrene, and Egypt (Ep. lxviii. 32) was marked by scenes of indescribable horror. In Cyrene, Dio states, the Jews devoured the flesh of their victims, clothed themselves in their skins, threw them to wild beasts, or compelled them to engage in gladiatorial combats. In Cyrene, two hundred and twenty thousand men perished; in Cyprus two hundred and forty thousand. One may say with Reinach, *Les chiffres et les détails de Dion inspirent la méfiance.*"

It will not be possible to assign the responsibility for these statements to the epitomator Xiphilinus. Unless they were found in Dio, he could not have ventured to place them here, since the epitome and the text were extant together for a long time.

In the Church History of Eusebius (IV. ii.) the revolt is described somewhat differently. Eusebius mentions the Cyprian revolt in his Chronicon (ii. 164). Here however he speaks only of the insurrection in Cyrene and Egypt. The name of the leader is given as Lucua, not Andreas, as Dio has it, and the whole event is described as an ordinary revolt, a στάσις, reviving the revolt of 68 c. e. At first the Jews were generally successful, driving their opponents to take refuge in the city of Alexandria, while they harried the land. At last the Roman prefect, Q Marcius Turbo, crushed them completely.

As far as Egypt is concerned, many papyri mention the revolt. Appian Arab. Liber (Fg. hist. gr. v. p. 65) gives us a first-hand view of the situation.

Both the papyri and Appian are in complete accordance with Eusebius' account, and emphasize the extent of the Jewish insurrection and the impression it produced upon others.

In Jewish writings the references to what must have been a matter of prime importance to all Jews are vague and confused. The punishment of the Mesopotamian Jews by Lusius Quietus [18] is mentioned, but beyond that we have only much later statements, in which a deal of legend-making has been imbedded. The " day of Trajan," which appears as a festival day, is connected by a persistent tradition with the permission to rebuild the temple, alleged to have been given by that emperor. The Roman and Greek writers know nothing of this, and in Jewish tradition likewise the permission is represented as abortive, and the "day of Trajan" ceased, according to another story, to be observed when the martyrs Papius and Lollianus were executed.[14]

However, it must be noted that for Palestine in particular details are lacking. Indeed we might well believe that Palestine itself took no part in it whatever. The expedition of Quietus to Mesopotamia may have been an ordinary military expedition against the Parthians' territory, with whom the Romans had been then at war. There is evidence that the Jews of Parthia were almost autonomous, and a foray into the section which they happened to control would not be considered as anything more than an attack on other Parthian dominions. The Mesopotamian provinces of Parthia were then under the theoretical rule of Rome, but the precarious character of the conquest was apparent to everyone, so that the first act of the conqueror's successor, Hadrian, was to abandon both Mesopotamia and Armenia. The revolt of the Mesopotamian Jews was, in consequence, a somewhat different thing from that of the Jews in Cyprus or Cyrene.

Perhaps the difficulties in Cyprus, Cyrene, and Egypt are to be considered nothing more than magnified race riots, which, however, assumed the dimensions of a real war, and demanded systematic military operations to suppress them. But the friction between the Jews and Greeks of Salamis or Alexandria could scarcely have resulted in such serious outbreaks, if the conditions that led to the revolt of 68 c. e. were not still operative. The fall of the temple did not paralyze the

Jewish propaganda. We find it as vigorous afterward as before. The Messianic hopes, which were one form of the prevailing spiritual unrest, had not died out in the East among Jews or non-Jews.[15] The calamity of the empire, which the death of Nero seemed to bring with it, did not after all take place.

Our sources represent the era begun by Vespasian, except for a few years of Domitian's reign, as one of general and increasing felicity. These sources, however, are in the highest degree suspect, and while the period between Vespasian and Marcus Aurelius represents an undoubted rise in administrative and legal development, they represent a deterioration in the economic condition due to the gathering pressure of the huge state machinery itself. The increase of the more degraded forms of superstition marks the spiritual destitution of the time.

The Jewish communities in Cyprus, Egypt, and Cyrene consisted largely of craftsmen and small merchants. Perhaps among them were a number of former Palestinian rebels, sold as slaves in the neighboring markets, and since ransomed. The conditions, the active Messianic hope, the presence of former soldiers, were themselves provocative of riot, and the outbreaks in the places indicated are scarcely surprising. We hear only of those that became formidable insurrections. It is possible that slighter ones have failed wholly to be recorded.

But during the reign of Hadrian there broke out an unmistakable insurrection in Palestine, which more clearly than its predecessors showed the motive force of these movements. In 131 C. E. a certain Simeon bar Kosiba led his people again to war on the all-overwhelming power of the empire. The occasion for the revolt is variously given, but that it was in the eyes of those that fought in it vastly more than an attempt to shake off a foreign yoke is shown by the Messiahship to which Simeon openly laid claim, and for which he had the invaluable support of the head of the Palestinian schools, the eloquent and passionate Akiba.[16]

Dio[17] states that the immediate instigation of the revolt was the building on the ruins of Jerusalem the new city and temple that were to be the official home of the colony of Aelia Capitolina, a community founded by Hadrian and composed perhaps of native Syrians, since it did not possess the *ius Italicum,* the full rights of citizenship.[18] This statement is much more probable than that of Eusebius, which reverses the order of events, and makes the founding of the Colonia Aelia Capitolina a consequence and not the cause of the revolt.[19]

The rebellion of 68 had enormously depopulated Judea. Those that were left had neither the power nor the inclination to try conclusions with the legionaries again, and, as we have seen, remained passive when closely related communities rose in arms. But the hopes they nourished, no doubt systematically fostered by the powerful communities in Mesopotamia and the Parthian lords of the latter, were none the less real for their suppression. The erection of Aelia was the

signal. Just as the desecration of the temple by
Epiphanes was the last measure of oppression, which
brought upon the king the vengeance of Heaven,
so this second desecration, the dedication of the holy
hill to one of the *elillim,* one of the Abominations of
the heathen, roused the frenzy of the people that witnessed it to such a pitch that the chances of success
could no longer be considered. At the same time, assur-
ances of ultimate help from Parthia were perhaps not
lacking. Among those who streamed to aid the rebellious Jews were doubtless many of Rome's hereditary
enemies, since of other rebellions within the empire at
that time we have no evidence.

The Jewish tradition speaks of a systematic and
cruel persecution instituted by Hadrian. The details
mentioned are very much like the remembered incidents
of the persecution by Epiphanes. We must keep in
mind that every one of the statements connected with
this persecution is late, and is in so far of dubious historical value.[20] As a matter of fact the character of
Hadrian makes the reality of the persecution in the
highest degree improbable. No doubt the revolt was
punished with ruthless severity, and for the permanent prohibition against the entrance of a Jew into
Aelia Capitolina there is excellent evidence;[21] but to
attempt to root out Judaism as Antiochus had done is
something that simply cannot be credited to Hadrian,
if only for the fact that the overwhelming majority of
Jews did not dwell in Palestine at all, and all the alleged
persecutions of Hadrian are localized only in Palestine.

In Hadrian's letter of 134 c. e., to his brother-in-law Servianus, the Jews of Egypt are referred to in a manner quite irreconcilable with the theory that Judaism was then a proscribed religion.[22]

In this connection we may mention a decree which, according to Jewish tradition, constituted one of the most deeply resented of Hadrian's persecutions—the prohibition of circumcision. Here again the late biographer of Hadrian, Spartianus, makes this edict precede and not follow the war; but the reliability of the *Historia Augusta,* of which Spartianus' biography is part, is not very high. We have the *Historia Augusta,* if it is not wholly a fabrication of the fourth century, only in a recension of that time, so that its testimony on such a detail is practically valueless.[23]

As a matter of fact, all bodily mutilation had been under the ban of the Roman law, but that prohibition applied only to Roman citizens. In practice circumcision had been openly carried on both by Jews who were Roman citizens and by their converts, in disregard of this provision, probably under the tacit assumption that the privileges of the Jewish corporations covered this as well. Primarily the prohibition was directed against castration, but it was quite general. The only formulation which the edict against these practices had received was in the Sullan Lex Cornelia de Sicariis et Veneficis (above, p. 241). This was a *lex per saturam,* or miscellaneous statute. Under one of its captions, any act, perhaps any act performed with a weapon or instrument of any kind, that resulted in

bodily injury, was prohibited. A senatorial decree of
the year 83 C. E. specified castration as one of the
mutilations referred to; similarly abortion was punished
as a violation of the Lex Cornelia.[24]

Hadrian's rescripts seem to have dealt on several
occasions with this law. His obvious intention to
extend the statute may have caused him to use terms
of general effect. Perhaps an isolated case of the practice of circumcision among people outside of those to
whom it was an ancient custom may have been followed by indictment and punishment. If Hadrian
really had attempted to carry out this prohibition generally, he would have provoked a rebellion in Egypt as
well as in Judea, since in Egypt the priests practised it
likewise.[25] The rescript of Antoninus, a few years later,
which expressly exempted Jews from the broad condemnation of the practice, simply restated established
law.[26] Indeed it may well be that the occasion of Pius'
rescript was rather one that restricted the Jews than
one that enlarged their privileges. Even in the case
of the severest form of mutilation, it is forbidden if it is
done *promercii aut libidinis causa*. A similar insistence
on criminal intent must have been present in the case of
the lesser mutilation involved in the Jewish rite. There
could of course never have been any question that circumcision was not performed *promercii aut libidinis
causa,* and therefore there seems to be little reason for
the rescript of Pius, unless we assume it to have been a
direct attempt to check the spread of Judaism by making the performance of the rite in the case of non-

Jews criminal *per se,* without proof of wrongful intent.

Paul, writing about seventy-five years later, states the limitation on the performance of the rite even more broadly, by including within it slaves of non-Jewish origin.[27] In all circumstances there does not seem to have been any real effort to enforce it. The Jewish propaganda went on in spite of it, not surreptitiously, as in the case of the still-proscribed Christians, but quite frankly. The statement of Paul is the stranger because of the open favor shown by Paul's master, the Syrian Severus Alexander, toward all foreign cults, including that of the Jews. The Sentences of Paul may have been written before the decree of the emperor which his biographer mentions, by which, he says, Severus strengthened the privileged position of the Jews, *Iudaeis privilegia reservavit.*[28] When one contrasts this with the immediately following statement, *Christianos esse passus est,* " He allowed the Christians to profess their faith," it is plain that in the case of the Jews there is no question of mere toleration, but of the recognition of an established position, and that is not quite in accord with the statement in Paul's Sentences, according to which the spread of Judaism was rigorously checked, even to the extent of modifying one of the fundamental concepts of the law—the unlimited character of the master's dominion over his slaves.

As has been said, the authenticity of the *Historia Augusta* is dubious, but the number of details offered to show the interest of both Alexander and his predecessor Elagabalus in Judaism and Christianity is too

great to be ignored. The Sentences of Paul, it must be
noted, have come down to us only in the abridged and
perhaps interpolated form in which they are found in
the Lex Romana Wisigothorum, a code issued by
Alaric II in 506, and called therefore the Breviarium
Alaricianum. At that time, however, proselytizing on
the part of the Jews had been expressly prohibited by
a rescript of Theodosius (Ccd. Theod. 16, 8, 9, 19) of
415. Even then it was completely ineffective, but at any
rate the rite of circumcision was definitely under a
legal ban.[29]

Whether or not a qualified restriction on the spread
of Judaism has been changed in our texts of the Sentences into a general and all-embracing one, it is
impossible to say, but that some such change has taken
place may be called even likely, by reason of the point
just raised; viz., that it is wholly contrary to the spirit
and principles of the Roman law to impose any restrictions whatever on the master's authority.

We have examined the decrees that regulated the
rite of circumcision, merely because general inferences
have been drawn from it—inferences that are in no
sense justified. The Roman law regarded bodily
mutilation, when practised as part of a religious rite,
and especially for sordid purposes, as against public
policy. It was a *privilegium* of the Jews, that to the
members of their organizations the general rule of the
law did not apply, and the various statements quoted
from the jurists were simply judicial decisions limiting,

by a well-known principle of interpretation, the exercise of the privilege to the narrowest possible bounds.

The rebellion of Bar-Kosiba was probably the last time that the Jews confronted the Roman troops on issues that were even partly national. We hear that between 150 and 161, under Antoninus Pius, another rebellion broke out, but we have no other record of it than the notices in the *Historia Augusta*,[30] upon which little reliance can be placed. After the death of Commodus and Pertinax,[31] the eastern empire, including Palestine, sided with the local claimant Pescennius Niger, and Palestine became the scene of battles sufficiently important to justify the decreeing of a "Jewish triumph" to Caracalla. It is likely that these various "rebellions" were the more or less serious insurrections of bandits, who terrorized the countryside until suppressed by the authorities. This view derives some support from the fact that of one of these bandits who submitted to Severus we know the name, Claudius (Dio Cass. Ep. lxxv. 2). There is even no certainty as to whether those who took part in them were wholly or mainly Jews. At any rate, there were no national ends which they attempted to serve.

A fact, which may be accidental, and is certainly noteworthy, is that, of all the struggles of the Jews with their surroundings, after 68, none are localized in Asia Minor.

It was, however, in Asia Minor that the Jews were especially numerous and influential. To a certain extent their propaganda had become most firmly established

there, and their position was so intrenched that even
the hostile legislation of the later Byzantine emperors
found them in successful resistance. We find evidences
of certain laxity in the practice of Jewish rites, but
neither in 68 nor under Trajan or Hadrian did the
Asiatic Jews take part in the movements that con-
vulsed that section of the Jews of the empire. And yet
it was in the cities of Asia that the Jews in earlier days
did meet hostility and direct attacks, and needed the
assistance of the Roman central government, to be
maintained in the position which they claimed for themselves.[32]   However, in that most ancient and fertile
nursery of beliefs and mysteries, the Jewish mystery
evidently found a grateful soil and, as we have seen,
sent its roots deep.[33]

CHAPTER XXI

THE LEGAL POSITION OF THE JEWS IN THE LATER EMPIRE

The empire established by Augustus was, as has been set forth (above, p. 259), a more or less abstract thing. It was the *imperium,* or supreme authority, which a single community, the city-state of Rome, exercised over all the other communities existing within certain not over sharply defined geographic limits. This *imperium* was, by Roman statute or series of statutes, almost completely delegated to a single individual. The delegation however was not quite complete, and the legal theory that made it incomplete remained to work no little mischief in a crisis like the death of Nero or Domitian or Commodus.

When Diocletian reorganized the empire in 286 c. e., the theory was completely changed. The *imperium* was now a *dominium;* it was the authority that a single man possessed over all the inhabitants of a region greater even than it was under Augustus, and that authority was in point of law as limitless as that of a master over his slaves.

Between Augustus and Diocletian the reign of the Severan emperors, particularly the promulgation of the Edict of Caracalla, the Constitutio Antonina, which extended Roman citizenship to almost all the free

inhabitants of the empire, may be considered the turning-point of the tendency toward absolutism.[1] It broke
finally and completely with the legal theory that the
populus Romanus was a paramount community within
a complex of other similar and inferior communities.
From that time on nearly all those who could possess
rights and obligations at all, whether in regard to one
another or to the state, were members of the paramount
community, and the delegation of the *imperium* to the
princeps, which had until then been subject to the
remote but still conceivable possibility of revocation,
became irrevocable by the sheer impossibility of con-
ceiving the *populus* as acting in the only way the
populus could legally act, by direct vote when assembled
in mass in the Campus Martius

In the period between Caracalla and Diocletian the
vast political machine snapped at many points. Diocletian's skill enabled it to go on for a considerable time,
and yet the changes he instituted were administrative
rather than social. Internally the new *populus Romanus*
took its form in the third century.

A calculation of doubtful value makes the population
of the empire at that time about 85,000,000.[2] Of these
about half were slaves, *i. e.* at law not participants in
the empire at all. The other half were nearly all *cives
Romani,* Roman citizens, and it is the position of these
cives that now concerns us.

Upon the *civis Romanus* devolved the task of maintaining a frightfully expensive governmental machinery. The expense consisted in the fact that a huge

army had to be maintained on what was practically a war footing all the time, because, as a matter of fact, war with the barbarians on the northern frontier and with the Parthians in the East was always going on. Compared with that, the expenses of the court itself, although considerable, were scarcely important; but an important item was the vast horde of civil employees which the execution of so tremendous a budget necessitated. Then the local civic centers, generally the remains of old independent communities, had an organization of their own that was partly ornamental, but in all circumstances costly. That is to say, a very large share of the available wealth of the empire was diverted into unproductive channels, since it was devoted to the purpose of maintaining a machinery not altogether necessary to guard that wealth.

Many of the nations of modern Europe have a military budget relatively and absolutely greater than that of the Roman empire of the third century; but in these nations the economic system has a high degree of efficiency, compared with that of the older state, and the waste is incalculably less. The great difference lies in the slave system, which was the foundation of ancient society. The total absence of individual incentive wherever the slaves were worked in gangs—and that was, perhaps, true of the majority of slaves—made the efficiency and consequent productivity of each laborer much less.

We must further remember that human waste was also much greater, owing to the absence of all measures to restrict it.   Only the most elementary of sanitary precautions existed, and they were directed against definite diseases of plainly infectious character.   With a great percentage of the population undernourished, the ravages of any disease with epidemic tendencies must have been enormous.   Even in the absence of any plague, such a scourge as consumption alone must have been much more generally destructive than it is now. As has been recently suggested, malaria in Italy had a heavy account to answer for in producing the physical debilitation of the *populus Romanus,* and was therefore a real factor in the gradual decay of the Roman state.[3]

The incidence of the state burdens was not regulated as it is at the present time.   Taxes were imposed within certain districts, and upon each district devolved the duty of satisfying the impost.   For a long time Italy had been free from such a burden, but even this exceptional position was abrogated by Constantine in 300 C. E.

How each district accomplished its task was a local matter, and was determined by its individual development.   Until the reorganization effected by Diocletian, the old national units had in the main been kept intact. That is to say, Egypt remained what it had been under the Ptolemies and for thousands of years before—a strongly centralized kingdom, rigidly bureaucratic, but measurably well organized.   Asia, again, was a group of independent cities and certain larger districts, principally rural, the kingdoms of Bithynia, Cappadocia, Galatia, etc.   The tax which the particular province had

23

to deliver was apportioned among the various units according to their apparent capacity. Here and there a poll-tax existed, levied upon every inhabitant alike, and on the existence of this poll-tax far-reaching theories have been constructed.

The obligation of the individual toward the state was determined by one fundamental fact, viz., domicile, or right of residence. Before the Constitutio Antonina there was only one class of inhabitants that possessed an almost unlimited right of residence, the *cives Romani*. But even these could not live indiscriminately in Egypt, for example, which was at all times an exceptional province, and was considered a sort of imperial appanage. As a matter of fact, it is in Egypt that we see the first development of the *colonatus,* destined to be of so fundamental importance in the creation of the feudal system. It may be that the *colonatus* was found practically everywhere in the Hellenistic states, but its growth in Egypt goes back to Pharaonic times, and its fullest expansion was found there.

The principle of the *colonatus* was the permanent obligation of the agricultural free laborer to remain on the soil he tilled. Originally it applied only to the state lands, but in the third century these state lands became largely private property, and the serf-like *coloni* went with them. All over the empire there were still, in spite of the *latifundia,* or agriculture on a big scale, a large number of peasant proprietors; but with the impossibility of competing with the production of the *latifundia,* these peasant proprietorships were soon converted into holdings resembling the *colonatus,* or actually that.

Now, as long as the *civis Romanus,* as a prerogative of his position, paid no tax, his right of residence was unqualified. When he too had to submit to a direct tax, the place where he resided became a matter of prime importance. The tax that was imposed upon any given locality could be met only if all those subject to tax, living there, paid their dues. Consequently those who by birth were domiciled there could not remove themselves without lessening to that extent the power of that district to meet its state obligations. At first, to be sure, this cannot have been a matter of first-rate importance. Changes of domicile after all were rare, and took place principally among the wealthier classes, a fact that made it easy to insure that no loss would accrue to the community abandoned. But as conditions of ordinary living deteriorated, the practice of deserting one's legal residence became more frequent, and needed the intervention of the central authorities, since the local magistrate had no jurisdiction whatever beyond the strictly circumscribed limits of his commune. As soon as it was possible for a commune to claim from its members, wherever they happened to be, their contribution to the communal tax, there arose the corollary that for all practical purposes the tax-paying member might not leave the place where his tax was due. The *colonatus* had been applied to the urban laborer.

But the chaining of the individual to his commune was not sufficient unless his paying power was maintained. The same motives that impelled men to evade their fiscal duties by change of domicile, would make them idle and sullen paupers in the places where they were forced to remain. It was a part of the state system which the Severan emperors introduced to make the paying power of the citizen certain by means of the compulsory guilds.[4] These latter were natural outgrowths of former voluntary associations. The formation of guilds of laborers, either free or consisting partly of freemen and slave laborers, was as old as the state itself. The evident superiority of training which such groups insured alone justified them. From time to time certain privileges and exemptions were conferred upon them—always in return for definite state functions[5] which they took upon themselves as well as the industrial functions which were their reason for existence. Indeed, in the municipal towns the *collegiati,* or members of these publicly sanctioned industrial guilds, formed an order of citizenship second only to that of the decurions, or municipal senate.

While the various *collegia* were at first voluntary associations, it is evident that the sons of members would tend to follow the callings of their fathers without statutory command to that effect. When, however, the dues of the corporation to the state became onerous, the voluntary choice of a calling might leave certain *collegia* quite deserted. At what time this danger became so serious that special legislation was required, we do not know, but there is a vague and textually uncertain passage in the Life of Alexander Severus, in the *Historia Augusta,* which indicates that a reorganization of the trade-guilds was undertaken by that emperor. If it was so, the appearance soon afterwards of the compulsory guild in full development makes it likely that the compulsory principle was officially recognized or perhaps extended then.

But it was not merely the artisans of the empire that were included in any organization or reorganization of the *collegia.* Like all other corporate bodies the trade-guilds, if not wholly religious in form, possessed a common cult or ceremony, and this common possession made it easy to consider them as not essentially different from *collegia* directly and solely religious—the Greek θίασοι, for example. In these, the voluntary principle remained even after the compulsory guilds were fully developed, although in point of fact they were generally rigidly hereditary at all times. Here too, after Alexander Severus, there must have been a certain legal restriction placed upon arbitrary withdrawal from such cult-organizations, even if their ritual was openly and unmistakably foreign, such as that of the Jews, the orgies of Atthis, or the mysteries of Mithra. Some restriction would be necessary, because membership in these organizations, as far as they were tolerated by law, involved the payment of certain dues to the state, and the state could not see with equanimity the obligation to pay these dues discarded and no new ones assumed in its place.

The dues to the state did not consist altogether, and soon not even principally, in the actual taxes levied upon a community, and portioned among its constituent members, whether individuals or corporations. Indeed these latter were paid to what seems to us a wholly disproportionate extent by a small and wealthy class in the community. The taxes, whether they consisted of ground-rent for state lands, harbor-dues, or taxes on certain sales, were principally paid by the large traders and investors, who were in every case the governing body of the local communes. In provinces where a poll-tax was levied, and where a tribute was imposed as on conquered territory, which the province really was, these direct taxes, when brutally executed on the peasant's grain, were oppressive enough, but in many parts of the Roman world they were in effect λει-τουργίαι, "liturgies," *i. e.* the burdens assumed by or imposed upon private persons of making large contributions in service to the state in proportion to their means. The principle of the liturgy was common to most Greek states, and was capable of indefinite extension.

And there was one state burden rapidly increasing in gravity, which was generally met on the principle of the liturgy, although the state too, as early as the time of Trajan,[8] was compelled to attempt it in part. That was the care of incompetents, by which term we may understand all free individuals who could not support themselves wholly by their personal efforts, *i. e.* widows and orphans, as well as destitute freemen. The proletariat of the empire not only had no share in its burdens, but itself formed the empire's chief economic burden.

The organization of the system was of very old standing. From time immemorial the minor children and the women of a family and of a clan had been under the legal control and care of the family's head. In the developed system of law, the technical terms were *tutela* and *cura,* the former being the guardianship of a child until fourteen, the latter the guardianship of a youth until twenty-five, as well as the care of an adult incompetent. This system of guardianship was further extended, but always remained the same in principle. It was the duty of the family to provide for its destitute members, and the legal extension the system underwent was simply that of widening the family circle. Not merely close relatives but remoter kinsmen were drawn into it as far as the obligations of guardianship were concerned; and in default of kinsmen, the guild, society, or commune assumed the wardship of minors, and was answerable for their maintenance.

It is easy to understand how important this item of state service became, when we recall how large a part of the municipal budgets in England during many centuries was concerned with the care of the poor. But after the disintegration of the slave system on its economic side, the number of persons for whose care this provision had to be made must have been much greater than it was in England at any time. If nothing else, the minute care with which the burdens of wardship were apportioned, the precautions against their evasion, the great part its discussion played in legal literature,[1] will make it evident that wardship of minors was a vitally important matter, and its administration one of the chief functions of citizenship in the empire. Many groups of men were practically exempted from all other state dues, provided the guardianship of minors within that group was assumed.

The maintenance of the poor is almost a corollary of the compulsory wardship of women and minors. The artisan whose efforts no longer sufficed to maintain his family often absconded, or in very many cases succumbed physically to his tasks, leaving in either case a family for whose wardship his kinsmen or colleagues had to provide. The state foundations instituted and maintained by Trajan and his successors were probably abandoned during the third century, when the *tutela* was systematized and minutely regulated.

All in all, every member of the state as such had certain fiscal duties to the state, *munera,* and his performance of these *munera* determined his place in the state. The social cleavage between the *honestiores,* the " better classes," and the *humiliores,* " the lower classes," was of very great importance in criminal law, since the severity of the penalty varied according to the class to which the convicted criminal belonged; but we are not told on what basis the judge determined whether any given man was *honestior* or *humilior,* and the whole distinction seems somewhat un-Roman.[8] For other purposes the various honors and ranks which multiplied in spite of the sinking significance of the many constituent communities were much less important than the drastically enforced classification of citizens by the taxes they paid.

The Jews of the Roman empire were to be found in all the classes that existed. As long as innumerable forms of local citizenship existed, distinct from citizenship in the Roman state, Jews might be met in all those groups. But when the Constitution of Caracalla merged all the local forms of citizenship in the *civitas Romana,* practically all the Jews then living in the empire became Roman citizens, although it is highly likely that the old names did not at once disappear.

Only one exception is known to have been made by Caracalla. A certain class of inhabitants known as the *dediticii* were excluded from his general grant. To analyze the exact position of these *dediticii* would demand more detailed argument than can here be offered, especially since it is a highly controversial matter. Recently it has been urged that all those who paid a poll-tax, particularly in Egypt and Syria, were classed as *dediticii* and consequently excluded from Roman citizenship. For this, however, there is not the remotest evidence. In the Institutes of Gaius[9] there is an unfortunate lacuna where the matter is discussed, but from what is said there, it is likely that as early as the Antonines the *dediticii* in Rome were a class of freedmen suffering legal disabilities for proven offenses, and that there were few others. The exemption of the *dediticii* from the benefits of the Edict of Caracalla was therefore perfectly natural, and did not in the least imply the exemption of those who paid the poll-tax in Egypt and Syria, among whom were many Jews.

As Roman citizens domiciled in the various quarters
of the empire, the Jews were subjected to the obligations that went with that domicile. So in Egypt a great
number of Jews paid a poll-tax, although many of them,
especially in Alexandria, were exempt. In Syria and
Asia, where many communities still had tribute to pay,
the Jewish members of those communities were equally
assessed.

But besides being legally domiciled in some definite
place, the Jews in every place formed cult-organizations.
Apostasy in the case of the Jew meant no more than the
abandoning of this organization, " separating himself
from the congregation." [10] Those who did so found
themselves at once obliged to perform the rites of the
state worship in the many cities where such rites were
legally enforced, or to enter other cult-associations,
since it was only as a member of the Jewish corporation
that he secured the privilege of abstention.

These Jewish corporations were known as " synagogues," a term more properly denoting the meetings of
the societies. The word was used of other associations
as well as of the Jewish. A word of kindred origin and
meaning, *synodos,* was almost a general term for corporation everywhere." However " synagogue" became
gradually appropriated by the Jewish *collegia,* and in
inscriptions in which the word occurs it is generally
safe to assume a Jewish origin.

Like all other similar corporations or guilds, the
Jewish synagogues had special *munera.* One which
was almost unique was the Jewish tax, the *fiscus*

Iudaicus, or didrachm, which, since 7c, had been levied on all the Jews, originally for the support of the Capitoline temple, but probably long merged into the general fiscus, or imperial treasury It is unique, because there does not seem to have been any other tax which, like this one, was wholly devoid of local basis, and did not depend on domicile at all. Otherwise membership in the Jewish synagogue conferred a highly valued and general exemption. The Jews could not be required to perform any task that violated their religious conviction. This privilege is formulated in a constitution of Caracalla, but it seems rather a confirmation of one already existing than a new grant.[12]

According to this privilege, Jews were immediately relieved from all dues connected with local or state worship or with the temples. As many Jews were in a financial position that would ordinarily invite the imposition of just these liturgies, that meant a very great relief. All other liturgies including the *tutela* both of Jews and of non-Jews, we are expressly told the Jews were subject to.

We know further that the demands upon them did not end there. In Palestine the organization of the Sanhedrin had maintained itself, although only in the form of several schools under the general presidency of the Nasi, whom Romans and Greeks called the Patriarch. The maintenance of these schools and those who labored in them was a religious duty which most Jews voluntarily assumed. The money was collected by *apostoli,* " envoys," despatched to the various Jewish synagogues for that purpose.[13]　The early Christian emperors believed, or professed to believe, that the payment of this tax was a grave burden to the poorer Jews, and that irregularities were committed in its enforcement.　The Jewish sources, all of which are Palestinian, naturally show no trace of this complaint; nor is it likely that there was much foundation for it except in certain localities already grievously burdened by constantly increasing dues.

Besides these various classes into which the tax-paying Jewish citizens fell, there were also Jews who did not share in the support of the state at all.　Jewish slaves existed in the third and fourth centuries too, but they can scarcely have been numerous.　A Jewish slave belonging to a Jewish master was practically only a servant bound for a term of years.[14]　Within a relatively short space of time he could demand his freedom by Biblical law.　If his master was a pagan, a religious duty devolved upon all other Jews, and particularly the local synagogue, to redeem him.[15]　Often, to be sure, that duty could not be carried out.　Not every master would sell, and not every synagogue was financially able to supply the necessary funds.　In general, however, it added another motive to those already existing that made emancipations frequent.

The social position and occupations of the Jews throughout the empire are only slightly known.　For Egypt and Rome we have fuller documents than elsewhere, except for Babylon, which was outside the empire.　We have no means of determining whether the facts found in Egypt and Rome are in any way typical. One negative statement may however be safely made. They were only to a very slight extent merchants or money-lenders. In most cases they seem to have been artisans. The inscriptions in the Jewish catacombs show us weavers, tent-makers, dyers, butchers, painters, jewelers, physicians.[16] In Egypt we meet sailors and handicraftsmen of all description.[17] Vendors, of course, on a small and large scale were not wholly lacking. Indeed it would be impossible to understand the individual prosperity of some Jews or of some communities except on the assumption of commercial occupations and success. However, in general, commerce was principally in the hands of Syrians and Greeks, especially the former, whose customs and cults spread with them over the Mediterranean.

We may say, in conclusion, that the economic and political position of the Jews in the empire was unique in one sense. There were no other groups that had exactly the same rights, or were subject to exactly the same demands as the Jews. But in another sense that position was not at all unique. Many other groups of men had rights somewhat like those of the Jewish synagogues, and played a part in the social economy similar to theirs; and, as individuals, there was probably nothing to mark out the Jew from his fellows in the community.

We cannot tell how far and how long the Jews would have been able to maintain their position. There seems however to have been nothing in the conditions of the

Diocletianic empire that threatened the stability of the synagogues in the form in which they were then found. The religious basis of the state—the maintenance of a common cult for the whole empire—had practically been abandoned. At one time, under Aurelian,[18] the emperor's devotion to the solar cult had almost made of that the state religion. But in general it may be said that the absolutism of Diocletian rendered such bonds unnecessary. Where all men were born subjects or slaves ("slaves of their duties," *servi functionum,* the guild-men are called explicitly [19]) of the same master, it could be considered indifferent whether they all maintained the same theology.

But whether the Jews might have maintained their position or not, if the conditions had remained the same, is a purely hypothetical question. When Christianity became the state religion, under Theodosius,[20] a step was taken that Jews must perforce regard as retrogressive. In ancient times participation in the common *sacra* was of the essence of membership in a state.[21] That principle was, however, tolerantly enforced. In the first place the mere existence of private *sacra* was not deemed to imperil the public *sacra.* Secondly, exceptions and exemptions that did not take offensive forms were freely allowed. But when Theodosius established Christianity, he consciously strove to make the ecclesia coterminous with the empire. "As well could those be saved who were not in the ark with Noah," Cyprian [22] had cried, "as they be saved who are not in the church." What was originally a group of elect, a company of saints (ἅγιοι), "the salt of the earth," [22] had been expanded into a world-filling community.

Not only was the ancient theory revived, but it was revived without the qualifications that had made the ancient theory a livable one. No other *sacra* could be permitted to exist. Not to be in the ecclesia, was not to be in the empire. Only the practical impossibility of really enforcing that theory restrained the zealous and triumphant leaders. Of course, the development of law was continuous. The new basis of citizenship was never actually and formally received as a legal principle. Yet gradually the limitation of civic rights, which non-membership in the church involved, operated to work an exclusion from citizenship itself. In a very short time those who were not within the church were in a very real sense outside the state, merely tolerated sojourners, and subject to all the risks of that precarious condition.

SUMMARY

What has been attempted in the foregoing pages is an interpretation of certain facts of Jewish, Roman, and Greek history within a given period. For that purpose it has been necessary to analyze fully the terms used, and in many cases rather to clear away misconceptions than to set forth new points of view. A brief retrospect is here added.

The Jews, as one of the Mediterranean nations, began to come into close contact with Greek civilization about the time of Alexander. Greece was then entering on a new stage in her development. The Macedonian hegemony produced a greater degree of political unity than had been previously achieved, but above all a real cultural unity had been created, and was carried by arms and commerce over the East. To this the Jews, as other nations did, opposed a vigorous resistance; and this resistance was successful in so far as it allowed the creation of a practically independent nation, and particularly it stimulated the independent development of Jewish institutions, especially religious ones.

In religion the Jews came into further and more extensive conflict with their Greek environment. For many centuries all the East had known a great spiritual unrest, from which had grown various religious movements. Of all these the common goal was the attainment of a personal immortality, the " salvation of the soul." Among the Jews too this movement had been active, and had produced concrete results in sects and doctrines. The Jewish aspect of this general movement would have remained a local development, had it not been given a wider field by the unusual position of the Jews, due to their dispersion.

For this dispersion various causes can be assigned. Perhaps the most potent single cause was the fact that the Jews, who rigorously opposed exposure of infants, and encouraged in other ways the growth of their population, increased too rapidly for the very limited resources of their small and niggardly territory. At any rate the kingdoms of the successors of Alexander found Jews as colonists in many of the new foundations in Asia, Syria, and Egypt, especially the last, where, as a matter of fact, Jews had lived from pre-Persian times. Within these new and, in many cases, old communities the doctrines preached in Palestine became a means of propaganda, and enabled the Jews to do more than maintain themselves in the exceptional position which their highly specialized religion necessitated.

The Jews were by no means the only religious group in the Greek communities with proselytizing tendencies. But they were unique in so far as they were permanently connected with an existing national group, with which they maintained relations. This made friction of some sort inevitable at first, since some community of religious observances for all citizens of a single state was axiomatic for ancient times. How-

24

ever, the anomaly of the Jewish position became less glaring in course of time.

The first stage of Jewish influence is marked by two things, a constantly increasing dispersion and an equally increasing propaganda that reached all stages of society.

The advance of the power of Rome at first did not change these conditions. In fact that advance materially assisted both the dispersion and its propaganda, since the support of Rome was an invaluable asset for the Hasmonean kingdom. Even the conquest by Pompey had no other effect than to accelerate the indicated development, especially within Italy and Rome itself.

But the relations of the Jews with the Greco-Roman world entered upon a second stage, the stage of armed conflict, when the national and religious aspirations of certain classes of Jews, which culminated in the Messianic hope, came into contact with the denationalizing tendencies of the imperial system. This conflict was in no sense inevitable, and might easily have been avoided. In addition to the internal movements that provoked the series of rebellions between 68 and 135, there was a constant excitation from without. The hereditary enemies of the Greek East and its successor, the Roman Empire—the Persians and their kinsmen and successors, the Parthians—maintained not only their independence but also their hostility, and the fact that the Jews lived in both empires, and that Parthian Jews communicated freely with the others, presented a channel for foreign stimulation to revolt.

The third stage of Jewish relations consists of an adjustment of the Jews to the rapidly centralizing empire, of which the administrative center was moving eastward. The center of wealth and culture had always been in the East. The reforms of Hadrian and his successors prepared the way for the formal recognition of the new state of things in the Constitutio Antonina, the Edict of Caracalla, which gave Roman citizenship to almost all the freedmen of the empire. This is the great period of Roman law, when, in consequence of the enormously extended application of the civil law, a great impetus was given to the scientific analysis and application of juristic principles. Out of this grew the bureaucratic system perfected by Diocletian, and begun perhaps by Alexander Severus, in which as told in the last chapter, the attempt was made to classify every form of human activity in its relation to the state.

A new stage of Jewish relations begins with the dominance of Christianity; and that, as was stated at the beginning of this study, lies outside of its scope.

NOTES

INTRODUCTION

[1] To what extent the Jews of the present day or those of earlier times may be considered racially pure, depends upon what criteria of race are adopted. At present there is no general agreement among ethnologists on this subject. The historical data are very uncertain. At all events absolute racial unity of the Jews of the Dispersion cannot be maintained. The facts of their vigorous propaganda and their extensive slave-property are too well attested. But it is wholly impossible to determine how far the admixture went.

[2] The best edition of Philo is the still unfinished one which is being prepared by two German scholars Wendland and Cohen. In this the *Apologia* has not yet appeared. Earlier editions are those of Mangey (1742) and Hohze (1851).

Philo's works were translated into English by C. D. Yonge (Bohn's Library, London, 1854).

[3] In Greek the two commonest editions of Josephus' works are those of Niese (1887-1895) and of Naber (1896). Neither completely satisfies all the demands that may be made for the adequate presentation of the text.

The old English translation of W. Whiston, so widely circulated both in England and America, is very inaccurate. The revision of this translation by A. R. Shilleto (1889-1890) has only slightly improved it.

[4] The references to the Jews in the inscriptions and papyri have not, as yet, been collected. Mr. Seymour de Ricci planned a collection of the Greek and Latin inscriptions to be called *Corpus Inscriptionum Judaicarum*. This Corpus was, at least partly, in manuscript form in 1912, but no part has been published. Mr. de Ricci's article on " Inscriptions " in the Jewish Encyclopedia, and Johannes Oehler, Epigraphische Beiträge zur Geschichte des Judentums (Monatsschrift f. Gesch. u. Wiss. d. Jud. 1909, xvii. 292-302, 443-452, 524-538) give a practically complete collection.

Chapter I

GREEK RELIGIOUS CONCEPTS

[1] It is nowhere directly stated that the power of a god did not extend beyond a definite locality. But the numerous local epithets applied to the various gods indicate it. We need mention only such typical references to the θεοὶ ἐγχώριοι as Aesch. Septem. 14, Soph. Trach. 183, and Thuc. ii. 74.

[2] Cf. Dionysus in the "Frogs" of Aristophanes, Herakles and Poseidon in the "Birds." The other comic poets, even Epicharmus, the oldest, dealt with even greater freedom with the gods. Even the scanty fragments of Cratinus and Amphis indicate that fact. In Sicily, an entire dramatic genre, that of the Φλύακες, contained practically nothing but situations in which the divine personages of the myths were the subjects of the coarsest fun.

[3] Such heroic friendships as that of Achilles and Patroclus were perverted early in the imagination of Greeks. Cf. Aeschylus, in Athen. xiii. 601 A, and Aeschines, i. 142. So also the story of Apollo and Admetus became a love story for Alexandria; Callimachus H. ii. 49.

[4] The subject has been discussed in full by de Visser, De Graecorum deis non referentibus speciem humanam (Leyden, 1900;) 2d ed. in German, 1903. So at Phigaleia, in Arcadia, Demeter had the form of a horse; the Brauronian Artemis was a bear; Apollo Lykeios was sometimes adored in the form of a wolf.

[5] Aegean and Mycenean are both used to designate the civilization that preceded that of historical Greece. Aegean, however, has, to a large extent, superseded the older term. For the specifically Cretan form of it, Minoan is generally employed.

[6] In spite of the apparently well-defined personalities of the Homeric gods and a poetic tradition of many centuries, the sculptors of later times found it necessary to indicate the subject of their labors, either by some well-known attribute, such as the caduceus, or a sacred animal, or a symplegma representing a scene of a known legend. Without these acces-

sories, archeologists often find themselves at a loss when they are required to name the god intended. Cf. Koepp, Archäologie ii. 88 seq.

[7] It is not suggested that prayer could not exist without sacrifice. But where sacrifice did take place, the act of worship did not lie in the sacrifice alone, or in the propitiatory allocution that accompanied it, but in the two together.

[8] Cf. Apollo Soter, Soph. O. T. 149, Dionysus Soter, Lycophr. 206, Zeus Soter, Aristoph. Plut. 1186 etc.

[9] Max Müller, Lectures on the Science of Language, *passim*. The term is rarely used by recent investigators.

[10] For the sacrificial act when addressed to gods, the word was θύειν; addressed to heroes, ἐναγίζειν. Herod. ii. 44. The color of the sacrificial animal for heroes was usually black, and no part of the flesh was eaten. Cf. Sch. Hom. Il. i. 459.

[11] For heroes whose position in the state was as high as that of gods, we have only to refer to the eponyms of the Cleisthenic tribes at Athens, Theseus, Cecrops, Erechtheus, etc

[12] Local deities, such as Pelops at Olympia (Sch. Pind. Ol. i. 149), Archemorus at Nemea (Arg. Pind. Nem. i), Tlepolemus at Rhodes (Sch. Pind. Ol. vii. 146).

[13] Cf. Suidas. s. v. Ἀναγυράσιος, Alciphro, iii. 58.

[14] The doctrine of Socrates cited by Xenophon, Memor. iv. 7, represents popular Greek feeling on the subject of theological speculation.

[15] Xenophanes of Colophon (sixth cent. B. C. E.) cited in Sex. Emp. adv. Math. ix. 193. The lines are frequently quoted, and are to be found in any history of philosophy.

[16] A monotheistic or pantheistic tendency showed itself in the attempt on the part of poets like Aeschylus and Pindar to absorb the divine world into the personality of Zeno. Cf. Aesch. Heliades, 71 :

> Ζεύς ἐστιν αἰθήρ, Ζεὺς δὲ γῆ Ζεὺς δ' οὐρανός,
> Ζεύς τοι τὰ πάντα χὥτι τῶνδ' ὑπέρτερον.

[17] The solar myth theory was especially advocated by Max Müller in his various books and articles. Most of the older writers on mythology, *e. g.* in the earlier articles of Roscher's

Lexikon, accept it as an established dogma. There can be no reasonable doubt that the celestial phenomena of sun, moon, and stars exercised a powerful influence on popular imagination.

[18] Dionysus came into Greece probably from Thrace and Macedon about the tenth century B. C. E. By the sixth century there was no Greek city in which he was not worshiped. As far as any center of his worship existed, it may be placed in Boeotia. Cf. Farnell, Cults of the Greek States, chs. iv. and v.

[19] We find Aphrodite firmly established among Greek gods from the earliest times. It may be that the Semitic or Oriental connections which have been found for her (cf. Roscher, s. v. Aphrodite, Roscher's Lex. i. 390-406) are due to the readiness with which she was associated with Oriental female deities. That fact, however, is itself significant.

[20] The merchants of Citium formally introduced into Athens the worship of their local Aphrodite; Dittenberger, Syll. no. 551. Sarapis, Isis, and Sabazios also early found their way into Athens.

[21] The statement that ἀσέβεια was a negative offense, that its gravamen consisted not in introducing new divinities, but in neglecting the established ones, is made by Wilamowitz (Antigonus von Karyst, p. 277). It is, however, only qualifiedly true. The Greeks found purely negative conceptions difficult. Impiety, or ἀσέβεια, was not the mere neglect, but such a concrete act as would tend to cause the neglect of the established gods. The indictment against Socrates charged the introduction of καινὰ δαιμόνια, but only because that introduction threatened the established form. The merchants of Citium (cf. previous note) might introduce their foreign deity with safety. No such danger was deemed to lie.

[22] The stories of Lycurgus (Il. vi. 130) and of Pentheus (Euripides, Bacchae) are a constant reminder of the difficulties encountered by Dionysus in his march through Greece. Then, as has always been the case in religious opposition, the opponents of the new forms advanced social reasons for their hostility (Eurip. Bacchae, 220-225).

[23] The Egyptian origin of the Eleusinian mysteries is maintained especially by Foucart, Les grands mystères d'Eleusis.

[24] The Homeric Hymn to Demeter dates from the close of the seventh century B. C. E., perhaps earlier. In it we find the Eleusinian mysteries fully developed, and their appeal is Panhellenic.

[25] Homer certainly knows of no general worship of the dead. But the accessibility of the dead by means of certain rites is attested not only by the Νέκυια (Od. x. 517-520), but by the slaughter of the Trojan captives at the funeral of Patroclus (Il. xxiii. 174). The poet's own attitude to the latter is not so important as his evidence of the custom's existence.

[26] In later times any dead man was ἥρως, and his tomb a ἡρῷον; C. I. G. 1723, 1781-1783.

[27] The kinship of gods and men was an Orphic dogma, quickly and widely accepted. Pindar formulated it in the words ἓν ἀνδρῶν, ἓν θεῶν γένος; Nem. vi. i. Cf. Plato, Timaeus, 41 C.

[28] Od. iv. 561.

[29] Hesychius, s. v. Ἁρμοδίου μέλος.

CHAPTER II

ROMAN RELIGIOUS CONCEPTS

[1] Adolph Bastian presents his theory of Grundideen in his numerous writings. It has, however, been found difficult, if not impossible, even for anthropologists to present the details of that theory with either definiteness or clearness.

[2] Cf. W. Warde Fowler, Roman Religion, in Hasting's Dictionary of Religions (consulted in proof).

[3] The relation, or the contrast, between magic and religion has been a constant subject of discussion since the publication of Tylor's Primitive Culture. For the present the contrast stated in the text may suffice.

[4] Sei deo sei deivae sac (C. I. L. vi. 110); sive deo sive deae (ibid. iii, 1212); sei deus sei dea (ibid. x v. 3572). Cf. also Not. d. Sc. 1890, p. 218.

⁵ Such a story as that of Mars and Nerione may belong to genuine Roman mythology. The enormous spread of Latin translations of Greek poems, and the wide popularity of Greek plays, rapidly drove out all the native myths which had attained no literary form.

⁶ Livy V. xxi. 3, 5.

⁷ Macrob. Sat. III. ix. 7-8.

⁸ The authenticity of this particular application of the formula has been questioned; Wissowa, s. v. Evocatio (deorum); Pauly-Wiss. vi. 1153. The proofs that the formula has been extensively modified are not conclusive. The *evocati di* received a special form of ritual at Rome. Festus, p. 237, a, 7. Cf. Verg. Aen. ii. 351-352.

⁹ For the Dioscuri, Livy, II. xx. 13. Apollo, Livy, III. lxiii. 7; IV. xxv. Both introductions are placed in the fifth century B. C. E. The historical account of the reception of Cybele and of Asclepius, Livy, Per. ix. and xxix. 10 seq.

¹⁰ The *lectisternium* is generally conceded to be of Greek origin. The ceremony consisted in formally dressing a banquet table and placing thereat the images of some gods, who reclined on cushions and were assumed to be sharing in the repast.

¹¹ Cic. De Nat. Deor. i. 119.

Chapter III

GREEK AND ROMAN CONCEPTS OF RACE

¹ The extreme of racial fanaticism will be found in H. S. Chamberlain, Grundzüge des neunzehnten Jahrhunderts.

² Aristophanes, Acharn. 104, Ιαοναῦ and the Schol. *ad loc.:* ὅτι πάντας τοὺς Ἕλληνας Ἰάονας ἐκάλουν οἱ βάρβαροι.

³ After the defeat of the Persians, the victors set up a tripod at Delphi, about the stem of which a bronze serpent was coiled. About this serpent ran an inscription, τοίδε τὸν πόλεμον ἐπολέμεον, "The following took part in the war." Then follows the list of the Greeks beginning with the Lacedemonians. Here, if anywhere, a collective term denoting the common origin of all these nations might have been expected.

[4] Euripides, Iph. Aul. 1400; Aristotle, Pol. I. ii. 4; ὡς ταὐτὸ φύσει βάρβαρον καὶ δοῦλον ὄν.

[5] Isocrates, Pan. 181.

[6] Demosthenes, In Mid. 48 (xx. 530).

[7] Daniel xi. 3.

[8] Besides the flings at barbarian descent scattered throughout the orators (cf. Dem. In Steph. A. 30), Hellenic origin was required for all the competitors in the Olympian games. Herodotus, v. 22.

[9] The secretary of Appius Caecus was a certain Gnaeus Flavius, grandson of a slave, who became not merely *curule aedile*, but one of the founders of Roman jurisprudence. (Livy, IX. xlvi.). Likewise the Gabinius that proposed the Lex Tabellaria of 139 B. C. E. was the son or grandson of a slave, *vernae natus* or *nepos.* (Cf. the newly discovered fragment of Livy's Epitome, Oxyr. Pap. iv. 101 f.) The general statement is made by the emperor Claudius (Tac. Ann. xi. 24), in a passage unfortunately absent in the fragments of the actual speech discovered at Lyons.

[10] Cicero, In Pisonem (Fragments 10-12). Aeschines, In Ctes. 172.

[11] Muttines, a Liby-Phoenician (cf. Livy, XXI. xxii. 3, *Libyphoenices mixtum Punicum Afris genus*), becomes a Roman citizen (*ibid.* XXVI. v. 11).

[12] Ennius ap. Cic. de. Or. iii. 168.

[13] Mucius defines *gentiles, i. e.* true members of Roman *gentes,* as follows (ap. Cic. Topica, vi. 29) : *Gentiles sunt inter se qui eodem nomine sunt, qui ab ingenuis oraundi sunt, quorum maiorum nemo servitutem servivit, qui capite non sunt deminuti.* Literally taken, that would exclude descendants of former slaves to the thousandth generation. But Pliny demands somewhat less even for Roman knights. The man is to be *ingenuus ipse, patre, avo paterno* (H. N. XXXIII. ii. 32).

[14] Gallic was still spoken in southern Gaul in the fourth century C. E., Syriac at Antioch in the time of Jerome, and Punic at Carthage for centuries after the destruction of the city.

[15] The racial bond upon which modern scientific sectaries lay such stress was constantly disregarded in ancient and

modern times. The Teutonic Burgundians found an alliance with the Mongol Avars against the Teutonic Franks a perfectly natural thing.

CHAPTER IV

SKETCH OF JEWISH HISTORY BETWEEN NEBU-CHADNEZZAR AND CONSTANTINE

[1] The Carduchi, Taochi, Chalybes, Phasiani (Xenophon, An. IV. iii. 6), make friends with the Greek adventurers, or oppose them on their own account without any apparent reference to the fact that the army of the Ten Thousand was part of a hostile force recently defeated by their sovereign.

[2] Herodotus, vii. 89: παρείχοντο δὲ αὐτὰς (sc. τὰς τριήρεας) οἴδε, Φοίνικες μὲν σὺν Σύροισι τοῖσι ἐν τῇ Παλαιστίνῃ, and he later defines the name specifically (*ibid.*): τῆς δὲ Συρίας τοῦτο τὸ χωρίον καὶ τὸ μέχρι Αἰγύπτου πᾶν Παλαιστίνη καλέεται.

[3] Aramaic Papyri Discovered at Assuan, edited by Sayce and Cowley, London, 1906. Aramäische Papyri . . . . zu Elephantine, ed. Sachau, Leipzig, 1911.

[4] Josephus, Antiquities, XI. vii. Reference to the same incident in Eusebius, Chron. (Ol. 103), Syncellus (486, 10), and Orosius (iii. 7) depends upon Eusebius. The general statement of pseudo-Hecataeus (ap. Joseph. in Ap. i. 22) is, of course, worthless as evidence.

Ochus was especially noted for his sacrilege. (Cf. Aelian, N. A. x. 23).

[5] After the death of Antiochus Sidetes, in 129 B. C. E., the various occupants or claimants of the Syrian throne are scarcely to be distinguished by nickname or number. They are uniformly imbeciles or puppets, and the last of them, Antiochus XIII, dies miserably at the hands of a Beduin sheik.

[6] In the Talmud John Hyrcanus is always יהוחנן כהן הגדל, but Alexander is יני המלך. On the coins John styles himself High Priest; but Jannai, on both his Hebrew and Greek coins, bears the title of King, יהונתן המלך and Ἀλεξάνδρου βασιλεως. Cf. Madden, Coins of the Jews. We have no record that the

royal title was specifically bestowed upon Jannai, either by the Seleucids or by the people. It is therefore likely that it was assumed without such authorization. The high-priesthood, on the other hand, was duly conferred upon Simon and his descendants.

CHAPTER V

INTERNAL DEVELOPMENT OF THE JEWS DURING THE PERSIAN PERIOD

[1] Cf. especially the Testaments of the Twelve Patriarchs, in the editions of Kautzsch or Charles.

[2] That the name is Sira and not Sirach, as it appears in the LXX, is generally accepted. It was the practice of Greeks to put a final X to foreign names to indicate that they were indeclinable. Cf. Ἰωσήχ (Luke iii. 26) for José.

[3] Ecclesiasticus xlviii. 24.

[4] Job iv. 7 seq.

CHAPTER VI

THE FIRST CONTACT BETWEEN GREEK AND JEW

[1] Σύριος means scarcely more than "Oriental" in Aeschylus (Persae, 81, Σύριον ἄρμα; and Ag. 1312, Σύριον ἀγλάϊσμα).

[2] Except Hittite and Amorite, these names have no non-Biblical occurrence.

[3] Caphthor is rendered Cappadocia in the LXX (Amos ix. 7), for no better reason, it may be, than the similarity between the first syllables. The Keftiu ships of the Egyptian monuments are scarcely other than Mycenean, and if they came from Crete, Minoan (Breasted, Ancient Records of Egypt, ii. 492). That the Philistines are of Cretan origin is, in the absence of monumental sources, a pure theory. It fits in well, however, with what we do know of them.

[4] The Jews were commanded by Ezra to put away their "strange wives" (Ezra x. 10) for the specific reason that the latter incited them to idolatry. Instances of intermarriage occur in the papyri from Elephantine (see ch. IV., n. 3).

[5] Datis and Artaphernes commanded the Persian troops defeated at Marathon, 490 B. C. E. Mardonius was defeated at Plataea in 479.

[6] Joel iii. 6. There is nothing in the extant Book of Joel inconsistent with a pre-Exilic date. Such slave raids as the Phoenicians are here accused of making, the Greeks made freely in Homeric times, and Greek merchants were already in every mart. In the famous picture of a golden age in Isaiah, Jewish captives are to be assembled " from Assyria, Egypt— and from the islands of the sea" (Isaiah xi. 11), a passage indubitably pre-Exilic. The " islands of the sea," however. are obviously Greek.

[7] In the lexicon of Stephen of Byzantium (s. v.) we read Σύροι κοινὸν ὄνομα πολλῶν ἐθνῶν. Strabo, writing in the time of Augustus, includes most of the nations of Asia Minor, such as the Cappadocians, etc., under that term (xvi. 2).

[8] The famous Harpy-tomb from Xanthus in Lycia, now in the British Museum, dates from the sixth century. It is, however, so highly developed a work that it presupposes a long history of mutual artistic influence between Greece, Ionia, and Lycia.

[9] One of the magnificent sarcophagi found in 1887 at Sidon by Hamdi Bey. They are all published in sumptuous form by Hamdi Bey and Reinach, Une nécropole royale à Sidon, Paris, 1892. An excellent and convenient description may be found in Hans Wachtler, Die Blütezeit der griechischen Kunst im Spiegel der Reliefsarcophage, Teubner, 1910 (Aus Natur u. Geisteswelt, no. 272).

[10] Strato, king of Sidon in 360 B. C. E. Athen. xii. 531. Cf. Gerostratos of Arados at about the same time.

[11] Herodotus, ii. 104 (cf. ii. 37).

[12] Aristotle states the fact in the Meteorologica, II. iii. 39, but does not mention the Jews.

[13] Textes, p. 8. n. 3.

[14] In the royal tombs at Sidon excavated by Hamdi Bey (see above, n. 9.), one of the monuments bears a long Phoenician inscription of a king of Sidon. It begins: " I, Tabnit, priest of Astarte and king of Sidonians, son of Eshmunazar, priest of Astarte, and king of the Sidonians."

[15] Plato, Euthyphro, 3 C., and *passim*.

[16] Aristotle, Rhetoric, III. vii. 6.

[17] Reinach, Textes, pp. 10-12. Müller, Frag. hist. graec. ii. 323, quoted in Josephus, In Ap. i. 22.

[18] The untutored philosophers of Voltaire's stories were quite in the mode of the eighteenth century, which had discovered the "noble savage," and were quite convinced that civilization was a retrogression from a state of rude and primitive virtue. It was, further, a convenient cloak behind which one might criticise an autocratic régime. Hence the flood of "Turkish," "Chinese," "Japanese," etc. "Letters," of which Montesquieu's Lettres Persanes are the most famous. Modern instances are "The Traveller from Altruria" of Mr. Howells, and Mr. Dickinson's "Letters of a Chinese Official."

[19] Cited by Diogenes Laertius, i. 9 (Müller, Frag. hist. graec. ii. 328).

[20] Reinach, Textes, p. 13; Müller, Frag. ii. 437; Clemens Alex. i. 15. Megasthenes had previously resided at the court of Sibyrtius, satrap of Arachosia (southern Afghanistan). Arrian, Anab. V. vi. 1.

[21] Clemens Alex. Str. v. (Sylberg) pp. 607 seq. Justin Coh. ad Graecos, 25.

[22] Cf. Ecclesiasticus l. 26; Zech. ix. 2.

[23] At Elephantine we learn from the papyri recently from there (Pap. 1, Sachau) that the Jews had a shrine consecrated to יהו, and that in 410 B. C. E. it was destroyed by the priests of a rival Egyptian temple.

[24] Reinach, Textes, p. 39. Müller, Frag. iii. 35.

CHAPTER VII

EGYPT

[1] This fragment, of the authenticity of which little doubt can be entertained, must be distinguished from the books attributed to Hecataeus about the Jews and Abraham. Josephus uses both in his "Defense" against Apion (i. 22 seq.), but their authenticity was questioned even in ancient times (cf. Herennius Philo, cited by Origenes, C. Cels. i. 15; Reinach,

Textes, p. 157). They are almost certainly Jewish works of the first century B. C. E.

The text of the real Hecataeus (Reinach, Textes, p. 14 seq.) is anything but certain. We have it only in a long citation by Diodorus, xl. 3. This book of Diodorus, however, has disappeared, and is found only in the *Bibliotheca* made by the Byzantine patriarch Photius in the ninth century C. E. (cod. 244).

² There were in Egypt a number of colonies of military settlers. They are distinguished by certain privileges, and, in legal terminology, by the term τῆς ἐπιγονῆς, placed after the words of nationality. Just as there are Πέρσαι τῆς ἐπιγονῆς, so there are Ἰουδαῖοι τῆς ἐπιγονης. In the Hibeh Papyri, i. 96, of 259 B. C. E., we read an agreement between the Jew Alexander, son of Andronicus, decurion in the troop of Zoilus, and Andronicus, a Jew τῆς ἐπιγονῆς. The groom Daniel (?) in a papyrus of the second century B. C. E. (Grenfell, An Alexandrian Erotic Fragment and Other Papyri, no. 43.) and the farm laborer Teuphilus (Grenfell-Hunt, Fayûm Towns and their Papyri, no. 123) are also humble men, and probably in the same stage of cultivation as other men of their calling.

³ Elephantine Pap. (ed. Sachau), no. 6.

⁴ Osiris appears as a theophoric element, not only in Egyptian names and in those of Grecized Egyptians, but also in purely Phoenician names, and joined to Semitic elements. So Osirshamar, from Malta, and Osiribdil, from Larnaca (Notice des Mon. Phén du Louvre, nos. 133, 162).

⁵ Reinach, Textes, pp. 20 seq. Müller, Frag. ii. 511-616.

⁶ Tac. Hist. V. ii.

⁷ Reinach, Textes, p. 362. Photius Bibl. no. 279.

CHAPTER VIII

JEWS IN PTOLEMAIC EGYPT

¹ Naucratis was founded, on the Canopic mouth of the Nile, about 550 B. C. E.

² However completely oligarchical in practice the government became, the sovereignty of the dēmos was recognized in theory. In the ancient doom ascribed to Lycurgus (Plutarch,

Lyc. 6), which may be said to form the constitution of Sparta, occur the words δάμῳ δὲ τὰν κυρίαν ἦμεν καὶ κράτες.

³ Fränkel, Inschriften, v. Perg. no. 5, 18 *et passim.*

⁴ Mitteis und Wilcken, Grundzüge und Chrestomathie der Papyruskunde, I. v. 1, pp. 14 seq.

⁵ Mitteis-Wilcken, *op. cit.* p. 15.

⁶ Xenophon, De Reditibus, ii. 4-7.

⁷ Josephus often refers to the Jews of Alexandria as οἱ ἐν Ἀλεξανδρείᾳ Ἰουδαῖοι (Ant. XIII. iii. 4) or οἱ ἐν Ἀλεξανδρείᾳ κατοικοῦντος Ἰουδαῖοι (Ant. XIV. vii. 2), but he refers similarly to the Greeks there (Ant. XVIII. viii. 1), and plainly understands κατοικεῖν simply as " inhabit.' The question is fully discussed in Contra Ap. ii. 5, where the general statement is made that Jews might and did become Alexandrian citizens, but that Egyptians were at first excluded.

⁸ Jewish Μακέδονες, Berliner Griechische Urkunden (B. G. U.), iv. 1068 (62). In other classes of citizenship, B. G. U. iv. 1140; iv. 1151, 7. For humbler classes of Jews cf. ch. VII., n. 2. A Jewish house-slave is manumitted in Oxyrhyncus Pap. ix. 1205.

⁹ The discussion is fully set forth by Brandis, s. v. Arabarches in the Pauly-Wissowa Realenzyklopädie, ii. 342. The word " alabarch " or " arabarch " impressed the Romans somewhat as " mogul " impresses the English, and was used with the same jocular intent. Cic. ad Att. II. xvii. 3. Juvenal, Satires, i. 130.

¹⁰ Apuleius, Met. xi. 30. Drexler in Roscher's Lexikon Myth., s. v. Isis, ii. 409 seq. gives a list of the cities through which the worship of Isis spread.

¹¹ Sarapis was not Osiris-Apis, but a deity of Sinope in Asia Minor, duly " evoked " into Alexandria by Ptolemy. The matter is left an open question by Cumont, Les religions orientales dans le paganisme romain, p. 112, but the general consensus of opinion is in favor of the theory just mentioned. The opposition referred to in the text was less an aggressive one than it was an assertion of the distinction between Greeks and Egyptians. It broke down with the fourth Ptolemy, and Sarapis was more or less officially identified with Osiris.

[12] Alexandronesus.   Cf. Reinach, in Mélanges Nicolle, p.
451 ; Pap. of Magdola, n. 35.

[13] Greek Pap. of the Brit. Mus. iii. 183, the ἄρχοντες Ἰουδαίων
προσευχῆς pay their water tax.

[14] B. G. U. iv. n. 562.

[15] The cartouches representing the Ptolemies contain all the
royal titles of the Pharaohs.

[16] Mitteis-Wilcken, Grundzüge und Chrestomathie, I. p. 42.

CHAPTER IX

THE STRUGGLE AGAINST GREEK CULTURE IN PALESTINE

[1] Ecclesiasticus xxxi. 12-30 ; vi. 2-4.

[2] Cf. ch. III., n. 14.

[3] A full bibliography is given in Schürer, Geschichte der
Juden[4], iii. 472 seq.

[4] Flinders Petrie Pap. iii. 31, g, 13.

[5] By Mishnic tradition Antigonus was a pupil of Simon the
Just (Abot i. 3).   A later legend makes him the founder of
the Sadducees (Abot R. N. v.).   The saying of Antigonus is :
" Be not like servants who minister to their master for the
sake of a reward, but be like servants who minister to their
master without the expectation of reward, and let the fear
of Heaven be upon you."

[6] Andronicus (Hibeh Pap. i. 96), Helenus and Trypho (B.
G. U. iv. 1140), Dionysius (Dittenberger, Syll. no. 73).

[7] Cf. Oesterley's edition of Ecclesiasticus, pp. xxiv-xxv.

[8] Josephus, Ant. XII. iv.

[9] Abot i. 4 ; Shab. 46 a ; Eduy. viii. 4 ; Pes. 15 a.

CHAPTER X

ANTIOCHUS THE MANIFEST GOD

[1] Polybius, XXVI. i. 1 : Ἀντίοχος ὁ Ἐπιφανὴς μὲν κληθεὶς
Ἐπιμανὴς δ' ἐκ τῶν πράξεων ὀνομασθείς.   Cf. also Athenaeus, v.
5 (193), and x. 10 (439).

[2] Ptolemy Euergetes II (Athenaeus, x. 10, 438 D).

[3] It is usual to speak of the Seleucid kingdom as Syria. That, however, conveys a wholly wrong impression of either the pretensions of the house or the actual extent of its dominion. Seleucus himself actually maintained his authority within what is now Hindustan and was styled "king of Asia," where he was not called simply "the king" as Alexander and the Persians had been before him. Even when Antiochus the Great gave up all his Asiatic possessions north of the Taurus, he did not renounce his claim to the Persian and Oriental patrimony of Alexander.

[4] Zeitschr. d. deut. morg. Gesell. xxiii. 371; Nöldeke, Die sem. Spr. 41 f.; Zeitschr. f. Assyr vi. 26. Cf. also Gardner, Greek and Scythic Kings of Bactria and India.

[5] The full title is Θεὸς Ἐπιφανής, as it appears upon coins.

[6] The στρατηγός ἐπὶ τὰ ὅπλα, i. e. "general of infantry," was at that time practically equivalent to the chief magistracy. Athenian coins of the year 175 B. C. E. bear his name and the elephant which was the heraldic emblem of his house. Reinach, Rev. d. et. gr. 1888, 163 f.

[7] Josephus, Ant. XII. v.

[8] The titles ἀγορανόμος and δήμαρχος are translations of "aedilis" and "tribunus," which Antiochus sought to transfer to his capital. Polyb. XXVI. i. 5-6. Livy XLI. xx.

[9] Livy (loc. cit.), Polyb. (loc. cit.). Athenaeus, x. 438 D and E.

[10] Hybristas is mentioned in Livy XXXVII. xiii. 12.

[11] Polyb. XXXI. xi. 3; Josephus, Ant. XI. ix.

[12] I Macc. i.

[13] Cf. ch. I., n. 22.

[14] Cf. the article Druidae, Pauly-Wissowa Realenzykl.

[15] Isocrates Nicocles (III), 54. King Nicocles of Salamis in Cyprus, the type and exemplar of a benevolent despot, states to his subjects: ἑταιρείας μὴ ποιεῖσθε μήτε συνόδους ἄνευ τῆς ἐμῆς γνώμης. αἱ γὰρ τοιαῦται συστάσεις ἐν μὲν ταῖς ἄλλαις πολιτείαις πλεονεκτοῦσιν, ἐν δὲ ταῖς μοναρχίαις κινδυνεύουσιν.

[16] Jerome in Dan. xi. 21 f.

[17] So the Spartans actively assisted the oligarchical party in Megara, Argos, Sicyon, and Achaea (Thuc. iv. 74; v. 81; v. 82).

Chapter XI

THE JEWISH PROPAGANDA

[1] Cumont, Les religions orientales dans le paganisme romain, gives the best and clearest account of the spread of these foreign cults. The Cabiri came from Samothrace. They were generally referred to as Θεοὶ μεγάλοι, and are found in many parts of the empire.

[2] Athenian criminal statutes often contain in the penalty clause καὶ τὸ γένος αὐτοῦ. Cf. Glotz, La solidarité de la famille dans le droit Ath. Cf. for Teos C. I. G. 3044.

[3] Homer, Odys. xi. 489-491.

[4] Frequently pictured relief (Gardner, Greek Sculpt. p. 136) formerly in the Sabouroff Coll. Pl. i., Ath. Mitth. 1877. Taf. xx-xxiv.

[5] Il. iii. 243-244; v. 638-651; xviii. 117-119.

[6] Cf. the translation of Menelaus, ch. I, notes 28, 29.

[7] Hymn in Dem. 480-482.

[8] Ben Sira knows of no life after death except Sheol. Perhaps it is better to say that he refuses to acknowledge any. His repeated affirmations have the air of consciously repudiating a doctrine advanced by others. The author of Wisdom (iii. 4) is sure of an immortality of the elect. It is in the apocryphal literature generally, in Enoch, the Testaments of the Patriarchs—most of them written in the first century B. C. E.—that the scattered and contradictory references to a future life are to be found.

[9] Josephus, Wars, II. viii. 14. His words are (οἱ Σαδδουκαῖοι) ψυχῆς τε τὴν διαμονὴν καὶ τὰς καθ' Ἄδου τιμωρίας καὶ τιμὰς ἀναιροῦσι. The passages in Josephus are our only contemporary authority for the sects and their differences; and Josephus was a Pharisee. The word ἀναιροῦσι would in this context naturally have the meaning "deny," but it might also simply indicate that the Sadducean belief on the subject was, in his opinion, so vague or so qualified as to render their whole transcendental scheme ineffectual. It is, however, more natural to give the word its dialectic sense (Cf. Plato, Rep. 533 c).

[10] Joseph. Ant. XIII. x. 10. Kid. 43 a.

[11] The vision of a Messianic age in Isaiah ii. 4, and Micah iv. 1, expressly includes the gentiles. This is the more important as it is highly likely that both Micah and Isaiah are here quoting an ancient and widely-accepted prophecy.

[12] There is no direct evidence about the extent of proselytizing in pre-Maccabean times. But there are two forms of proselytizing which always seemed natural and even inevitable to a man of ancient times. The slave, and the stranger actually resident under the roof of a head of a household were, however foreign in blood, practically members of that household, and it was a small step when they were brought formally into it by appropriate ceremonies. So the first Biblical reference to circumcision especially notes that not merely Abraham but all his household, the slaves born there and those bought of strangers, were circumcised (Gen. xvii. 23, 27).

The גר, μέτοικος, the sojourning stranger, is expressly held to the observance of the religious prohibitions. Ex. xii. 43; Lev. xvii. 12. And the relative frequency with which such a stranger became a full proselyte is indicated by Ex. xii. 48, and Num. ix. 14. It is true that the נכר or "stranger in blood" is treated with extreme rigor by Nehemiah, xiii. 30, but it is this same נכר who is referred to as a proselyte in Deutero-Isaiah (Is. lvi. 3, 6).

[13] Ab. R. Nat. ii. 1.

[14] Josephus, Ant. XV. viii.

[15] Josephus, Wars IV. iv.; VII. viii.

[16] Cf. Catullus, LXIII. The archigallus was not permitted to be chosen from Roman citizens till the time of Claudius.

[17] This genre seems to have first taken literary form at the hands of Bion of Borysthenes, a pupil of Crates, who was himself a pupil of Diogenes.

[18] Wisdom of Solomon xiv. 12-14. Cf also the entire thirteenth and fourteenth chapters of Wisdom.

[19] In Dan. x. 13-20 angels, or "princes," are the patrons of the various nations, as also in the Testaments of the Patr. (Test. Naph. 9). That fact of itself indicates a belief in the reality of the divine protectors of the heathen nations. And the "devils," דים ע (Deut. xxxii. 17), and שעירים (Lev. xvii. 7), are very likely the local gods.

[20] Philo, De Specialibus Legibus, ch. 7.

[21] We have already noted the ancient prophecy cited in Is. ii. 4 and Micah iv. 1. The fullest statement of this universalist aspiration is in Malachi i. 11, and i. 14.

CHAPTER XII

THE OPPOSITION

[1] The Messenians also expelled the Epicureans (Athen. xii. 547), and Antiochus (VI) Dionysius, or rather Tryphon in his name, expelled all philosophers from Antioch and all Syria (Athen. *ibid.*). The latter document has been questioned by Radermacher, Rh. Mus. N. F. lvi. (1901), 202, but on insufficient grounds. It is probably genuine, but the king referred to is uncertain. It will be remembered that the Epicurean Philonides claimed to have converted Epiphanes and to have been a favorite of Demetrius (Crönert, Stzb. Berl. (1900), 943, and Usener Rh. Mus. N. F. lvi. (1901), 145 seq.) Alexander Balas professed Stoicism.

[2] Josephus, Ant. XVIII. ix.

[3] Dio Cassius, lviii. 32; Ens. Chron. ii. 164. The account in its details is not free from doubt.

[4] Josephus, Ant. XIV. x.

[5] Senatusconsultum de Bacch. C. I. L. i. 43, n. 196. Bruns Fontes, n. 35, ll. 14-16.

[6] Cf. the instances cited in Cumont, Les rel. or. dans le pag. rom., p. 122, and the articles on Isis in the Pauly-Wissowa Realenzykl, the Dar.-Saglio Dict., and Roscher's Lexikon.

[7] In Greek διαβολή. Cf. Aristotle, Rhetoric, II. iii. 30; Syrianus, In Hermogenem, ii. (134, 3). Of this διαβολή, a favorite form was ἐπηρεασμός, "mockery" (Arist. *op. cit.* II. ii. 3), and "Commonplaces," κοινοὶ τόποι, on the subject are cited in Aristotle (*op. cit.* III. xv. 1).

[8] Reinach, Textes, p. 49.

[9] Eratosthenes was head of the Alexandrian Academy.

[10] Apollo is the god named and ascribed to Dora, which, as Josephus remarks, is not in Idumaea at all. Nor does Apollo appear as the god of Dora on the coins of that city. Accord-

ing to Josephus (Ant. XV. vii. 9) the Idumæan god was named
Koze, who might of course have been identified w th the Seleu-
cid patron Apollo. It may be a title connected with קצין
(Josh. x. 24, Micah iii. 1, 9).

[21] An inscription forbidding the approach of gentiles has
been found at Jerusalem, and is now in Constantinople:
μηθένα ἀλλογενῆ εἰσπορευεσθαι ἐντὸς τοῦ περὶ τὸ ιερὸν τρυφάκτοι καὶ
περιβόλου· ὃς δ' ἂν ληφθῇ ἑαυτῷ αἴτιος ἔσται διὰ τὸ ἐξακολουθεῖν
θάνατον.

[22] Reinach, Textes, p. 56. For an estimate of the importance
of Posidonius for his time, cf. Wendland, Hellenist. Kult. p.
60 seq. and 134 seq.

[23] Molo in Reinach, Textes, p. 60 seq.   Damocritus, ibid.
p. 121.

[14] Reinach, Textes, p. 131.

[13] Plutarch, Moralia, ii. 813; Reinach Textes, p. 139.

[16] Pseud-Opp. Cyn. iv. 256. Lact. Inst. i. 21-27.

[17] Cf. also Aelian Var. Hist. xii. 34. Strabo, xv. 1057.

[18] Pseudo-Plut. Sept. Sap. Con. 5. Apul. Met xi. 6. Ael. Hist.
An. x. 28.

[19] Juvenal, Sat. xv. 1-3. *Quis nescit Volusi Bithynice qualia
demens Aegyptos portenta colat? crocodilon adorat pars hæc,
illa pavet saturam serpentibus ibin; ei. also latrator Anubis*
(Verg. Aen. viii. 698, Prop. iv. 11, 41).

[20] It is not to be inferred that ancient historians as such were
unreliable. In those times, as in ours, the value of an historical narrative must be judged by estimating the character
and capacity of the writer and the means at his disposal. Many
modern historians have been special pleaders, some consciously,
like Froude and von Treitschke, and most have been impelled
by personal sympathies and antipathies of many kinds.

It is, however, a fact that the writers of antiquity consciously used falsehoods in what they believed to be details,
if they supposed that they could thereby more forcibly present
the essential character of a transaction, or better enforce a
moral lesson. The extreme danger of such a practice need
not be insisted on, nor did all writers engage in it. But
Panaetius and Cicero (Cic. De Orat. ii. 59; De Off. ii. 14),

Quintillian (ii. 26-39) and the Church Fathers, unhesitatingly defend it (Eusebius, Praep. Evan., John Chrysost. De Sac. i. 6-8, Clemens Alex. Strom. vii. 9).

[21] Polybius shares the general estimate of Syrians (XVI. lx. 3), but that does not prevent him from acknowledging the loyalty and devotion of the people of Gaza, whom he classes as Syrians.

CHAPTER XIII

THE OPPOSITION IN ITS SOCIAL ASPECT

[1] Horace, Sat. I. v. 100.
[2] Apuleius, Florida, i. 6.
[3] Anthol. Pal. v. 160. Reinach, Textes, p. 55.
[4] Fg. hist. gr. iii. 196; Reinach, Textes, p. 42.
[5] Journ. Hell. Stud. xii. 233 seq.
[6] Pausanius, X. xii. 9; Suidas, s. v. Σαμβήθη; Sibyllina, iii. 818.
[7] Valerius Maximus, I. iii. 3.
[8] Shab. vi. 2, 4, but cf. Demai iii. 11, and Erub. i. 10.
[9] Cf. above, ch. VII., n. 2.

The letter of Dolabella to the Ephesians, cited in Josephus, Ant. XIV. x. 12, makes it perfectly clear that if the Sabbath restriction had actually been enforced in the sense indicated, Jews would have been wholly useless for the army. But we have seen that they not merely fought their own battles, but engaged freely as mercenaries. We can therefore understand the passage in Josephus only in the sense of an attempt to escape conscription with the other Ephesians, by alleging an extreme application of the Sabbath principle.

The other passage in Josephus (XVIII. iii.) is in direct contradiction with other sources, and will be discussed later.

[10] Saguntum, Livy, XXI. xiv. Abydus, Livy, XXXI. xvii. Cf. also Livy XXVIII. xxiii.

[11] Cic. De Nat. Deor. ii. 28, 71, *his fabulis spretis ac repudiatis*. . . . .

[12] Reinach, Textes, p. 17. Cf. above, p. 93.

[13] The word itself does not occur in Homer. However, Od. ix. 478, the taunt is flung by Odysseus, the blind monster,

σχέτλι᾽, ἐπεὶ ξείνους οὐχ ἅζεο σῷ ἐνὶ οἴκῳ
ἐσθέμεναι τῷ σε Ζεὺς τίσατο καὶ θεοὶ ἄλλοι.

[14] Arrian, Anab. I. ix. 9-10.

[15] Il. iii. 207; Od. iii. 355; vii. 190.

[16] Plutarch, Lycurgus, xxvii.; Ael. V. Hist. xiii. 16; Thuc. i. 144.

[17] Juvenal, Sat. xv. 93-131.

[18] Cf. the undoubted instances of the Gallus-Galla, Graecus-Graeca sacrifices at Rome. See article, Gallus et Galla, in Pauly-Wissowa Realenzykl, especially the unwilling testimony of Livy, XXII. lvii. 6.

[19] The Tauric Artemis was considered a barbarian goddess, but received the veneration of Greeks, and of her we read, Eur. Iph. Taur. 384, αὕτη δὲ θυσίαις ἥδεται βροτοκτόνοις. The sacrifices of the Trojan captives at the funeral of Patroclus, the sacrifice of Polyxena, Astyanax, and Iphigenia are sufficient evidences of the familiarity of the practice to Greeks. An historical instance is the atonement-sacrifice of Epimenides at Athens. Diog. Laert. i. 111, 112; Athen. xiii. 602 C.

[20] For the Gauls, cf. Strabo, iv. 198; the Thracians, vii. 300; the Carthaginians, Verg. Aen. i. 525.

[21] The question of the Molech sacrifices in Palestine is too uncertain and complicated to be treated here in full. Doubtless some Jews at various times sacrificed to Molech; but some Jews in Greek times sacrificed to heathen gods, or, at any rate, adored them while still professing Judaism, and throughout the Middle Ages individual Jews indulged in superstitious practices severely reprobated by the rabbis. The passage in Jeremiah (xxxii. 35) does not necessarily imply that those who took part in these rites deemed themselves to be worshiping Jehovah.

[22] Reinach, Textes, p. 121.

[23] Sat. xv. 78-82 and 93 seq.

[24] Sat. xiv. 103.

[25] It is a curious and instructive fact that Chinese have charged Christian missionaries with precisely this same crime, *i. e.* of kidnaping and killing children as part of their religious ceremonies.

Chapter XIV

THE PHILOSOPHIC OPPOSITION

[1] Cf. the whole Lucianic dialogue on Images, 459-484, and Zeus Tragoedus, 654 seq.

[2] Cicero, De Nat. Deorum, i. 23, 63. Athenag. Supp. xii.

[3] Josephus, Contra Ap. ii. 37.

[4] Euthyphro, viii. 3 (7A).

[5] Sophocles, Oed. Rex, 661.

[6] Cf. ch. XI., n. 19. Also II. Chron. xi. 15. The שׂדים are mentioned in Psalms cvi. 37 as deities to whom human sacrifices are made.

[7] Isocr. Pan. 155-156; Lycurgus, In Leocr. 80-81.

[8] For the Boeotians cf. the common ὗς Βοιωτία; Pind. Ol. vi. 153; id. Fr. iv. 9, and Hor. Epp. II. i. 244; for Egyptian *perfidia*, Val. Max. v. 1, 10; for Abdera, Juv. Sat. x. 50; Mart. x. 25, 4; for the Cretans, the famous Κρῆτες ἀεὶ ψευσταί, Call. Hymn in Jov. v. 8., a proverb also quoted from Epimenides by Paul, Ep. ad Tit. i. 13. One may also note in this connection the Greek proverb, τρία κάππα κάκιστα · Καππαδοκία καὶ Κρήτη καὶ Κιλικία.

[9] Livy, XXXIV. xxiv. 4.

[10] Plautus, Rud. v. 50, *scelestus, Agrigentinus, urbis proditor.*

[11] Cicero, Pro Fonteio, 14, 30.

[12] Cicero, Pro Scauro, 17, 38.

[13] Pliny, Hist. Nat. Praef. 25.

[14] Africanus, ap. Eus. Praep. Ev. x. 10, 490 B, Clemens Alex Strom. i. 22.

[15] Reinach, Textes, p. 122.

[16] Cf. ch. VIII., n. 14.

[17] Cf. ch. XII., n. 12.

[18] Strabo, i. 66; Cic. De Rep. i. 58.

[19] Cicero, Paradoxon, iii.: ὅτι ἴσα τὰ ἁμαρτήματα. *Parva, inquit, est res. At magna culpa; nec enim peccata rerum eventis, sed vitiis hominum metienda sunt.*

[20] Cumont, Les rel. orient. pp. 157 seq.

Chapter XV

THE ROMANS

[1] The first Greek historians to deal with Roman history are Hieronymus of Cardia and Timaeus, both of the fourth century B. C. E.

[2] Pliny, Nat. Hist. III. lvii.

[3] Psalms of Solomon, ii.

[4] Livy, XLIX. v.: *Syros omnis esse, haud paulo mancipiorum melius propter servilia ingenia quam militum genus.*

[5] Cf. ch. III., n. 9.

[6] Servile origin has been ascribed to such a family as the Sempronian, and is assumed for the praenomen Servius, as for the nomen Servilius.

[7] Macrob. Saturn. II. i. 13.

[8] The reading of the last phrase in the mss. is *quod servata,* which is scarcely consistent with the rest of the passage. Bernays, Rh. Mus. 1857, p. 464 seq., conjectured that it was a Jewish or Christian marginal gloss which found its way into the text, a supposition by no means to be dismissed as cavalierly as Reinach does (Textes, p. 241, n. 1). A Christian scribe might easily have been moved by the taunt *quam dis cara,* to retort with the triumphant *quod servata!* It will be remembered that the Christians accepted as part of their own all the history and literature of the Jews till the birth of Christ, and resented as attacks upon themselves any slur against the Jews of pre-Christian times. Cf. the very interesting passage in Lactantius, Div. inst. iv. 2.

[9] Cic. In Vat. 5, 12.

[10] It may be worth while to indicate briefly the relation between the senatorial authority and the executive power at Rome. Unless the senate acted at the instance of the magistrate himself, a *senatusconsultum* was an advisory resolution, passed upon motion and suggesting to the holder of executive power, or *imperium,* a certain course of action. The words were generally: *Placet senatui ut A. A., N. N. consules, alter ambove, si eis videretur, illa faciant.* In practice, it is true, such a resolution was almost mandatory. A strong magistrate, however, or a rash one, might and did disregard it.

While, accordingly, a magistrate might neglect a course of action prescribed by the senate, there was nothing to hinder any action on his part (whether or not there was senatorial authority for it), except the veto power residing in the tribune or in an equal or superior magistrate. The only restrictions were made by the laws concerning the inviolability of the person of a *civis Romanus,* and of the *aerarium.*

[11] The *contio* was a formal assembly of citizens, called by a magistrate holding *imperium.* The purpose was generally to hear projected legislation either favorably or unfavorably discussed. No one spoke except the magistrate or those whom he designated. The *contio* took no action except to indicate its assent by acclamation, or its dissent equally emphatically. At the actual legislative assembly, for which the *contiones* were preparations, no discussion whatever took place. The law was presented to be accepted or refused. It will be seen that a mass of Orientals who less than two years before had been Aramaic-speaking slaves can scarcely have been a power in such gatherings as these.

[12] Philo, Leg. ad. Gaium, 23.

[13] The language of the inscriptions in the various Jewish cemeteries at Rome is almost always Greek, as is that of most of the monuments in the Christian catacombs. Latin is rare and generally later. But these monuments belong to Jews who lived several generations after 63 B. C. E. As far as Palestine is concerned, both inscriptions and literature leave no doubt that the masses spoke only Aramaic or Hebrew.

[14] Caesar, Bell. Gall. II. xxxiii. 7; III. xvi. 4.

[15] Foucart, Mém. sur l' affranchissement des esclaves.

[16] Suet. Div. Iul. 84, 76, 80.

[17] The pretensions of the senatorial party to be the only true Romans were not altogether unfounded. The terms *boni* and *optimates* which they gave themselves were perhaps consciously adapted from the καλοὶ κἀγαθοι of Athens. The importance of *nobilitas* as a criterion of true Roman blood lay in the fact that it attested lineage in a wholly unmistakable way. We may compare the insistence of Nehemiah upon documentary evidence of Israelitish blood (Neh. vii. 61, 64).

[18] Pro Flacco, 15, 36, compared with 26, 62 seq.

[19] Cf. ch. XIV., notes 11, 12.

[20] The chief political asset of the triumvirs was the orientalized plebs of the city, whose origin and poverty would combine to make them bitterly detest the organized tax-farmers. Now Crassus, one of the triumvirs, was himself the head of a powerful financial group. It may be that the tax-farmers persecuted by Gabinius belonged to a rival organization, or that Crassus had withdrawn from that form of speculation before 60 B. C. E. In the case of Flaccus, the complaint of the tax-financier Decianus was a pretext, or else Decianus may have been forethoughtful enough to have joined the right syndicate.

[21] Cicero ad Att. ii. 9.

[22] Augustinus, De Civ. Dei, iv. 31, 2.

CHAPTER XVI

JEWS IN ROME DURING THE EARLY EMPIRE

[1] Myths are understood by modern anthropologists exclusively as a " folk-way," with the effects of single creative imaginations almost wholly eliminated. However, the better-known Greek myths are not at all folk-devised. As far as the Romans are concerned, it has so far been impossible to pick out a definite story which does not appear to have been derived from an existing Greek myth by quite sophisticated methods.

[2] The phrase referred to is *Ubi bene ibi patria,* although just this form of it may not be ancient. However, the idea, that a fatherland might brutally ill-use its citizens and still claim their loyalty, was something that the average Greek scarcely recognized even in theory. When Socrates propounds some such doctrine in Plato's Crito, 51 B, he is consciously advocating a paradox. It was regarded as a noble ideal somewhat beyond the reach of ordinary men. Its disregard involved no moral turpitude.

In Cicero, Tusc. v. 37, 108, the phrase runs, *Patria est ubicunque est bene.* That is an evident adaptation of a Greek phrase, such as the one in Aristoph. Plut. 1151, πατρὶς γάρ ἐστι πᾶσ' ἵν' ἂν πράττῃ τις εὖ.

[3] Livy, Epit. lvi. Eunous, the leader, called his followers *Syri,* and himself King Antiochus. Cf. Florus, ii. 7 (ii. 9),

Diodorus fr. xxxiv. 2, 5. Atargatis was the *Dea Syria* that played so important a rôle in the life of the empire.

⁴ The philosophic schools had the usual corporate names of θίασος, σύνοδος, and the like. Or like other corporations they have a cult name in the plural, οἱ Διογενισταί, οἱ Ἀντιπατρισταί, οἱ Παναιτιασταί (Athen. v. 186). For the International Athletic Union, ἡ περιπολιστικὴ ξυστικὴ σύνοδος, cf. Gk. Pap. in Brit. Mus. i. 214 seq.

⁵ Cf. ch. III., n. 9.

⁶ Cf. Menippus in Lucian's Icaromenippus, 6 seq. Menippus does not spare his fellow Cynics (*ibid.* 16).

⁷ Macrobius, Sat. II. i. 13. The jest has unfortunately not come down to us.

⁸ The book we know as the "Wisdom of Solomon" is unquestionably the finest in style and the profoundest in treatment of the Apocrypha. Such passages as i.; ii. 1 seq.; ii. 6; iii. 1 seq. can hardly have appealed to any but highly cultured men.

⁹ Until the time of Claudius, we are told by John Lydus, no Roman citizen might actively participate in the rites of Cybele. Cf. Dendrophori, Pauly-Wissowa, p. 216. Claudius removed the restriction, perhaps to make Cybele a counterfoil to Isis.

¹⁰ The story in Livy, XXXIX., viii. seq. is a case in point. The abominable excesses which, as Hispala testifies, took place among the Bacchae (*ibid.* 13) are almost certainly gross exaggerations.

This hostility to new-comers was not a sudden departure from previous usage. Sporadic instances are mentioned in Livy's narrative. As early as 429 B. C. E., he tells us, *Datum negotium aedilibus ne qui nisi Romani dii neu quo alio more quam patrio colerentur* (Livy, IV. xxx. 11). The notice is of value as an indication that the general Roman feeling was not always so cordially receptive as is often assumed.

¹¹ Valerius Max. I. iii. 3.

¹² Cf. Cic. ad Att. iii. 15, 4; Asconius ad Pison. 8.

¹³ Suetonius, Div. Iul. 42. Josephus, Ant. XIV. x. 8. Suetonius (*ibid.* 84) states that many *exterae gentes* enjoyed his favor. The Jews may have been only one group among many. However, the statement is indirectly made by Suetonius and

directly by Josephus, that they received his special protection
to a striking extent. We have only the political support given
the triumvirs and Caesar personally to fall back upon for a
motive.

[14] I undertake with some diffidence to revive a conjecture
made before without much success, that the 30th Sabbath
was the Day of Atonement. One remarkable misunderstanding
of the Sabbath institution was that it was a fast-day. When
we consider the number and activity of the Roman Jews, it
seems scarcely credible that so many otherwise well-informed
persons supposed that the Jews fasted once a week. Augustus
in his letter to Tiberius seems to do so (Suet. Aug. 76). Pomp.
Trogus (Justinus), xxxvi. 2, explicitly states it. Cf. also Petronius (Bücheler, Anth. Lat. Frg. 37) and Martial, iv. 4. But
at least one man, Plutarch, not only knew that it was not so,
but was aware that, if anything the Sabbath was a joyous
feast-day (Moralia ii., Quaest. Con. v. 2). To this testimony
must be added that of Pers us, Sat. v. 182 seq. It is in the
highest degree surprising that Reinach (p. 265, n. 3) could
have accepted the theory that the *pallor* alluded to is the faint-
ness brought on by fasting. The tunny fish on the plate should
have convinced him of his error. It may be remembered that
fish in all its forms was one of the chief delicacies of the
Romans. Tunny, however, was a very common fish, and one
of the principal food staples of the proletariat.

Persius writes from personal experience. Of the other
writers it is only Pompeius Trogus who makes the unqualified
statement that the Sabbath as such was a fast-day. When
Strabo writes that Pompey is said to have taken Jerusalem
τὴν τῆς νηστείας ἡμέραν τηρήσας (xvi. 40), he is assumed to
have been guilty of the same confusion. But it is not easy
to see why he should have hesitated to say the Sabbath if he
meant the Sabbath. Nor is it so certain that Josephus is
mechanically copying Strabo (Reinach, p. 104. n. 1) when
he says (Ant. XIV. iv. 3) that Jerusalem was taken περὶ τρίτον
μῆνα τῇ τῆς νηστείας ἡμέρᾳ. The details of Josephus are vastly
fuller than those of Strabo, and he is not guilty of the latter's
error regarding Jewish observance of the Sabbath in times of
war (Ant. XIV. iv. 2). Besides, the siege lasted several weeks

—more than two months—so that Pompey's manoeuver, if it depended wholly upon the Sabbath, might have been performed at once.

Hilgenfeld's supposition (Monatsschrift, 1885, pp. 109-115) that the day was the Atonement, is better founded than Reinach would have us think. In the mouth of Josephus, ἡ τῆς νηστείας ἡμέρα can scarcely have any other sense. And if Josephus believed that Jerusalem fell on the Kippur, he believed so from more intimate tradition than the writings of Strabo.

Now, ἡ τῆς νηστείας ἡμέρα, the great fast of the Jews, must have been as marked a feature in their life two thousand years ago as to-day. While all the other feasts have individual names, it does not appear that this one did. יום הכפורים (Lev. xxiii. 27; LXX, ἡμέρα ἐξιλασμοῦ) seems rather a descriptive term than a proper name. Josephus (Ant. IV. x.) has no name for it, although he has for the others. In the Talmud, it is ימא, "the Day," יומא רבא, "the Great Day," צומא רבא, "the Great Fast." In Acts xxvii. 9 we meet the phrase ἡ νηστεία, "the fast κατ᾽ ἐξοχήν." Similarly in Philo, De Septenario, all the festivals have names except this, which is referred to simply as "the Fast." It must be, however, evident that with the institution of other fasts, ἡ νηστεία would hardly be adequate. As a distinctive appellation, some other name had to be chosen.

In the Pentateuch the term (שבת שבתון) is used of ordinary Sabbaths (Ex. xxxi. 15, xxxv. 2, Lev. xxiii. 3) as well as of the Atonement (Lev. xvi. 31, xxiii. 32). But the LXX expressly distinguishes the application of it to ordinary Sabbaths from its application to the Atonement. The former, it renders σάββατα ἀνάπαυσις, the latter σάββατα σαββάτων. This latter term may therefore be considered the specific designation of the Atonement Day, and it is so used by Philo, De Septen. 23, σάββατον σαββάτων, τῶν ἁγίων ἁγιώτεραι (ἑβδόμαδες).

We may, therefore, assume that in the Greek-speaking Jewish community of Rome, σάββατα σαββάτων, "the Great Sabbath," was the common designation—or at least a familiar designation—of the Day of Atonement. In that case it could scarcely be otherwise than familiar to those who had any dealings whatever with the Jews.

Fuscus pretends to share a very general observance, and on the strength of it to be disinclined to discuss any personal matters with his friend. Can that day have been a simple Sabbath? The tone indicates a rarer and more solemn occasion. Besides, we are definitely told that it is a special Sabbath, the "thirtieth."

The Jews at that time seem to have reckoned their festivals by strict lunar months (Josephus, Ant. IV x.) and their civil year by the Macedonian calendar. The thirtieth Sabbath, if we reckon by the Roman calendar, might conceivably have fallen on the Atonement. By the Macedonian or Athenian it could not have done so. However, as the Roman calendar was a solar one, the correspondence of the thirtieth Sabbath with the Atonement can only have been a fortuitous one in a single year. *Tricesima sabbata* can hardly apply to that.

It is just possible that the reason for the word "thirtieth" is to be found in the widely and devoutly pursued astrology of that time. The number thirty had a certain significance in astrology, Firmicus Maternus, IV. xvii. 5; xxii. 3. If for one reason or another the *mansio* of the moon, which coincided with the second week of the seventh lunar month (cf. Firm. Mat. IV. i. seq. for the importance of the moon in astrology), bore the number thirty, then *tricesima sebbata,* to initiated and uninitiated, might bear the portentous meaning required for the Horatian passage.

Whether that is so or not, the only Sabbath which we know to have been specially singled out from the rest of the year, was this σάββατα σαββάτων, the Day of Atonement. Whatever reason there was for calling it the thirtieth, the mere fact of its being particularly designated makes it likely that Horace referred to that day.

Nearly every one of the festivals in Tishri has already been suggested for the phrase, but these results have been reached by elaborate and intricate calculations, which bring the thirtieth Sabbath on the festival required. The main difficulty with all such calculations has been noted. The coincidence can only have been exceptional, and an exceptional coincidence will not help us here. Some especially rigorous Jews undoubtedly fasted every week like the Pharisee in Luke xviii. 11-20, but that was intended as a form of asceticism. The custom

26 ·

survived in some Christian communities, notably in Rome,
which elevated it almost to a dogma, so that Augustine had to
combat the point with especial vigor. (Ep. xxxvi., and Casu-
lanum, Corp. Scr. Eccl. xxxiv. pp. 33 seq.) It may be interesting
to remember that from a passage of this epistle referring to
this Sabbath fast (xiv. 32) is derived the famous proverb,
"When you are in Rome, do as the Romans do."

[15] Sat. I. iv. 18.

[16] Sat. I. v. 97.

[17] Apellas is a common name for a slave or freedman. Cic.
ad Fam. vii. 25; C. I. L. x. 6114. That a Jew should bear a
name derived from that of Apollo, is not at all strange. Cf.
ch. IX., n. 6.

[18] Cf. Ep. I. vi. 1 seq. The *nil admirari* of the first line is
Horace's equivalent for the ἀταραξία of Epicurus.

[19] As is stated in the text, the *peregrina Sabbata* and the
septima festa, which is merely a metrical paraphrase for *Sabbata,* are treated here as of annual occurrence. The word
redeunt itself points to that. It has been suggested in Note
14, that the great annual Sabbath was the Day of Atonement.
If that is referred to here, the application is very natural. The
season of the Tishri festivals coincided in the Mediterranean
with rather severe storms. These generally began after the
Day of Atonement, so that among Jews sailing was rarely
undertaken after that day. This is strikingly shown by Acts
xxvii. 9. But the equinoctial storms, while sufficient to make
a sea-voyage dangerous, do not seem to have caused serious
discomfort on land. The reference, accordingly, must in each
case be understood from its context. In the first the courtship
is to be begun, *tu licet incipias,* at the great Sabbath, to take
advantage of the exquisite autumn of Italy. In the second, the
voyage is not to be deferred even for this same Sabbath,
which ordinarily marked the danger line of navigation.

[20] Vogelstein u. Rieger, Gesch. der Jud. in der Stadt Rom,
p. 39 seq.

[21] Reinach, Textes, p. 259.

[22] Pliny, Hist. Nat. XXIX. i. 6. Plaut. Amphitruo, 1013.

[23] Cf. Garrucci, Cimitero . . . . in Signa Randanini; F. X.
Kraus, Roma Sott. p. 286 ff.; Garucci, Storia del arte Cristiana,
VI. tav. 489-491.

Chapter XVII

THE JEWS OF THE EMPIRE TILL THE REVOLT

[1] Verg. Ecl. i. 6-7; Georg. i. 503; Horace, Odes, I. ii. 43; Ovid, Ex Ponto, ii. 8.

[2] Xen. An. IV. i. 2-3.

[3] Cic. ad Att. i. 1.

[4] While notoriously corrupt governors like Cotta (130 B. C. E.), Cic. Pro Mur. 58, and Aquilius (126 B. C. E.), Cic. Div. in Caec. 69, were acquitted, a rigidly honest man like Rufus was convicted under such a charge. Dio Cassius, fr. 97.

[5] Ditt. Or. inscr. no. 456, l. 35; from Mytilene, 457, 659.

[6] The Edict of Caracalla, called the Constitutio Antonina or Antoniniana, has been known in substance for a long time. Recently fragments of its exact words in Greek were discovered in a papyrus (Giessen, Pap. II. (P. Meyer), p. 30 seq):
δίδωμι τοῖς συνάπασιν ξένοις τοῖς κατὰ τὴν οἰκουμένην πολίτειαν Ρωμαίων μένοντος παντὸς γένους πολιτευμάτων χωρὶς τῶν δεδειτικίων
The exact effect of the decree is not yet quite clear. It seems evident that the *dediticii* were excluded.

[7] Dio Cassius, xxxvi. 6.

[8] Suet. Aug. 93.

[9] Josephus, Ant. XIV. x.; XII. iii. 2.

[10] The "heterodox Jewish propaganda" is of course Christianity. The success of Paul and other missionaries in Asia Minor is best indicated by the churches of Asia to which Revelations is addressed.

[11] Horace, Ep. II. ii. 184. The sumptuous present of Aristobulus, which formed part of Pompey's triumphal procession, Josephus, Ant. XIV. iii. 1. Pliny, Hist. Nat. XXXVII. ii. 12, must have made the Jewish kings symbols of enormous wealth. None the less, Herod's unsparing severity toward his own sons was also well known, and it is said to have elicited from Augustus the phrase *mallem Herodis porcus esse quam filius*—Macrob. Sat. II. iv. 11—a jest which, as Reinach points out (Textes, p. 358), is of doubtful authenticity, and certainly not original.

[12] Josephus, Ant. XX. iii.

[13] Judea herself was free from tribute, but Herod was responsible for certain Arab revenues. Besides, he received from

Augustus a number of Greek towns (Josephus, Wars, I. xx.
seq.), and his kingdom included further Batanaea south of
Damascus, Galilee, and Peraea, the Greek cities across the
Jordan and south through Idumaea. All this was held by him
as the acknowledged beneficiary of Rome (Josephus, Ant. XV.
vi. 7).

[14] Josephus, Ant. XV. i. 2.

[15] Josephus, Ant. XVII. vi. 6.

[16] Cf. ch. XI., n. 15. Cf. also Josephus, Ant. XVII. x.

[17] Not merely composed of Herod's old soldiers (Josephus,
Ant. XVII. x. 4). Matt. xxii. 16; Mark iii. 6; xii. 13.

[18] Madden, Coins of the Jews. Cf. also Josephus, Ant.
XVIII. iii. 1.

[19] Josephus, Ant. XX. viii. 11.

[20] Josephus, Ant. XX. v. 4.

[21] Josephus, Ant. XV. xi. 15.

[22] Josephus, Ant. XVI. vii.-viii. seq. The many children of
Herod's ten wives were in almost constant intrigues against
him and one another.

[23] Strabo, xvi. 755.

[24] It is necessary at every point to note the uncertain character
of our evidence. The *Historiae Philippicae* of Pompeius
Trogus written under Augustus would have been of inestimable value for us, if we had them in full. But we possess them
merely in the summary of Justin (third century?), which gives
us all the substance, but little or none of the personality of the
writer. And in this case the loss is the more serious because
Trogus seems to have had a keener feeling for the dramatic
character of events and a broader sympathy than many other
ancient historians.

[25] Josephus, Ant. XVII. x. 9.

[26] This is the Varus made famous in the Teutoburg battle.
The insurrection mentioned in the text is the *polemos shel
Varos* of the Seder Olam.

[27] Caesar, Bell. Gall. iii. 10.

[28] Josephus, Ant. XVII. x. 9.

[29] Nicolaus of Damascus, philosopher and historian, was
Herod's principal Greek adviser and the advocate of the Jews
in many public controversies. As far as we can judge from

fragments, his History of the World, in no less than 114 Books, was a loosely connected compilation rather than a work of literary merit.

[30] Josephus, Ant. XVIII. i. 1 and 6.

[31] A complete investigation of this subject is contained in Domaszewski, Die Religion des römischen Heeres.

[32] Cagnat. in Dar.-Sagl. Dict. des ant. s. v. legio, p. 1084.

[33] The signa were actually worshiped by the soldiers. They are the *propria legionum numina*. Tac. Ann. i. 17. Cf. Cagnat., *op. cit.* p. 1065. Domaszewski, *op. cit.* p. 115.

[34] To the sense and tact of this typical Roman official the averting of a crisis in the history of Palestinian Jewry is due. The rebellion which Gaius would undoubtedly have provoked might have dragged other parts of the world with it, and at that time the conditions were less favorable for re-establishment of the empire than in 68 c. e.

[35] Josephus, Ant. XVIII. vii. 2.

[36] Josephus, Ant. XIX. vi.

[37] That Tacitus shows a strong antipathy to the Jews can scarcely be questioned. It is in these chapters (Hist. v. 2. seq.) more than most others, that we are able to see the rhetorical historian of ancient times almost in the act of preparing his narrative. The sources of Tacitus are open to us. That he used Manetho and Apion instead of Josephus and Nicolaus is itself ample indication of the complete lack of conscience with which such a writer could select his evidence according to the thesis he meant to establish.

[38] Cagnat. Inscr. Gr. ad res Rom. pertin. ii. n. 176.

[39] Cf. for the Jewish feeling toward him, Jos. Ant. VI. i. 2; Ketub. 17a; Pes. 88b. He is represented as a rigidly observant and pious Jew. However, the born companion of the young Gaius and the voluptuaries of the imperial court must have undergone an overwhelming change of heart if he was really worthy of the praise lavished upon him.

[40] Josephus, Ant. XIX. vii.

[41] Josephus, Ant. XX. i. One of the slain rioters is named Hannibal.

[42] Josephus, Ant. XX. v.

[43] Josephus, Ant. XX. viii.

CHAPTER XVIII

THE REVOLT OF 68 C. E.

[1] Cf. Livy, Books XXXIX and XL.

[2] Tac. Ann. iii. 40 seq.; *ibid.* ii. 52; iv. 23. In 52 C. E., Cilicia rose in revolt; *ibid.* xii. 55. The Jewish disturbances of the same year are alluded to in Tac. Ann. xii. 54—a passage omitted in Reinach.

[3] Josephus, Wars, II. xvi.

[4] The entire life of this curious impostor, as portrayed by Lucian, is of the highest interest. The maddest and most insolent pranks received no severer punishment than exclusion from Rome.

[5] C. I. L. vii. 5471.

[6] For the Armenian, British, etc., rebellions, see Suet. Nero, 39, 40. In at least one other part of the empire, prophecy and poetry maintained the hope of an ultimate supremacy, something like the Messianic hope of the Jews. This was in Spain, and upon this fact Galba laid great stress. Suet. Galba, 9: *Quorum carminum sententia erat, oriturum quandoque ex Hispania principem dominumque rerum.*

[7] Suetonius speaks first of the joy shown at his death, then of the grief. It is, however, easy to see that the latter manifestation was probably the more genuine and lasting.

[8] Josephus, Ant. XX. viii. 11; Vita, 3.

[9] We learn from the same passage that a great many accounts of Nero existed, and many of them were favorable. The implication further is that these accounts were written after his death. We have only the picture drawn by Tacitus and Suetonius. If we had one written from the other side, like Velleius Paterculus' panegyric of Tiberius (Vell. Pat. ii. 129 seq.), we should be better able to judge him.

[10] Gittin 56a.

[11] Reinach, Textes, pp. 176-178.

[12] Neither the arch nor the inscription exists any longer. A copy of the inscription was made, before the ninth century, by a monk of the monastery of Einsiedeln, to whose observation and antiquarian interest we owe more than one valuable record.

[13] The phrase *Iudaica superstitione imbuti,* already quoted,

shows what the term would be likely to suggest to Roman minds. In Diocletian's time, when the Persians were the arch-enemies of Rome, and Persian doctrine in the form of Manicheism was widely spread over the empire, the emperors did not hesitate to call themselves *Persicus*. But *Persicus* never meant an adherent of a religious sect.

[14] *Idumaea* is used for *Iudaea* in Statius Silvae, iii. 138; v. 2, 138; Valerius Flaccus, Argon. 12.

CHAPTER XIX

THE DEVELOPMENT OF THE ROMAN JEWISH COMMUNITY

[1] Philo, Leg. ad Gaium, 24.

[2] We may compare such expressions as *magica arte infecti*, Tac. Ann. ii. 2; Cic. Fin. III. ii. 9.

[3] Long before the attempts made in the nineteenth century to rehabilitate all the generally acknowledged historical monsters, historians had looked askance at the portrait of Tiberius drawn by Tacitus. For a recent discussion, cf. Jerome, The Tacitean Tiberius, Class. Phil. vii. pp. 265 seq.

[4] Suet. Tib. 36. The *mathematici* are strictly the astrologers whose science was called μάθησις. Cf. the title of Firmicus Maternus, *Matheseos libri*. The governmental attempt to suppress the *mathematici* was a total failure, but the law's attitude toward them may be seen from the rescript of Diocletian (294 C. E.): *ars mathematica damnabilis interdicta est* (Cod. Just. IX. xviii. 2).

[5] Nero assigned Sardinia to the senate as ample satisfaction for Achaea, which he took under his own jurisdiction.

[6] Acts xi. 26; xxvi. 28. Ιησοῦ χρήστου in the inscription quoted in n. 10. In this case the identification of names may be due to iotacism.

[7] Cf. the well-known rhetorician Philostr. Vita. Soph. ii. 11, and in Rome itself Inscr. gr. Sic. et Ital. 1272; and *ibid.* 2417, 2.

[8] The question of the authenticity and date of the Acts does not belong to this study. A thorough discussion will be found in Wendland, Die urchristlichen Literaturformen,[3] p. 314 seq.

[9] Acts xi. 19; xiii. 5, 50.

[10] συναγωγή = ἐκκλησία. Le Bas, 2528 (318 c. e.), a Marcionite association.

[11] There was a jurist Tertullian of whom some fragments have been preserved in the Digest (29, 2, 30; 49, 17, 4). He has on plausible grounds been assumed to be the same as the Church Father. There can be no question that the latter had legal training. As for the cruelties described by Tacitus, it may be said that Eusebius has no word of them, even in his denunciation of Nero. (Hist. Eccl. II. xxv.)

[12] All the Church Fathers mention these outrageous charges. Pliny (Ep. x. 96) refers vaguely to wickednesses charged against them, but the *flagitia cohaerentia nomini* are more likely to be the treasonable machinations which the Christian associations were assumed to be engaged in than these foul and stupid accusations. It will be remembered that Tertullian (*loc. cit.*) is more eager to free the Christians from the charge of treason than of any other. Treason in this case, however, meant not sedition or rebellion, but anarchy, *i. e.* attempts at the destruction of the state. The attitude of medieval law toward heresy gives a good analogy.

[13] It would scarcely be necessary to refute this slander, if it had not recently renewed currency; Harnack, Mission and Ausbreitung. Tertullian knows nothing of it, nor Eusebius, although the latter refers in the case of Polycarp to Jewish persecution of Christians (Hist. Eccl. IV. xv. 29). Tertullian, on the contrary, implies that an enemy of the Jews would be likely to be a persecutor of Christians (Apol. 5).

[14] Like most men of his time he bore two names, his native name of Saul and the name by which he was known among Christians, Paul. This is indicated by the phrase Σαῦλος ὁ καὶ Παῦλος (Acts xiii. 9), which is the usual form in which such a double name was expressed.

[15] The mother church at Jerusalem consisted exclusively of Jews until the time of Hadrian (Euseb. Hist. Eccl. IV. v. 2).

[16] Quint. Inst. X. i. 93.

[17] Maecenas, too, was of the highest Etruscan nobility. Horace, Sat. I. vi. 1 seq. The antiquity of Etruscan families was proverbial among the Romans.

[18] Mommsen seeks to make his crabbed style a racial characteristic. The statement is quite gratuitous. His peculiarity of expression is amply explained by his youth, his lack of literary practice, and his absorption in his philosophical pursuits.

[19] Pers. v. 176. Reinach, Textes, p. 264.

[20] Strabo apud Jos. Ant. XIV. vii. 2: καὶ τόπον οὐκ ἔστι ῥᾳδίως εὑρεῖν τῆς οἰκουμένης ὃς οὐ παραδέδεκται τοῦτο τὸ φῦλον μηδ' ἐπικρατεῖται ὑπ' αὐτοῦ. Seneca apud Aug. De Civ. Dei, vi. 10: *Cum interim usque eo sceleratissimae gentis consuetudo valet ut per omnes iam terras recepta sit; victi victoribus leges dederunt.*

[21] Besides the capital passage (Sat. xiv. 96) Juvenal speaks of Jews in Sat. iii. 10 seq., 296; vi. 156, 542.

[22] Cf. Garrucci, Cimitero . . . . in Signa Randanini; Rossi, Roma Sotteranea, especially the Indices. As late as 296 C. E. the epitaph of the Bishop of the Roman church is given in Greek.

CHAPTER XX

THE FINAL REVOLTS OF THE JEWS

[1] Perhaps the "egg laid on the Sabbath" would have excited less comment, if the fact were kept in mind that a decision in a specific case can hardly fail to be particular.

[2] C. I. L. ix. 1. 26.

[3] Laius outraged Chrysippus, son of Pelops, who had been left in his care. The Euripidean lost play on Oedipus seems to have adopted that version. Pisander, Schol. Eur. Phoen. 1750: πρῶτος δὲ Λάιος τὸν ἀθέμιτον ἔρωτα τοῦτον ἔσχεν.

[4] Cf. Philo, De Spec. Leg. 7.

[5] Tosefta Ab. Zar. ii 6.

[6] Ziebarth, Kulturbilder aus griechischen Städten, p. 73.

[7] In very much earlier times Jews left dedications in the temple of Pan Euhodus. Ditt. Inscr. Or. 74: Θεύδοτος Δωρίωνος Ἰουδαῖος σωθεὶς ἐκ πελάγους. Cf. 73 Πτολεμαῖος Διονυσίου Ἰουδαῖος.

[8] This became a standing formula and in inscriptions is regularly abbreviated N. K. C. (Valerius Probus, 4), *i. e. non kalumniae causa.* The use of *k* for *c* testifies to the antiquity of the formula.

[9] Suet. Domit. 12.

[10] Dio Cassius (Xiph.), lxvii. 14.

[11] Passed in 81 B. C. E. This law punished offenses as diverse as murder, arson, poisoning, perjury, abortion, and abuse of magisterial power. In every case it was the effect of the act that was considered.

[12] Reinach, Textes, p. 197, n. 1.

[13] The *polemos shel kitos* of Mishnah Sota ix. 14 and the Seder Olam.

Quietus was a Moorish chieftain of great military ability. He seems to have hoped for the succession to the throne. After the end of the revolt he was transferred to his native province, Mauretania, by Hadrian, and was ultimately executed for treason.

[14] Meg. Taan., Adar 12; Grätz, Gesch. der Juden,[3] iv. 445 seq.

[15] In the case of non-Jews, the Messianic hope was simply the dread of an impending cataclysm. As far as this dread was connected with the failure of the Julian line, it proved groundless. But the Jewish Apocrypha and Pseudepigrapha of this time are full of prophecies of the end of the world. It was the general belief that the world was very old, and that a fixed cycle, then rapidly coming to its end, determined the limits it would reach.

[16] Jerus. Taan. iv. 7, p. 68 d. Ekah Rab. ii. 1.

[17] Dio Cassius (Xiph.), lxix. 12; Reinach, Textes, p. 198.

[18] Dig. 50, 15, 1, 6.

[19] Euseb. Hist. Eccl. IV. vi. 4.

[20] Gen. Rab. lxiii. (xxv. 23) makes Hadrian the typical heathen king, as Solomon is the typical Jewish king. His name is followed, as is that of Trajan, by a drastic curse. But there are traditions of a kindlier feeling toward him. Sibyl. v. 248. In the Meg. Taan. the 29th of Adar.

[21] Eusebius, Hist. Eccl. IV. vi., quoting Aristo of Pella. Jerome in Ezek. i. 15. It is here that the famous passage of Jerome occurs, which describes the Jews as "buying their tears." Cf. also Itiner. Burdigal. (Hierosolymitanum), I. v. 22.

[22] Vopiscus, Vita Saturn. viii.; Reinach, Textes, p. 326. The authenticity of this letter has been questioned, but the transmission, although indirect, is better documented than in most

such cases. Hadrian is known to have written an autobi-
ography, and Phlegon, his freedman, who also wrote his life,
no doubt used it. Spartianus, Hadr. i. 1; iv. 8.

[23] The writers Spartianus, Capitolinus etc., dedicate their
work to Diocletian or Constantine. It was suggested by Dessau, Hermes, 24, 337, that these writers never existed, and were
invented by a forger of a century later. Mommsen, Hermes,
25, 298, assumed their existence, but regarded the extant works
as revised at the time mentioned by Dessau. Other investigators, except H. Peter, accept Mommsen's conclusions.
Whether they are authentic or not, these biographies are alike
wretched in style and thought.

[24] Paul, Sent. V. xxiii. 14; Dig. 48, 8, 3, 2; 8, 8. The date is
not certain; Dig. 48, 8, 3, 4.

[25] B. G. U. 347, 82.

[26] Dig. 48, 8, 11. pr.

[27] Paul, Sent. V. xxii. 3.

[28] Lampridius, Vita Alex. 22.

[29] Jews made converts even after the prohibition of Theodosius (Jerome, Migne Patrol, 25, p. 195; 26, p. 311). One
further ground for doubting the statement of Paul as it appears
in the extant texts is the following: In the Digest (48, 8, 4, 2)
it is only the physician and the slave that are capitally punished
for castration. The owner of the slave (ibid. 48, 8, 6) is punished by the loss of half his property. Further, the penalty for
circumcision is stated to be the same as that for castration.
That was the case not only in Modestinus' time, who lived after
Paul, but as late as Justinian, since it is received into the Digest.
Yet Paul, according to the extant text, makes the circumcision of
alien slaves a capital crime (V xxii. 4). The discrepancy can
scarcely be reconciled.

[30] Capitol. Antoninus Pius, 5.

[31] 193 c. e. It was on this occasion that the Pretorians
offered the imperial purple to the highest bidder.

[32] Josephus, Ant. XIV. x.

[33] The legend of Polycarp assumes a large and powerful
Jewish community. In late Byzantine times, the Jews of Asia
Minor were still a powerful factor. The emperor Michael
II, a Phrygian, was suspected of Jewish leanings; Theophanes
(Contin.), ii. 3 ff.

CHAPTER XXI

THE LEGAL POSITION OF THE JEWS IN THE LATER EMPIRE

[1] The theory advanced by Wilcken-Mitteis (Grundzüge und Chrestomathie der Pap. vol. I.) that all who paid a poll-tax were *dediticii,* and therefore excluded from the Const. Ant. is wholly gratuitous. There is no evidence whatever connecting the *dediticii* with the poll-tax.

[2] There are few reliable statements in the extant texts for estimating the population. Beloch's work on the subject puts all the data together, but nothing except uncertain conjectures can be offered.

[3] Lanciani, Ancient Rome, pp. 50-51; Pelham, Essays on Roman History, pp. 268 seq.

[4] Lampridius, Alex. 33: *corpora omnium constituit vinariorum . . . . et omnino omnium artium.*

[5] These are the *collegia, idcirco instituta ut necessariam operam publicis utilitatibus exhiberent* (Dig. 50. 6, 6, 1). They are the transportation companies and others engaged in caring for and distributing the *annona,* the fire companies and the burial associations of the poor. Cf. C. I. L. vi. 85, 29691; x. 1642, xiv. 2112.

[6] The *institutio alimentaria* commemorated on the marble slabs (*anaglypha*) in the Forum and by the bronze tablets of Veleia and the Baebiani (C. I. L. ix. 1147; xi. 1455). It had begun with Nerva: *puellas puerosque natos parentibus egestosis sumptu publico per Italiae oppida ali iussit* (Aur. Vict., Nerva, xii.).

[7] An entire article of the Digest (26, 1) is devoted to the *tutela.* Another one (27, 1) deals with *excusationes,* which are mainly exemptions from the burden of the *tutela.*

[8] The distinction is thoroughgoing in the penal clauses cited in the Digest. It was already established in Trajan's time (Plin. Ep. X. lxxix. 3). It is implied in Suetonius, Gaius, 27: *multos honesti ordinis.* It is doubtful, however, whether the distinction was already recognized in the time of Caligula.

[9] Gaius wrote about 150 C. E., probably in the eastern provinces.

[10] Abot ii. 5. The saying of Hillel has no direct reference to apostasy, and concerns rather arrogance or eccentricity of conduct. But it literally describes the act by which such a man as Tiberius Julius Alexander ceased to be classed as a Jew.

[11] Cf. Plutarch, Numa, 17 ; Dionys. Ha. iv. 43.

[12] Dig. 50, 2, 3, 3.

[13] Cod. Theod. viii. 14.

[14] Exodus xxi. 2 ; Josephus, Ant IV. viii. 28.

[15] Bab. Bat. 3b; Gittin 46b. The duty was regarded as of the highest urgency.

[16] Vogelstein and Rieger, Gesch. der Juden, p. 61 seq. Friedländer, Darstellungen der Sitt.⁷ i. p. 514.

[17] Ox. Pap. ii. no. 276.

[18] Aurelian reigned from 270-275 c. e. The *sol invictus* whom he adored was probably the Baal cf Palmyra. Cumont, Les rel. orient. pp. 170, 367, n. 59.

[19] Cod. Theod. xvi. 4.

[20] In 311 c. e. Galerius, and in 318 c e. Constantine and Licinius, legalized the practice of Christianity. In 380 c. e., by the edict of Thessalonica, most of the heathen practices became penal offenses.

[21] Every state as such had its characteristic and legally established state ritual. Many centuries later Gladstone, then "the rising hope of the stern and unbending Tories," stated, as a self-evident proposition, that a government in its collective capacity must profess a religion (The Church in its Relation to the State, 1839).

[22] Cyprian. De catholicae ecclesiae unitate, ch. x.

[23] Matth. v. 13. Cf. generally the Pauline Epistles, *e. g.* II. Corinth. xiii. 13.

BIBLIOGRAPHY

PERIODICALS

The Jewish Quarterly Review: First Series, London, 1889-1900. Second Series, Philadelphia 1910-date.

Revue de études juives, Paris, 1880-date.

Monatsschrift für Geschichte und Wissenschaft des Judenthums, Breslau, 1851-date.

ENCYCLOPEDIAS

Jewish Encyclopedia: New York, 1901-1906.

Encyclopedia Biblica: London, 1899.

Hastings' Dictionary of the Bible, 1901-1904.

Hastings' Encyclopedia of Religion and Ethics, 1908. Not yet completed.

Daremberg-Saglio: Dictionnaire des antiquités grecques et romaines, 1877. Not yet completed.

Pauly-Wissowa: Realenzyklopädie, 1894. Not yet completed.

Schaff-Herzog-Hauck: Realencyklopädie für protestantische Kirche und Theologie. 3d ed. Eng. tr. 1908.

GENERAL REFERENCE BOOKS

Grätz: Geschichte der Juden (1873-1895). Eng. tr., History of the Jews (1891).

Schürer: Geschichte des jüdischen Volkes im Zeitalter Jesu Christi (4th ed.), 1901.

Juster: Les juifs dans l'empire romain, 1914.

Wendland: Die hellenistisch-römische Kultur in ihren Beziehungen zum Judentum und Christentum, 1912.

Wendland-Poland-Baumgarten: Die hellenistische Kultur.

Friedländer: Darstellungen aus der Sittengeschichte Roms. Leipzig (7th ed.). Eng. tr. London, 1909.

Cumont: Les religions orientales dans le paganisme romain, 1912.

INDEX

The Lord Baltimore Press
BALTIMORE, MD., U. S. A.